About This Book

Why is this topic important?

Developing business acumen is an imperative for our profession. Without it we are in danger of becoming irrelevant. *Business acumen* is defined as the collection of knowledge, skills, and experience that transforms us into indispensable strategic partners in our organizations.

What can you achieve with this book?

This is the first book to provide step-by-step, practical advice on business practices guaranteed to help you win the support, respect, and attention of your organization. You will learn how to play a starring role in making your organization more competitive. This is an essential book for both new and seasoned professionals in the field.

Reading this book will show you how to start putting into practice three critical areas of business acumen:

1. Finance skills
2. Partnering skills
3. Communication skills

How is this book organized?

The book is broken into three sections—one for each area of business acumen, with four chapters devoted to each area. Each section and each chapter is complete in itself, a stand-alone piece that can be quickly used to strengthen your business acumen in that area. Case studies, thought-provoking interactive scenarios, tools, templates, quizzes, questions for reflections, and self-paced exercises provide lots of opportunities for you to experientially engage with the information you need to succeed. The book also includes a CD-ROM crammed with value-added materials for you to use in your daily practice.

About Pfeiffer

Pfeiffer serves the professional development and hands-on resource needs of training and human resource practitioners and gives them products to do their jobs better. We deliver proven ideas and solutions from experts in HR development and HR management, and we offer effective and customizable tools to improve workplace performance. From novice to seasoned professional, Pfeiffer is the source you can trust to make yourself and your organization more successful.

Essential Knowledge Pfeiffer produces insightful, practical, and comprehensive materials on topics that matter the most to training and HR professionals. Our Essential Knowledge resources translate the expertise of seasoned professionals into practical, how-to guidance on critical workplace issues and problems. These resources are supported by case studies, worksheets, and job aids and are frequently supplemented with CD-ROMs, websites, and other means of making the content easier to read, understand, and use.

Essential Tools Pfeiffer's Essential Tools resources save time and expense by offering proven, ready-to-use materials—including exercises, activities, games, instruments, and assessments—for use during a training or team-learning event. These resources are frequently offered in looseleaf or CD-ROM format to facilitate copying and customization of the material.

Pfeiffer also recognizes the remarkable power of new technologies in expanding the reach and effectiveness of training. While e-hype has often created whizbang solutions in search of a problem, we are dedicated to bringing convenience and enhancements to proven training solutions. All our e-tools comply with rigorous functionality standards. The most appropriate technology wrapped around essential content yields the perfect solution for today's on-the-go trainers and human resource professionals.

Essential resources for training and HR professionals

www.pfeiffer.com

Building
Business
Acumen for
Trainers

Building Business Acumen for Trainers

Skills to Empower the Learning Function

Terrence L. Gargiulo,
with Ajay M. Pangarkar,
Teresa Kirkwood,
and Tom Bunzel

Pfeiffer
A Wiley Imprint
www.pfeiffer.com

Published by Pfeiffer
An Imprint of Wiley.
989 Market Street, San Francisco, CA 94103-1741
www.pfeiffer.com

Library of Congress Cataloging-in-Publication Data

Gargiulo, Terrence L., 1968-
  Building business acumen for trainers: skills to empower the learning
function/Terrence L. Gargiulo, with Ajay M. Pangarkar . . . [et al.].
      p. cm.
  "The materials on the accompanying CD-ROM are designed for use in a group
setting and may be customized and reproduced for educational/training purposes."
  Includes bibliographical references and index.
  ISBN-13: 978-0-7879-8175-4 (cloth/CD)
  ISBN-10: 0-7879-8175-3 (cloth/CD)
1. Business education. 2. Management—Study and teaching.
  3. Employees—Training of. 4. Organizational learning. I. Title.
  HF1106.G355 2006
  658.3'124—dc22
                                              2006019146

Acquiring Editor: Matthew Davis
Director of Development: Kathleen Dolan Davies
Developmental Editor: Susan Rachmeler
Production Editor: Rachel Anderson

Editor: Elspeth MacHattie
Manufacturing Supervisor: Becky Carreño
Illustrations: Lotus Art

Printed in the United States of America

Printing   10 9 8 7 6 5 4 3 2 1

Contents

    The Introduction lays out the intended audience, major themes, and organization of this book. An introductory case study tells the story of the (fictitious) Pogo Insurance Company. Try to help Stanley, Pogo's manager of training and development, tackle the challenges he encounters. Use this case study to assess your business acumen in the areas of financial skills, partnering skills, and communication skills.

    In this review of the essential principles of business financial management, key terms and concepts are explained in clear, easy-to-understand language.

ix

CD-ROM Contents

Balance Sheet (Chapter 1)

Master Budget Templates (Chapter 2)
> Revenue Budget
> Materials Cost Budget
> Staff Budget
> Capital Budget
> Cash Flow Budget
> Master Budget

Break-Even Analysis Template (Chapter 2)

Preassessment Form (Chapter 3)

ROI Analysis Templates (Chapter 3)
> ROI Analysis
> 12-Month ROI Analysis

Vendor Selection and Evaluation (Chapter 4)

Vendor Evaluation

Vendor Selection

Request for Proposal Template (Chapter 4)

Assessment of Perceptions of T&D Form (Chapter 5)

Writing Exercises (Chapter 9)

Writing Exercise Answers (Chapter 9)

Report Writing Exercises (Chapter 11)

Report Writing Exercise Answers (Chapter 11)

Quarterly Report Example (Chapter 11)

Report Template (Chapter 11)

Acknowledgments

SPECIAL THANKS to Darlene Van Tiem, associate professor of performance improvement and instructional design in the School of Education at the University of Michigan-Dearborn, and Jeff Miller and Patti Radokovich, graduate students at the University of Michigan, for providing the case study presented in the Introduction and for authoring Chapter Eight, "Human Performance Technology and Business Acumen." Special thanks to Ajay M. Pangarkar, Teresa Kirkwood, and Tom Bunzel for their generous contributions of Chapters One through Four and Chapter Twelve.

I am indebted to Renee Stoll, manager of Training, Education, and Employee Development at TDS Telecom for sharing so many of her insights and invaluable experiences with us.

I am grateful for all the time, energy, and support of so many people. The Pfeiffer team of Matthew Davis, Kathleen Dolan Davies, Elspeth MacHattie, and Rachel Anderson exceeded every hope and expectation. And my family . . . well, they deserve medals of honor for being so patient and loving.

For the T&D community—
May our shared passion for learning and for developing
people's potential give us the resolve to stretch in new
directions and become major leaders in our organizations.

Introduction

BUSINESS ACUMEN is the collection of knowledge, skills, and experiences that transforms us into indispensable strategic partners in our organization. My drive to write this book rose from many late-night passionate discussions with my training and development (T&D) colleagues, as we racked our brains on ways we could do a better job of increasing our relevance and value in our organizations. There was always more than one doomsday seer among us who would insist that our days in organizations were numbered. In their eyes our beloved profession was on its way to becoming a dying art, soon to be relegated to fond memories of the "good old days." According to them it was inevitable that our crucial work was on its way to becoming a transparent, outsourced function, gradually fading into the background of our organizations' infrastructure. "No," I would scream as I jumped up and down. Then I would whip out a pen and start writing on anything I could get my hands on. Napkins turned into canvases contoured with grand visions and plans.

These legitimate concerns for our profession transformed themselves into a huge opportunity in my eyes. Here was the wake-up call. I asked myself, What do we need to do differently as a profession to move beyond the confines of our domain and help our organizations succeed in achieving their objectives? As I interviewed people in our profession I discovered the critical missing ingredient for concocting a new brew of success was *business acumen.* Like so many other experts we are often so mired in our own vocabulary and frame of reference that we forget that what comes easily to us—the things we know well and the lingo we speak—are foreign to anyone outside our area. What is apparent to us is not apparent to others. We might even occasionally feel defiant and say to ourselves, "Hey if these folks don't understand the value of learning and performance then that's their problem, not mine." Wrong!

We need to speak the language of business and we need to meet other people on their turf. So what does that mean? What does that look like? That means gaining a better understanding of the nature of the work of other functional areas and how it contributes to the organization's vitality. After extensive research, experimentation, review of the different competency models for our industry, and dialogues with business leaders, I developed a simple framework for identifying the knowledge, skills, and experiences that transform us into indispensable strategic partners in our organization. The framework is built on three pillars; financial skills, partnering skills, and communication skills. This book follows that structure. There are four chapters focused on each area. This is an essential book for anyone old or new working in the T&D field who wants to strengthen his or her competencies in these areas. Throughout this book I use the term *T&D,* but our profession has many other labels, disciplines, and nuances that are impossible to capture in any one designation. Moreover, no single book can possibly provide an exhaustive treatment of all the facets of business acumen, but this book will give you a solid foundation.

We begin with a scenario, or case study, to set the stage. Sandwiched in this case are three groups of questions, one for each area of the framework for business acumen (financial skills, partnering skills, and communication skills). Take a moment to pause and reflect on the questions. Following the case there are some suggestions for answering the questions.

This Introduction ends with a self-assessment tool. Use it to identify the areas of the book you want to concentrate on. The self-assessment also provides a high-level glimpse of the book's topics and the chapters that address them.

Without any further ado, let's get started . . .

The Pogo Insurance Company: Quagmire or Opportunity?

The Pogo Insurance Company is a large group insurer with decentralized regional claim operations. It provides health and disability benefits to the workers in various companies throughout the United States. With 24,000 employees, Pogo's revenues are derived largely from premiums and service contract fees paid by corporate policyholders, and its operating expenses consist mainly of claim-related costs incurred by its home and field operations. The marketing centers generate sales revenue and the claim operations incur expenses. Profit, or shareholder value, is the result of resourceful management of expenses and the creative expansion into new markets and acquisition of new corporate clients.

In this very competitive market new and existing business is acquired and retained by providing the best service at the lowest cost. In Pogo's quest for expansion, local marketing and office staff aggressively dedicate their efforts to landing newer and larger accounts.

As each new account is signed up, claim management prepares to service the new business. This involves assessing and allocating physical and human resources and training a new set of claim approvers on how to process claims cost effectively.

Current Situation

Today, the largest challenge to most businesses is the rising cost associated with providing medical coverage and benefits. Medical care spending and health care inflation far surpass costs associated with other goods and services. Superior service, defined as the delivery of a high-quality, low-cost product, becomes the overriding factor for companies in choosing an insurer to administer benefits for their employees. An inefficient, inadequately trained staff makes it impossible for insurers to compete successfully in this environment.

At the time of the events this case focuses on, Pogo's Northeast regional office employed 500 workers, including claim approvers and administrative, clerical, and supervisory and management staff. With little advance notice the Hartford central office had been awarded a contract to administer medical and dental benefits for Northwest Networks, a technology company in Seattle.

People, processes, systems, and associated resources had to be in place in three months. Hartford had directed that existing physical space be staffed with the sufficient claim approvers to begin processing claims by the October 1 deadline.

To complicate the situation, several months later Hartford would also be rolling out new technology and programming for administering all health savings accounts, including those of the new client, Northwest Networks. This technology would affect how the newly staffed office handled Pogo's complex, consumer-directed health insurance plans, and it would also have an impact on Pogo's ability to curb medical care spending while offering tax advantages for its customers.

Scenario

In anticipation of the October 1 deadline, in mid-August forty-five new employees had been hired and set to begin a training program in a Seattle office space with just fifteen computer terminals. For Norma, the Pogo trainer, an already stressful situation was made worse by the need to develop additional training materials and to accelerate the training so that the new trainees were prepared to process incoming claims for the last quarter of the year. In addition, she had to get up to speed on all the new benefit provisions for the client, Northwest Networks. With the pressure of training new claims adjusters at three per terminal while the trainer was absorbing the material herself in off hours, this training program was obviously faltering.

Fortunately, Stanley, Pogo's manager of training and development, co-opted additional auditing support for Norma, but did so at the expense of taking four trained claim approvers away from established processing modules elsewhere in the division. Claim backlogs, increased lag times, and cost overruns were now starting to encumber claim staff and were threatening service to existing accounts.

At the same time the senior corporate level, in the person of Ozzie, Pogo's Northwest regional vice president, was strongly resisting requests from Tim, Seattle's claim operations manager, for more space and resources. As an executive his job depended on containing expenses to meet operating efficiency goals and to make sure that each cost per claim transaction met Pogo's stated objectives by year's end.

"Enough is enough," an exasperated Tim complained to his managers. "We need more accurate projections of our operating expenses, and I am being pressured to reduce expenses by an even greater percentage next year. This means more work with fewer people while maintaining—or increasing—our productivity! While we're training new staff in our Seattle office, I need to accurately project a 2006 budget and to keep to our 0 percent cost increase mandate. I need all of your input, numbers, and analyses in ten days!"

Tim reminded his team that "for this year we have barely been able to maintain our average processing time of fifteen days and average cost per claim transaction of $50. With just four months to go in 2005, we project incurred operating expenses of $50 million and health care costs of $250 million on local revenues of $300 million. Since the only parameters we directly control are our operating expenses, we'll need to run at peak efficiency in 2006 to do any better than break even." Looking around the room he saw that it was sinking in—without a miracle many of these people were going to lose their jobs.

In the midst of this turmoil Pogo's training manager, Stanley, was faced with both the "big picture" of corporate needs and his own mandate to get well-trained staff in place. He knew he could submit a budget to make a case for additional resources, which he thought might ease some of the problems hampering training. As manager of training and development he was eager to provide input.

Imagine that you are the training and development manager in this situation, and consider the following questions.

Question Set One: Finance Skills

- What cost factors need to be considered in preparing a budget for the training and development (T&D) area?

- What areas or people within the organization might be involved before preparing the T&D portion of the budget?

- What competencies can be applied in this situation, and how do they link to specific solutions?

- What would be the probable consequences of your chosen actions?

- What additional data or financial information could be used to develop meaningful information for forecasting training expenditures?

After Stanley's budget was submitted and just two weeks before the October 1 deadline, Stanley expressed his misgivings to Tim: "Massaging our numbers for next year does nothing to resolve our immediate training issues. Norma is doing the best she can, but she's got three people to each computer and needs to teach them a whole new set of procedures as well as provide background on the client. You know, Northwest Networks has its own set of needs—they want a nutritional and exercise program."

Stanley wondered quietly to himself, "What other surprises are waiting around the corner?" He'd heard rumors that Tim was busy "putting out fires" with his staff.

After all, Tim had to deliver the numbers, meet quality standards, and keep the office running smoothly. It also occurred to Stanley that the problems affecting the training department might have their roots in other parts of the company.

For example, Stanley was aware of the rift between the marketing and claims departments. He had heard that Ann, the marketing manager, sometimes didn't return Tim's phone calls and e-mails.

Tim was always complaining of being out of the loop when a new account was acquired, which caused a last-minute rush to train people to service the barrage of new claims that suddenly poured in.

"Why doesn't anyone see the big picture, open some channel of communication?" Stanley wondered. As things stood, Tim got the new business notice as an afterthought, Stanley received the request for training at the last possible minute, and then Norma was forced to train people too quickly with limited resources. Often there was not even enough time to vet the trainees and make sure they knew what they were doing.

As Stanley thought about it, he knew it didn't stop there. Surely Harriet, the human resource manager, felt whipped around by eleventh-hour requests to recruit new people, let alone keep up with recruiting and selection with the constant turnover of personnel. Now this latest directive to hire and train forty-five new people to process claims for 40,000 Northwest Networks employees and their families fit an all-too-familiar pattern: poor coordination and planning was sure to result in inefficiency and lost revenue. Frustration and stress pervaded the Pogo workplace wherever Stanley looked.

Stanley realized the mess he was in. He could easily be blamed for the inevitable poor performance of the new employees, and he knew he had to take action.

Imagine that you are the training and development manager in this situation and consider the following questions.

Question Set Two: Partnering Skills
- What do you see as the central issues affecting outcomes thus far?
- What needs to be done to coordinate and integrate the efforts of the operations and marketing functions?
- What decisions and actions would you take and at what point? What are the pros and cons of taking such actions?
- What would be the probable consequences of your chosen actions?

Over a couple of drinks Tim and Stanley agreed among themselves that their initial efforts to heal the rift between marketing and claims were a good start. But both of their overworked staffs were showing signs of caving under the pressure—absenteeism and arguments in the workplace had increased noticeably.

Stanley finally said, "We just can't keep putting out fires. We both know we need to begin dealing with the underlying real issues. Let's get all the department heads together to discuss the situation. Together we should be able to decide how to solve our problems."

After some days of deliberation and a phone discussion with Ozzie, the regional VP, Tim brought Stanley into his office to discuss his new ideas. He told Stanley that Ozzie had agreed that given the glitches occurring in the system between marketing and operations, between IT and operations, and even between customer service and the processing areas, something needed to be done. All of them needed to work toward the same objective: acquire new customers and retain current ones by providing prompt, efficient claim service.

"As you said the other night, Stan, we need a systematic approach to improving performance in the workplace," Tim summed up.

Stanley continued with a more focused analysis: "We need improvement in a lot of important areas: organizational development, reengineering, and training, just to name three. The way I see it, since Harriet and I are the HR and T&D professionals here, we need to define and model those competencies we want to see in our staff. Also, we have to effectively communicate to employees how our business makes its money and coherently explain our business model. Once they have a high-level understanding of how the overall business works the staff may begin to have some ideas of their own as to how we can continually improve our performance and address issues as they arise. It is increasingly vital for our employees to understand these issues, and it's obviously in the company's best interest to ensure that everyone understands his or her own specific role in the big picture."

Impressed by these insights, Tim formally delegated the change initiative to Stanley. If the outcome is successful, the potential for positive implementation and change in the Northwest region appears significant. Stanley welcomed the challenge and felt empowered by playing a key role in potentially affecting the company's profitability and the work conditions of his colleagues.

After his initial euphoria and confidence, he began considering all the possibilities and ramifications. He realized that rolling out a comprehensive communication plan to set the stage for success was just the beginning, but it was a necessary first step in getting this business initiative off to a good start.

Although you do not have enough information to adequately answer all the following questions, these are the kinds of questions that you would be considering if you were in Stanley's shoes.

Question Set Three: Communication Skills

- If you had to write a business case for investing in this new initiative, what communication style and tone would you use?
- How might financial concepts play into a communication strategy?
- What would be the probable consequences of your choosing various forms of communication?

Stanley reviewed the events of the past weeks and the impact on the company and wrote down a few high-level goals so that he could continue to lead a change initiative owned and shared with the other departments:

- Sustain the budding partnership with marketing.
- Ensure the successful transfer of trainees into a processing module.
- Lengthen the lead time for acquiring needed resources.
- Effectively coordinate efforts with IT to ensure a smooth integration of programming changes.
- Deal with sagging morale.
- Repair quality control issues.

Review

The preceding case study illustrates many of the topics that are discussed in more detail throughout the remainder of this book. Before we move on, let's go over some potential actions and strategies. Don't worry; you'll have an opportunity to check your answers to the questions before moving on to an assessment inventory.

You might also be pleased to know that implementing these actions and improving communication had an immediate positive impact on Pogo's work environment and the bottom line. Even Norma, the beleaguered Pogo trainer, was able to provide marketing material to her students that enabled them to understand the big picture, and budget adjustments enabled her to expand the facility and creatively allocate more computer time to each trainee.

After the stress and disharmony were somewhat abated, a more relaxed Tim congratulated Stanley. Eventually Tim was named to coordinate a brand-new overseas division of the company, and he took Stanley along. On the way to Frankfurt, in first-class, they sipped some champagne.

Suggested Approaches to Question Set One: Financial Skills

Estimated expenditures for next year's training need to account for both fixed and variable costs.

The budget needs to include, at a minimum, costs for staff salaries proportionate to time spent in training activities, equipment, supplies, and apportioned rent, as well as expenses that vary according to the amount of business transacted, such as phone, travel, and ad hoc training expenses.

Accurately forecasting training expenditures will also depend on estimates of turnover and estimates of claim volumes from new business clients. Thus, in order to demonstrate business acumen, Tim and Stanley must be able to develop a budget and forecast training expenditures based on potential trends. This presents a great opportunity for Stanley to partner with the finance department or with Tim to get some ideas and coaching.

In analyzing their needs for next year, they would do well to build collaborative support with the marketing manager, Ann, and to get input from all their other internal clients. If they successfully leverage their partnership with Ann, they could build a business case for additional financial resources and set a workable course for effectively guiding and controlling finances.

Suggested Approaches to Question Set Two: Partnering Skills

The central issues affecting outcomes appear to be the rift between marketing and operations, a reactive rather than a proactive approach to dealing with problems, a short-term rather than a long-term planning perspective, and a narrow rather than a systems approach to running operations. Demonstrating business acumen in resolving issues would result in a sound strategy positively supporting Tim's ability to deliver desired outcomes.

In coordinating and integrating the efforts of operations and marketing, Tim should consider partnering with Ann. Their mutual interests could be served by working together to deliver outcomes that retain current customers as well as attract new business. By first taking steps to resolve their conflicts, Tim demonstrated his willingness to reestablish or build trust. Taking additional concrete steps to foster cooperation and collaboration would enable both managers to leverage and solidify their partnership.

Tim demonstrated his ability to drive results when he identified an opportunity for improvement. By partnering with Ann, for instance, he can articulate new, clear, and measurable goals with her and the management staff. The consequence of these actions would likely be a commitment to solutions that improves team and organizational performance for both operations and marketing.

Suggested Approaches to Question Set Three: Communication Skills

To demonstrate a vital foundational skill—communicating effectively—Stanley should take the following key actions: develop and articulate the business case for change, identify the proper mode and form of communication, and use the right style and tone in communicating this initiative. Incorporating financial concepts, such as return on investment (ROI) and operating efficiency, adds substance to communications; it gauges measurable progress, provides feedback to employees, and generally influences stakeholders to commit to attaining desired outcomes. Whatever form of communication Stanley uses in driving results, he should take into account his purpose, the audience, and the desired effect. Communicating effectively, whether by phone, e-mail, or any other mode of communication, needs to be developed as a core competency.

Over the life of this project, Stanley can improve the chances for a successful initiative if he, along with Norma and Harriet, strives to model personal development. When managers identify learning opportunities and embody relevant competencies, they demonstrate their commitment to changing outcomes. Both Stanley and Tim can visit and attend training classes.

Networking and partnering is a competency Stanley can use to leverage the communication strategy in a way that engenders confidence and attains desired results. To avoid a potential role conflict with Tim in carrying out this strategy, however, Stanley has to be sure to coordinate his actions and partner, or collaborate, with Tim throughout the course of this initiative.

Assessment

Exhibit I.1 contains a form for you to use to assess your current level of business acumen—your financial skills, partnering skills, and communication skills. Knowing how your answers stacked up against the suggested approaches to the case study questions will help you in completing this inventory. Here are some specific directions to guide you through it.

Assessment Directions

1. When making your responses, consider not only your own perceptions but also how your manager would rate your level of competency for each listed skill. Then place a checkmark in the box that best describes your perceived level of competency: *novice, proficient,* or *expert.* (Hint: How well did you identify and apply key actions in your answers to the case study questions?)

2. Use the "Go to Chapter" column as a guide to material that will help you explore developmental needs and further enhance your skills. For example, a pattern of "novice" ratings in the "financial skills" section of the assessment suggests that you need to brush up in this area.

Exhibit I.1. Business Acumen Self-Assessment

Rating	Definition
Novice	You are able to apply basic skills but need assistance or additional instructional resources to do the job.
Proficient	You are able to apply advanced skills but may need some assistance or additional instructional resources to do the job.
Expert	You are able to apply skills confidently and do not need assistance or additional instructional resources to do the job.

	Self-Assessment Ratings			
Skills	**Novice**	**Proficient**	**Expert**	**Go to Chapter**
Financial skills				
· Working knowledge of business financial terminology				1
· Ability to read and understand financial statements and analyses				1

Exhibit I.1. Business Acumen Self-Assessment, Cont'd

	Self-Assessment Ratings			
Skills	**Novice**	**Proficient**	**Expert**	**Go to Chapter**
Financial skills				
· Knowledge of how to perform three types of analyses of financial statements (vertical, horizontal, and ratio)				1
· Knowledge of the different types of budgets				2
· Ability to manage budget variances				2
· Knowledge of how to prepare break-even analyses				2
· Experience with return on investment (ROI) techniques				3
· Ability to decide between hiring and outsourcing				4
· Ability to write a request for a proposal				4
· Ability to select vendors for a project				4
Partnering skills				
· Ability to sell the value of your group's services to other parts of the organization				5
· Knowledge of how to conduct a stakeholder analysis				5
· Knowledge of how to influence stakeholders				5
· Ability to build partnerships with other parts of the organization				6
· Ability to build strong relationships with people on your team				7

Exhibit I.1. Business Acumen Self-Assessment, Cont'd

Skills	Self-Assessment Ratings			
	Novice	Proficient	Expert	Go to Chapter
· Knowledge of performance management methods				7
· Ability to develop performance-based solutions				8
Communication skills				
· Ability to write effective business communications (for example, memos, letters, e-mails)				9
· Ability to write business cases				10
· Ability to write reports				11
· Ability to write business presentations				12
· Ability to deliver business presentations				12

Now that you have assessed your business acumen using this model, let's begin with a focus on financial basics.

Section 1
Financial Skills

A Primer on Financial Basics

LEARNING PROFESSIONALS who lack basic business skills are at a distinct disadvantage. A poor comprehension of business issues and the complexities associated with the business world prevents us from seeing how our efforts fit into the organization or how they are valued. It is time we took control of our situation and answered the call to action: the call to demonstrate the impact learning can have on the business. Financial and nonfinancial performance measures are increasingly sought after by senior management, and this places training and development (T&D) professionals and their departments on the cusp of playing a crucial role in helping their organizations meet their objectives. Learning professionals are being asked to contribute directly to attaining strategic objectives, and to translate these objectives into learning-oriented solutions. To meet this challenge and opportunity as a learning professional you must

1. Gain the business knowledge to serve your organization adequately.

2. Know the business knowledge you need to know.

3. Know the information relevant to your efforts.

4. Know how to communicate the right information to those requiring that information.

As a learning professional you do not need to be fluent in the language of business, but if your T&D work is to be effective, it is essential that you be able to accomplish three things when speaking with your business associates. You should be able to

- Discuss how your training solutions affect the business results of your T&D department.

- Understand the implications and impacts your training efforts have for the whole organization.

- Communicate outcomes to the right people, in the right way, and at the right time.

Business can be a complicated and even confusing topic, especially for those not required to answer questions about operational and strategic business issues in the past. Training and development is one of those areas that traditionally has not had to account for its actions and activities. This situation did not leverage the real capacity of T&D. Today there is more opportunity for T&D to contribute to an organization's focus on the bottom line and a strategic vision.

The days when T&D was a passive voice are over. Every dollar budgeted and spent in a company must be accounted for in some way. This requires that all employees, including T&D people, have a clear understanding of business objectives and be capable of proposing and reporting investment initiatives. T&D now has to justify the resources it requires and must communicate its needs and results in a clear and concise way that is understood by the decision makers in the company. This is an opportunity for T&D to become a real strategic business partner to all parts of the organization. It is important for learning professionals to understand the term *strategic business partner,* as it requires a shift in thinking. Rather than maintaining the traditional, passive, functional role of waiting for requests to develop training solutions, T&D must align itself as an operational partner to other departments, becoming a proactive organizational member pursuing internal opportunities to improve the organization and propel it toward its goals.

The intent of this chapter is to prepare you to gain knowledge and an understanding of the essential principles in business financial management. What you need to know, understand, and communicate to decision makers is crucial to your efforts to build a lasting and results-driven learning culture. In short, this chapter is designed to encourage you to start talking the language of business.

In this chapter you will learn

- Why T&D needs to understand business
- The vocabulary used daily in business
- The types of financial statements and analyses
- How to conduct an analysis of your financial results

This is information you need to know to communicate effectively with peers and senior managers.

Why T&D Needs to Understand Business

Management is focused on results and performance, and T&D has an opportunity to support this focus. Only in recent years has T&D been given the opportunity to step up and contribute in a leadership role. Previously, management did not recognize or understand how to leverage the capability existing within T&D. The work of T&D was used to support the integration of new employees or to meet employee job skill development needs. Performance was never seen as part of training's focus or responsibility. But these perceptions are changing. Companies are under increasing pressure from shareholders who seek accountability for every dollar invested in the organization. The training community must prove that employee development is directly correlated with organizational performance.

Management's focus is to ensure the company maximizes profits through sound strategic decisions and improved performance. In managers' minds training is about making employees knowledgeable about immediate job requirements as quickly as possible. Any other skill or ability not directly related to the organization's objectives is considered inessential. This attitude continues to exist, but it is slowly changing as T&D proves its worth by linking its efforts directly to business results.

T&D has an opportunity to be an integral part of the new business imperatives for organizations. Improved performance is at the center of every business decision, and employee performance is seen by management as a way to develop a sustainable competitive advantage. In many organizations learning and performance is now either at the top of management's to-do list or is gaining attention.

Business accountability is critical, and the impact of every business investment is witnessed through the company's financial statements. Why are financial statements so important? Because they are the universally accepted method by which management can show tangible and proven results. These results, when described in an acceptable financial context, reflect the direct relationship between the inputs and the eventual outputs of a given event or investment.

▶ T&D'S GROWING ROLE AT A SOFTWARE DEVELOPMENT COMPANY

VEHD Inc. is a (fictitious) software development company that specializes in creating innovative help desk tutorials and assessment systems. VEHD has seen exponential growth and gained a reputation of being a market innovator. The company has grown from a start-up with a staff of 25 twelve years ago to having 1,000 employees today. Revenues peaked at $195 million four years ago and have been slowly decreasing. Training and development has never been a strong component of the company, as management always tried to hire the skills required. Teresa, CEO of VEHD, is strategically focused and understands market demands. She expects results from her management team and also expects employees to be current in their skills and roles.

Teresa quickly recognized that the company was losing focus and innovative capability. As revenues began declining she held a meeting with her senior management team to better understand what was happening to the company. Adam, the chief financial officer (CFO), did not think it was a result of poor salaries, because they had a generous compensation and benefits package. Eddie, the chief operating officer (COO), said that he felt that employee skills were adequate in the last few years but that recently performance and quality had been decreasing. Teresa knew they were right. She proposed to develop a solution that would incorporate skills improvement, innovation capability, and quality assurance aspects. She turned to Marelene, VEHD's director of learning and performance, and asked her to conduct a needs assessment and skills gap analysis and to submit a proposal that would link the outcomes to the company's objectives.

Marelene accepted the opportunity but faced a dilemma. She and the training department had been responsible solely for skills and job training. Now she was in a position to contribute to the company's objective and prove training's worth, but she did not know where to start, and she wondered what Teresa and the senior management team would want to see.

Marelene was in a quandary. She knew senior management was very serious about getting the company back to the position it was in four years ago, so she was aware that her solution had to meet the company's specific needs. Marelene decided that her next step was to interview the management team members to gather more data on what they expected from her solution.

She met first with Teresa, to learn about her priorities for the company. Teresa stated three critical goals for VEHD to achieve:

1. Be less defensive in sales, increase net profits, and gain back the market share VEHD had lost in the last few years.

2. Identify the key competencies for the essential customer support and sales jobs, and provide training to ensure that all skills were at a standard performance level.

3. Ensure that customers received quality products and proper support and service.

Marelene then met with Adam, the CFO, and learned that he wanted to see that the suggested solution proposed a clear budget and provided specific financial targets and measures to meet the company's needs. Adam was interested in seeing whether Marelene's proposed solution would provide the company with a proper return on investment, increase its net profit, and help it make effective use of the financial resources available. The next person Marelene met with was Eddie, the COO. Eddie's concerns were making sure that operations and production would not be affected by the demands of training, and he wanted to see an increase in efficiency and production output. Eddie also wanted to see more efficient use of equipment and other assets in company operations.

Marelene now felt that she had a starting point. She knew that she had to include result statements that were written with this kind of specificity: "We can expect sales to increase by 15% in 6 months; product defects to decrease by 45% in the next 12 months; customer complaints

to be reduced by 10% in 60 days." She decided to compile this information and returned to her office to begin developing a solution. There were
some issues mentioned by the management team that were new to her,
especially Adam's and Eddie's requests. ◄

The Daily Vocabulary of Business

Business and financial terms are commonplace in every company. It is important
that you learn and understand the basic business terms so you can communicate
clearly and precisely with your peers. As the role of learning and performance
grows and becomes an integrated component for management and its strategic
business decisions, it is essential for learning professionals to possess a fundamental
comprehension of business terminology and be financially literate.

Exhibit 1.1 presents business terms used regularly in companies and also used
in this book (it is not intended to be an exhaustive list, however).

Exhibit 1.1. Common Business and Financial Terms

Account fiduciary	Person or company entrusted with assets owned by another party (beneficiary). The fiduciary is responsible for investing the assets until they are turned over to the beneficiary.
Asset	Anything that can generate cash. Examples are accounts receivable (money that customers owe), inventory (stock or merchandise), equipment (furniture, fixtures, machinery, delivery trucks), and anything else that can generate cash.
Audit	Inspection and verification of financial accounts, records, and accounting procedures.
Balance sheet	Financial statement showing assets on the left side and liabilities on the right. A balance sheet provides an overview of a company's financial position at a given time.
Break-even point	Volume of sales or revenues at which total costs equal total revenues. Sales above this volume generate profits.
Budget	A forecast of revenues, costs, and expenses for a specific period of time, usually a one-year period.
Capacity	Ability to repay a debt.
Capital	Money available to invest out of the total accumulated assets available for production.

Exhibit 1.1. Common Business and Financial Terms, Cont'd

Cash flow	The actual movement of cash. It measures cash inflow minus cash outflow.
Cash flow projection	A forecast of the cash (checks or money orders) a business anticipates receiving and disbursing during the course of a given span of time—frequently a month. It is useful in anticipating the cash position of a business at specific times.
Cost of goods sold	Used interchangeably with *costs* and *COGS,* this is the total cost to produce a specified amount of finished product.
Current ratio	Current assets divided by current liabilities. This ratio should be 1.0 or greater for liquidity. If it drops below 1.0 the ability to pay bills is impaired. If it is greater than 1.0 there is a possibility that assets are not being used efficiently to generate new revenue.
Dept-to-equity	Total debt divided by total owner's investment. This ratio compares amount of assets acquired by debt to amount of assets acquired by owner's funds. If the ratio is greater than 1.0, it means more of the money to acquire assets came from outside sources, and the company needs to monitor its sales level closely to ensure its ability to service this outside debt.
Depreciation	Decrease in the value of equipment from wear and tear and the passage of time. Depreciation on business equipment is generally deductible for tax purposes.
Expense	Any cost. An *expense account* is an account used for travel and entertainment costs (often by salespersons or executives).
Fiscal period	A defined accounting period. The length of the fiscal period may be a month, a quarter, or a year.
Fiscal year	Any twelve-month period used by a company or government as an accounting period.
Fixed cost	Any cost of production that does not vary significantly with the volume of output.
Fixed expense	Any cost not related directly to the production of a product or service. Indirect costs include such things as rent, insurance, basic utilities, and basic telephone service.
Grace period	Time allowed a debtor in which legal action will not be undertaken by the creditor when payment is late.
Gross profit	Sales minus cost of goods sold. The total dollars available to cover general and administrative expenses such as utilities, advertising, rent, and so forth. *Gross profit* is also called *gross margin.*

Exhibit 1.1. Common Business and Financial Terms, Cont'd

Gross profit percentage	Gross profit divided by total sales. The percentage of every dollar earned that can be used to pay general and administrative expenses.
Income and expenses	Accounting motion picture; the inflow versus the outflow of money.
Income statement	Reveals the overall profitability of the company. It displays the total of what the company earns (sales and revenue) less the costs of producing the product (COGS) and the costs of operation (expenses and overhead). It accounts for all expenses.
Liabilities	Accounts payable (money owed to suppliers) plus all current costs of doing business (mortgage payments, insurance, taxes, salaries, utilities, and so forth).
Lien	A legal claim on the property of another party; the property may be sold or applied to payment to satisfy the underlying debt.
Liquidation	Sale of the assets of a business to pay off debts.
List price	Price at which manufacturers recommend retailers sell a product. The list price is often reduced at the point of sale by the retailer to promote sales.
Loss leader	Merchandise sold by a retailer at a loss in order to increase store traffic and sales of other items.
Marginal cost	Additional cost (or lower cost) associated with producing one more (or one less) unit of output.
Market share	A company's share or percentage of customers or potential customers out of the total customers for a product or industry.
Overhead	Business expenses not directly related to a particular good or service produced. Examples are insurance, utilities, and rent.
Preferred lenders	Banks that have a written agreement with the Small Business Administration (SBA) that allows them to make a guaranteed SBA loan without prior SBA approval. Preferred loans have a maximum SBA guarantee of 80 percent. (Call SBA district offices for more information.)
Profit sharing	Compensation arrangement whereby employees receive additional pay or benefits when the company earns or increases profit.
Pro forma	A projection or estimate of what may result in the future from actions in the present; estimate of how the business will turn out if certain assumptions are achieved.

Exhibit 1.1. Common Business and Financial Terms, Cont'd

Profit and loss statement	A detailed earnings statement for the previous full year (if the company is currently in business). Existing businesses are required to show a profit and loss statement for the current period to the date of the balance sheet.
Quota	The quantity of goods of a specific kind that a country permits to be imported without restriction or imposition of additional duties.
Revenues	The income of the company from the sale of its principle product or service.
Spreadsheet	Table of numerical data in which columns and rows are related by formulas.
Working capital	The amount of money a company requires to operate efficiently in the short term.

Marelene did some research on the terminology that her colleagues used during her interviews with them. Not having a financial background she had limited knowledge of net profit and budgets. What worried her more was determining how her solution would increase net profits and how to measure the use of financial resources, as Adam had requested. She also had to address Eddie's need to ensure the efficient use of the company's equipment and other assets.

Her research was fruitful. Marelene discovered the terms she needed to incorporate into her proposal and the measures that would meet the needs of Teresa, Adam, and Eddie. She noted the following as a reminder to herself about what she needed to include in her proposal:

- *Return on investment.* Provide a complete account for the financial requirements for the project. Show the team the returns the company can expect by investing this money, both in financial terms and in intangible benefits.

- *Net profit.* Develop an operating forecast that demonstrates the impact the solution will have on the company's net profit.

- *Return on assets.* Clearly show to Operations how the equipment and assets of the company will improve as employee skills improve. Calculate the financial measure to prove the increase in the use of the assets.

- *Forecasts.* Develop various scenarios of the impact of the proposed solution on VEHD.

- *Budget.* From the most realistic forecast develop a budget for the project.

Marelene also discovered that if she were to do all this effectively she would need to gather the company's financial statements and conduct a proper analysis. But how would she go about doing this? Where would she begin? Analyzing financial statements had never been a requirement for developing training solutions in the past. Marelene decided to set up a meeting with the finance department to learn more about the financial indicators and measures important to management and the organization. Finding the areas where T&D could have an influence would give her a better understanding of the issues affecting the company. She realized that this would also put her in a stronger position when speaking with the management team.

To understand her company's current financial framework and eventually arrive at financial outcome statements to include in her proposal, Marelene had to begin with the basics. Similarly, it is important for you to understand these terms and concepts as you prepare budgets, and it also vital that you demonstrate results and strategic impact in your training proposals.

Types of Financial Statements and Analyses

As I mentioned at the beginning of the chapter, the most tangible method of determining the impact any investment has on a business involves the dreaded F-word—financial statements.

Financial results are reported according to one of two methods, depending on the context in which the results will be used. The financial statements we usually see report historical financial results; these are also the results reported to shareholders in a public company. The financial reports developed for internal use by management are budgets and forecasts, also referred to as *pro forma statements* (or more simply, *pro formas*); they look ahead rather than back.

The budgeting process is a critical step in planning and controlling a company's day-to-day operations. The resulting budgets provide realistic expectations based on specific assumptions. Budgeting is a formal process that matches revenues with expenses in a future fiscal period. Great effort is made to create accurate and detailed budgets that are fully aligned with the strategic goals of the organization.

A financial forecast is not as restrictive as a budget. Forecasts are used before, during, and even the after the budgeting process. Both financial documents let management look at the future financial performance of the company. What a forecast offers over a budget is flexibility. Management can create a variety of these future scenarios without being restricted to limitations or ensuring that future revenues match with future expenses. These scenarios provide managers with a better understanding of the ways internal and external factors may affect the company.

Financial forecasts and budgets are popular tools with management as they provide justification for undertaking major investments and activities. I will discuss budgets and forecasts in more detail in Chapter Two.

Financial statements are at the heart of companies' reporting process. They provide the information you require to understand past performance. Through an analysis of the financial data reported you will gain a better appreciation of how your efforts affect the company's results. These financial statements are the basis for all financial and many nonfinancial decisions:

- Income statement
- Balance sheet
- Cash flow statement

Whether you are looking at historical financial performance or are building your budgets and forecasts, the structures of the statements are identical.

Let's look at each one in more detail.

Income Statement

It is important that learning professionals understand the components of the *income statement.* Any training activity will have an impact in some way on the results presented in the company's income statement as well as in a T&D income statement. The income statement is important as the sole indicator of profitability. Exhibit 1.2 illustrates the typical contents of an income statement.

The income statement, also referred to as the *operating statement,* is a record of a company's earnings or losses for a specific period. The purpose of the income statement is to summarize the operating activities of the company for a specific period of time. It shows all the money the company earned (sales or revenues) and all the

Exhibit 1.2. Sample Income Statement Format

Revenue

The proceeds that come from sales to customers.

Cost of Goods Sold

An expense that reflects the cost of the product or good that generates revenue. For example, if a loaf of bread costs 50 cents to make, then COGS is 50 cents.

Gross Margin

Also called gross profit, this is revenue minus COGS.

Operating Expenses

Any expense that doesn't fit under COGS such as administration and marketing expenses.

Net Income before Interest and Tax

Net income before taking interest and income tax expenses into account.

Interest Expense

The payments made on the company's outstanding debt.

Income Tax Expense

The amount payable to the federal and state governments.

Net Income

The final profit after deducting all expenses from revenue.

Source: Investopedia, 2006c.

money the company spent (costs and expenses) during this period. The difference between these two totals is the company's net profit (also called *net income* or *net earnings*) for the period. The income statement is prepared in a standardized style. A sample income statement for VEHD is shown in Table 1.1.

Table 1.1. VEHD Income Statement for Fiscal Years 2003 and 2004 ($000)

	2004	2003
Revenue or sales	$167,000	$185,000
Less: cost of goods sold	(60,000)	(66,000)
Gross profit on sales	**107,000**	**119,000**
Less: general operating expenses	(38,000)	(45,000)
Less: depreciation expense	(12,000)	(14,000)
Operating income	**57,000**	**60,000**
Other income	12,000	15,000
Earnings before interest and tax (EBIT)	**69,000**	**75,000**
Less interest expense	(20,000)	(22,000)
Less taxes	(15,000)	(18,000)
Net income (available earnings for dividends)	**34,000**	**35,000**
Less preferred and/or common dividends paid	(5,000)	(9,000)
Retained earnings	**29,000**	**26,000**

VEHD's income statement shows its revenue and expenditures for the fiscal periods of 2003 and 2004. This is the information necessary for you to understand VEHD's profit position.

The first part of the statement shows the business's revenues. This is the dollar amount of sales that the organization has made in the reporting period identified by the organization. (When T&D is viewed as a profit center, a sale for T&D might be, for example, the designing and deploying of a training solution for a business unit.) The revenue shown on the income statement is based on the actual sales. The *gross profit on sales line* shows the difference between the total revenue earned by the company's products less the cost of what it took to produce them. This figure is calculated as follows:

Gross profit on revenue or sales = Revenue or sales − Cost of goods sold.

Cost of goods sold is the cost of producing finished goods and services. Cost of goods sold includes the expense of purchasing raw materials and any labor costs required to produce products. When you subtract the total cost of producing goods and services (cost of goods sold, or COGS) from the revenue generated from selling them (revenue or sales) you arrive at the *gross profit on sales.*

Gross profit on sales reveals the profitability on the core business. Because gross profit is linked directly to the company's core operations, T&D's role is to develop operational learning and performance solutions to help increase the gross profit. Gross profit also reflects management's effectiveness. This is another area where T&D can play an active role in helping management to improve processes and performance.

Inexperienced businesspeople often use the terms *costs* and *expenses* interchangeably, but it is important to note that they do not mean the same thing. Costs are expenditures required to manufacture or produce the company's product or service. For example, if your organization is producing candles, then the wax, wick, and any other item required to complete a candle is considered a cost. An expense, however, is an expenditure not directly related to the creation or production of a product or service. For example, such items as sales salaries and commissions and office salaries and purchases are expenses. This is why the income statement separates COGS from expenses. COGS is usually included only in the income statement of production-oriented organizations. Service-oriented organizations do not generally include a COGS section in their income statement.

> Ron, VEHD's company controller, sat with Marelene to review the income statement. He explained to her that sales in the last twelve months (2004) decreased by $18 million compared to 2003 results. He also quickly pointed out that the cost of goods sold, the cost to produce what was sold, did not decrease as much, only by $6 million. Marelene believed that even though sales decreased significantly the news of the costs decreasing by much less was good news in comparison. Ron quickly reminded her that costs represent financial resources tied up in the purchase, inventory, and production of the goods VEHD is to sell. He contin-

ued on to explain that the costs should decrease by at least the same amount as the sales. Because Marelene was still somewhat perplexed, Ron decided to use the gross profit formula to clarify for her the comparative impact on the company for the two years:

2003: Gross profit = $185,000 – $66,000 = $119,000.
2004: Gross profit = $167,000 – $60,000 = $107,000.
Reduction in gross profit: $119,000 – $107,000 = $12 million.

The next section of the income statement shows the organization's operational activities. Referred to as *operating expenses,* it shows the expenses related to the operations and administration of the organization. All of the company's expenses are accounted for, including *paper expenses,* that is, expenses other than out-of-pocket (cash) expenses. The subtotal is the *operating income.*

Operating income is the company's earnings after deducting its cost of goods sold and its general operating expenses. Operating income does not take account of interest expenses or other financing costs. Operating income is particularly important because it is a measure of profitability based on what the company actually does, the goods or services it produces. In other words, it illustrates whether the reason for which the company exists is profitable. Operating income is calculated as follows:

Operating income = Gross profit – General operating expenses.

General operating expenses are normal expenses incurred in the daily operations of the business. Typical items in this category are administration expenses, marketing expenses, salaries, rent, and other relevant operational expenses. General operating expenses are often referred to as *overhead.*

Earnings before interest and taxes (EBIT) is also a common term used by management and external investors. It is the sum of operating and nonoperating income (or loss). As its name indicates, EBIT is a firm's income excluding interest and income tax expenses. EBIT is calculated as follows:

EBIT = Operating income (loss) + (–) Other income (loss).

The company's *net earnings* (also called net income or net profit) figure is also known as the *bottom line.* Net earnings is the amount of profit a company makes after all its expenses and costs are deducted from its revenues. When a company fails to make a profit, it then reports a net loss. Net earnings (or loss) is calculated as follows:

Net earnings (loss) = EBIT – Interest expense – Income taxes.

Interest expense refers to the amount of interest a company has paid to its debtors in the current year. *Income taxes* are federal and state taxes based on the amount of income a company generates.

Depending on the company's financial policy, a portion of the net income may be paid to its owners (shareholders). These payments are called *dividends*. The amount remaining after dividends are paid is reinvested in the company for future growth. When no dividends are paid, the total amount is reinvested. The amount reinvested is called *retained earnings.*

The income statement provides management with insights into what monies the company is making and spending. Management must continually improve this performance, and T&D can play an important role in that improvement. Through the income and pro forma statements, learning professionals can better understand the relationship between profitability and performance and use that understanding when developing targeted, performance-oriented learning solutions.

Thinking Like Management

- How can training and development improve the organization's bottom line?

- What is a proper level of investment in training and development?

- What impact will an investment in training and development have on the organization?

Marelene was quick to point out to Ron that the 2004 net income was not too far off the 2003 results, and she wondered why, then, was there so much concern over this result? Ron agreed with her that the 2004 bottom line was reasonable but explained that this result was due to effective management of the operating expenses. He went on to say that even though the bottom-line result was acceptable, the top line, the sales figures, had to be addressed. The company would need to examine how the cost of goods would be affected if sales were to continue to decline. Ron was eager to point out to Marelene that analyzing past financial performance is a reactionary view of what is happening in a company and that results must also be compared against future expectations [as discussed in Chapter Two].

Balance Sheet

A *balance sheet* shows the value of an organization at specific point in time through what it owns (*assets*), what it owes (*liabilities* or *debt*), and what it has invested (*equity*). The reason this form is called a balance sheet is that the assets of the organization (what it owns) must equal, or balance with, the sum of its liabilities (what it owes) and its equity (what it has invested) (see Exhibit 1.3 and Table 1.2):

$$\text{Assets} = \text{Liabilities} = \text{Shareholders' equity.}$$

This also means that the *owners'* or *shareholders' equity* is the net worth of the business—what the business is worth after all the liabilities are cleared. (Shareholders' equity is also called *working capital.*)

$$\text{Assets} - \text{Liabilities} = \text{Shareholders' equity.}$$

Exhibit 1.3. Sample Balance Sheet Format

Assets

Current Assets

Cash, accounts receivable, and other assets that can be converted into cash relatively quickly.

Property and Equipment

Not exclusive to equipment and property, it can be more accurately described as long-term operating assets (less depreciation on these assets).

Other Assets

Anything that doesn't fit in the above categories.

Liabilities and Shareholders' Equity

Current Liabilities

A company's liabilities that will come due within the next 12 months.

Long-Term Liabilities

Debt not maturing in the next 12 months. A good example is outstanding bonds that don't mature for several years.

Stockholders' Equity

Reveals how the remainder of the company's assets are financed, including common and preferred stock, treasury stock, and retained earnings.

Source: Adapted from Investopedia, 2006a.

**Table 1.2. VEHD Balance Sheet for the Period
Ending December 31, 2003 and 2004 ($000)**

	2003	2004
Assets		
Current assets		
Cash and cash equivalents	$10,000	$10,000
Accounts receivable	35,000	30,000
Inventory	25,000	20,000
Total current assets	**70,000**	**60,000**
Fixed assets		
Plant and machinery	$20,000	$20,000
Less depreciation	–12,000	–10,000
Land	8,000	8,000
Notes receivable	2,000	1,500
Total assets	**88,000**	**79,500**
Liabilities and shareholders' equity		
Liabilities		
Current liabilities		
Accounts payable	$20,000	$15,500
Taxes payable	5,000	4,000
Total current liabilities	25,000	19,500
Long-term liabilities		
Long-term bonds issued	15,000	10,000
Total liabilities	**40,000**	**29,500**
Shareholders' equity		
Common stock	$40,000	$40,000
Retained earnings	8,000	10,000
Total shareholders' equity	**48,000**	**50,000**
Liabilities and shareholders' equity	**$88,000**	**$79,500**

The assets of an organization are categorized in two ways: *current assets* and *fixed assets*. Current assets, also referred to as *liquid assets*, are items that the organization can convert to cash without losing value within a period of one year. Simple examples of current assets are actual cash in the bank, product inventory, and accounts receivable. All of these assets are convertible to cash at an equal or greater value within a period of twelve months.

Fixed assets, or *capital assets*, provide the organization with the capacity to carry out its operations effectively. They are not intended to be used for or converted to cash. Fixed assets are items such as equipment and buildings. Organizations are permitted to take account of the decrease in the value of a fixed asset over its predetermined expected useful life (the amount of time that an organization can realize efficient and productive use from the asset). This is called *depreciation*.

An organization's liabilities are also divided into two categories, *current liabilities* and *long-term liabilities*. As with current assets, current liabilities are what an organization owes within a period of one year, whereas long-term liabilities are amounts owed for a period of more than one year. An example of a liability that can fall into both categories is a bank loan. Assume that your organization has an interest-free $100,000 bank loan to be paid back within a five-year period. The current portion of the loan, what is to be paid within the current twelve-month period, is $20,000. The balance, $80,000, is the long-term liability portion.

The last component of the balance sheet is the equity (ownership) section. Shareholders' equity is essentially the sum of the financial investment made in the organization and all retained profits reinvested from previous periods. Reinvested profits (also called retained earnings, as mentioned earlier), are a portion of the net profit appearing at the bottom of the income statement described earlier.

The balance sheet reflects the overall value of the organization. This means that anything that is developed, purchased, and used in the organization will either increase or decrease the value of the organization and this change will be seen in the ending balance sheet.

Thinking Like Management

- How can we reflect the investment in training and development in the balance sheet?

- How has training and development contributed to increasing the value of the organization?

Ron took out the company's comparative balance sheet and began to review it with Marelene. It was clear that she felt intimidated by the statement, and Ron acknowledged to her that the balance sheet is difficult to grasp. Simply put, he explained to Marelene, any investment made in the organization is somehow reflected in the balance sheet. That means that any training directly affecting the company can be seen over time in the balance sheet. For example, if a comprehensive, effective sales training program were to take place, not only would the sales line of the income statement increase but both the cash and accounts receivable sections of the balance sheet would also increase as a result of this more effective salesforce.

Cash Flow Statement

The cash flow statement (the formal accounting name is the *statement of changes in financial position*) is the simplest and most misunderstood financial statement in business. The primary purpose of the cash flow statement is to summarize the sources and uses of the organization's cash during a defined period. Essentially, it answers the questions, Where does the cash come from? and, Where did the cash go?

The cash flow statement is usually divided into three sections (Exhibit 1.4). The first section is the *cash from operations,* which includes the increase or decrease of cash in specific operating activities. The second section, *cash from investing,* is the cash used for the purchase or the disposal of operating equipment or capital assets. The third section is the *cash from financing* and usually includes any borrowings or investments made or the amounts paid to the shareholders and financial lenders. Table 1.3 shows a sample cash flow statement for VEHD.

Exhibit 1.4. Sample Cash Flow Statement Format

Cash from Operations
Cash generated from day-to-day business operations.

Cash from Investing
Cash used for investing in assets, as well as the proceeds from the sale of other businesses, equipment, or other long-term assets.

Cash from Financing
Cash paid or received from issuing and borrowing of funds. This section also includes dividends that are paid to shareholder or investors in the business.

Exhibit 1.4. Sample Cash Flow Statement Format, Cont'd

Net Increase or Decrease in Cash

Increases in cash from previous year will be written normally, and decreases in cash are typically written in (brackets).

Source: Adapted from Investopedia, 2006b.

Table 1.3. VEHD Cash Flow Statement, 2003 ($000)

Operating cash flow	
Net income after tax	$34,000
Depreciation	10,000
Increase in accounts receivable	(5,000)
Increase in inventory	(5,000)
Decrease in accounts payable	4,500
Increase in accrued expenses	0
Total operating cash flow	43,000
Investing cash flow	
Purchase of equipment	0
Decrease in notes receivable	500
Total investing cash flow	500
Financing cash flow	
Increase in long-term bonds payable	(5,000)
Increase in term loan	0
Total financing cash flow	(5,000)
Total cash flow	$38,500
Cash at beginning of period	1,000
Cash at end of period	$39,500

The cash flow statement is constructed using the information from both the income statement and the balance sheet. The first step is to determine operating cash flow. You start with net income and add back any noncash items like depreciation. Then you determine the changes in the balance sheet accounts that are part of the earnings cycle.

The cash flow statement is one of the most important management tools a business can have. Many businesses look to their cash flow statement to tell them what's going on in the business. It tells them how much income they made, whether operations generated cash or used cash, what assets were acquired, and how everything was financed.

CD-ROM RESOURCE

Determining how increases or decreases in assets and liabilities affect your cash flow statement can be complex. Open the "Balance Sheet with Financial Ratios Templates" file on the accompanying CD for a cash flow worksheet that can help you prepare your own cash flow statement.

Thinking Like Management

- What is the actual cash requirement for the training and development initiative?

- Will the training and development initiative be part of the operating or investment activities?

- How will the training and development initiative be financed?

Marelene obtained copies of VEHD's income statement and balance sheet for 2003 and 2004. After reviewing them she began to understand the concerns of the senior management team. On the income statement she saw a number of items of concern, including a dramatic decline in sales and gross profit. She did notice that the company remained in a healthy cash position. She figured that her proposal needed to budget appropriately and that financing the project would not be an issue if the team believed it would improve the company's current situation.

How to Conduct a Financial Analysis

All business professionals have to account for their activities and investments in terms of specific financial results for the organization, and T&D professionals are no longer excluded. The financial outcomes that you will be measured against are

- Revenue
- Profit and loss
- Costs
- Expenses (variable and fixed)
- Net worth
- Cash flow

What Is Financial Analysis?

Financial analysis is the study of a business's operations through the comparison of various financial components. The ability to analyze and understand financial statements has always been one of the most important skills required by business professionals and now it is important to T&D as well.

Sound financial analysis takes the guesswork out of business management and forms the basis for solid decision making. This analysis will also provide you with the knowledge from which to plan your operations and business activities.

Why Conduct a Financial Analysis?

The financial objectives and performance of your company and your department are built upon past performance and future expectations. These objectives generally fall into three categories: profitability, growth, and liquidity.

Profitability

Profitability refers to a company's return on investment and use of assets. Financial analysis helps managers plan for future profitability through the strategic management of resources.

Growth

Growth in the company and in its departments requires careful planning and additional resources and funding. A financial analysis indicates how much cash a company or department needs to support forecast growth.

Liquidity

Liquidity refers to a company's ability to pay its financial commitments. This requires accurate forecasting of cash inflows and outflows. A financial analysis will show you if your liquidity level is right for your operations.

Any financial analysis is designed to track and compare performance in these three areas—both internally from year-to-year and externally, comparing the company's results to industry performance.

It is a company's financial statements that provide insight into expected results and show the actual impact of every investment. The financial data obtained from the balance sheet and income statement provide a detailed analysis of potential outcomes.

Types of Analyses

Analyzing your company's financial statements involves three distinct types of calculations, referred to as

- Vertical analysis
- Horizontal analysis
- Ratio analysis

Vertical analysis

A *vertical analysis* involves expressing each item on the financial statement as a percentage of a common base for a single fiscal period. Revenue or sales are usually used as the common base. In other words, revenue is assigned a value of 100 percent, and each item on the statement is compared to this total. For instance, the formula for a vertical analysis of the cost of goods sold is

$$\frac{\text{Cost of goods sold}}{\text{Sales}} \times 100$$

Using the data on the financial statement provided for VEHD, the cost of goods sold represents the following percentage of sales:

$$\frac{\$60,000}{\$167,000} \times 100 = 35.9\%$$

The resulting percentage can be compared to the percentage for a previous fiscal period to see if there are any significant or unexpected variations. A company or department could also compare its performance to industry standards to see how it is doing against comparable business operations or activities.

Table 1.4 displays a completed vertical analysis for VEHD for fiscal years 2003 and 2004. As you can see, the vertical analysis is completed for every line of the income statement. Going into this level of detail allows management and other company professionals to clearly identify the strengths or weaknesses in operations. When you equip yourself with this knowledge, you are better able to resolve poor areas of performance and further develop your strong points.

Table 1.4. VEHD Income Statement for Fiscal Years 2003 and 2004, Vertical Analysis ($000)

	Variance	Vertical Analysis	2004	Vertical Analysis	2003
Revenue or sales	−9.70%	100.00%	$167,000	100.00%	$185,000
Less: cost of goods sold	0.23	35.90	(60,000)	35.67	(66,000)
Gross profit on sales	**−0.23**	**64.10**	**107,000**	**64.33**	**119,000**
Less: general operating expenses	−8.25	22.75	(38,000)	31.00	(45,000)
Less: depreciation expense	−0.32	7.18	(12,000)	7.50	(14,000)
Operating income	**1.70**	**34.13**	**57,000**	**32.43**	**60,000**
Other income	−0.92	7.18	12,000	8.10	15,000
Earnings before interest and tax (EBIT)	**0.81**	**41.31**	**69,000**	**40.50**	**75,000**
Less interest expense	0.10	12.00	(20,000)	11.90	(22,000)
Less taxes	−0.70	9.00	(15,000)	9.70	(18,000)
Net income (available earnings for dividends)	**1.45**	**20.35**	**34,000**	**18.90**	**35,000**
Less preferred and/or common dividends paid	−1.80	3.00	(5,000)	4.80	(9,000)
Retained earnings	**3.31**	**17.36**	**29,000**	**14.05**	**26,000**

Horizontal analysis (variance analysis)

A *horizontal analysis* is a method of comparing revenues and expenses of the current financial fiscal period with results from a previous period, both in dollar amounts and percentages. This means that you analyze the same financial component for comparable fiscal periods. These calculations may made in terms of actual numbers (such as cost of goods sold, training expenses, or revenues) or ratios (such as debt-to-equity or current ratio). Horizontal analysis is sometimes referred to as a *variance analysis.* You gain a clearer perspective of whether you are headed in the right direction or whether you need to make corrections. (Variance analysis is discussed in greater detail in Chapter Two.)

For example, VEHD's revenues for 2003 were $185 million. In 2004, it had earnings of $167 million. The horizontal, or variance, analysis can reveal such critical increases or decreases in income from one fiscal period to the next. The horizontal analysis for VEHD shows that it had a decrease of $18 million in revenues, or –9.70 percent, from 2003. This requires immediate attention by management to determine what is causing the decrease. Table 1.5 highlights this part of VEHD's horizontal analysis. A horizontal analysis is useful in highlighting trends, both good and bad, which can be either reinforced with future activities or analyzed for improvement.

**Table 1.5. VEHD Revenues for Fiscal Years
2003 and 2004, Horizontal Analysis ($000)**

	2003	2004	$ (+/−)	% (+/−)
Revenues	$185,000	$167,000	−$18,000	−9.70%

The primary advantage to conducting a vertical or horizontal analysis is that it quickly identifies issues that may affect your operation's performance. The major drawback of these types of analyses is that they do not provide sufficient information to allow you to correct the situation identified.

> Marelene quickly realized that there was ample opportunity for T&D to help the company. After speaking with many of her management colleagues recently, she realized there was a concern among them that VEHD's position and competitiveness were slipping against industry rivals and standards. This was a position that Marelene understood how T&D could

address. She also recognized that the improvements against the industry standards would also contribute to the company as a whole, increasing revenues through improved performance and knowledge and reducing production costs through better knowledge and capacity utilization. This would significantly improve the company's gross profit margins and affect its net profit.

Ratio analysis

A *ratio analysis* is the study of the financial position of your company or operation through the numerical relationships between items in the company's financial statements—specifically, the income statement or the balance sheet. Ratios are derived by dividing one financial figure with another. A number of ratios have proven to be of great value in analyzing financial data and results. These ratios are referred to as key business ratios. They reveal specific aspects of profitability, growth, and liquidity. These ratios measure the ability of a company to pay its maturing obligations in the short term, reveal how quickly certain assets can be converted to cash, and analyze profitability and the solvency of the company or operation.

In using ratios it is important that you compare your results properly and perform your calculations the same way each time for consistency and comparability of measurements. A ratio analysis can quickly determine whether your organization or initiative is operating within specific performance criteria or within industry standards. However, you should not use one single ratio to gage the success or failure of your initiative. This is important because operational training initiatives are critical to improving organizational performance. Comparing ratio analyses of historical performance with the forecast results allows you act quickly on issues affecting your department or training initiatives.

Table 1.6 summarizes the major key business ratios, showing how they are calculated and what their purpose is.

Liquidity ratios *Liquidity ratios* provide an analysis of the operation's cash position in relation to its short-term financial obligations. The liquidity ratio of most relevance to T&D is the *current ratio* (see Table 1.6).

The current ratio is driven by balance sheet components. It demonstrates the organization's ability to meet its current (that is, short-term) liabilities from its current (liquid) assets. It is often used by business professionals and management and should be a part of your discussions and vocabulary.

Table 1.6. Ratio Analysis: Evaluation of Operating Results (Analyses of Profitability and Growth)

Ratio Type	Calculation	Purpose	Analysis
Net profit	$\dfrac{\text{Net profit}}{\text{Net sales}}$	To provide the amount of profit the company or department generates compared to its revenues.	Ideally, your ratio will be positive and as high as possible. A low or negative ratio requires further analysis of revenue levels, pricing strategy, and expenses.
Return on assets	$\dfrac{\text{Net profit}}{\text{Total assets}}$	To determine the effective use of all financial resources and assets.	When the ratio is high you are making effective use of financial resources and assets. When the ratio is low you are not investing your financial resources adequately. You should analyze your assets and look to converting them to cash.
Return on investment	$\dfrac{\text{Net profit}}{\text{Shareholders' equity}}$	To determine the effectiveness of the reinvestment of funds into the company, how well those funds are being used.	When the ratio is high the investment or reinvestment is returning acceptable results. When it is low you need to assess whether you are making effective use of your investment dollars.
Current ratio (working capital)	$\dfrac{\text{Current assets}}{\text{Current liabilities}}$	To analyze the company's or department's cash position in relation to its short-term financial obligations analysts use liquidity ratios. The liquidity ratio of most relevance to T&D is the current ratio.	The current ratio (CR) is a single number based on a denominator of 1. The CR must be greater than 1. A high number means that you have sufficient cash available to meet short-term obligations. A low number (or a number less than 1) shows that you are in a poor cash position or maybe insolvent.
Debt-to-equity	$\dfrac{\text{Long-term debt}}{\text{Shareholders' equity}}$	To show the extent to which the organization is financed by external creditors compared to the extent of the internal investment (from reinvestment of funds, owners, and shareholders).	The debt-to-equity (D/E) ratio is based on a denominator of 1. A result that is lower than 1 is seen as indicating a company that is in control and does not have too much debt. A result of more than 1 indicates that the company is leveraged and in an unhealthy financial position.
Debt-to-assets	$\dfrac{\text{Total debt}}{\text{Total assets}}$	To measure the extent to which the organization is using its debt in relation to the assets it owns.	The debt-to-assets ratio is based on a denominator of 1. A result that is lower than 1 is seen as indicating a company that is in control and does not have too much debt. A result of more than 1 indicates that the company is leveraged and in an unhealthy financial position.

In the balance sheet for VEHD in 2003, for example, we see that the company had total current assets of $70 million and current liabilities of $25 million (as shown in Table 1.2). Here is how we arrive at our current ratio result:

Current ratio = Current assets / Current liabilities.
Current Ratio = $70,000 / $25,000.
Current Ratio = 2.8 (meaning the company has $2.80 of
current assets to meet every $1 of current liabilities).

The current ratio is always a single number, and it is based on a denominator of 1. In this example, VEHD has $2.80 of current assets available to pay for every $1 of its current liabilities. This is an important ratio for financial reporting and maintaining credibility with lenders. This places the company in a healthy financial position, as it can meet its immediate financial obligations.

There is no ideal current ratio value. The general rule of thumb is that a company is in a healthier short-term financial position as the ratio increases. From a management perspective, however, a ratio that is too high shows ineffective use or reinvestment of surplus financial resources that could help in the growth of the company.

The *quick ratio* is essentially the same as the current ratio. Often referred to as the *acid test ratio,* it reflects the true liquid cash position of a company by removing certain cash-generating items such as inventory. Financial lenders and creditors consider items such as inventory to be nonsignificant and nonvaluable in the event of a company backrupty.

Debt ratios Debt for many businesses is a normal part of their daily operations. Debt is often perceived as a practical alternative to the organization's cash reserve for financing internal projects. Debt is acquired through external financing sources, that is, by using other people's money and paying a premium called *interest* for that use. When you use debt, you are *leveraging* external funds. This leverage is common when an organization is growing quickly and does not have the cash flow immediately available to maintain its growth or when the economic cycle makes it inexpensive to borrow external funds, allowing the organization to maintain its own cash for future needs.

As appealing as debt financing is for organizations, there is a danger of having too much, of being *overleveraged.* In this position the lenders of the borrowed funds have more control than the actual owners of the organization.

There are two types of debt ratios: the *debt-to-equity* ratio and the *debt-to-asset* ratio. The debt-to-equity ratio compares the extent to which the organization is financed by external creditors to the investment made internally by the organization (reinvestment of funds, owners, and shareholders). Using the financial data from the VEHD balance sheet, this ratio is calculated as follows:

Debt-to-equity ratio = Long-term debt / Shareholders' equity.
Debt-to-equity ratio = $40,000 / $48,000.
Debt-to-equity ratio = 0.84.

The debt-to-assets ratio illustrates the extent to which the assets are financed by external creditors. Again using VEHD data, the formula is as follows:

Debt-to-assets ratio = Total debt / Total assets.
Debt-to-assets ratio = $40,000 / $88,000.
Debt-to-assets ratio = 0.45.

As with the liquidity ratio we analyze these results in relation to the denominator of 1. A result lower than 1 is seen as indicating a company that is in control and does not have too much debt. A result in excess of 1 indicates that the company is in a leveraged position. This means that if the creditors wanted to take control or call back their financing, it would place the company in an unhealthy financial position. So for VEHD's debt-to-equity ratio, we find $0.84 for $1 of total equity and for the debt-to-asset ratio we find $0.45 for every $1 in total assets. In both cases we see that VEHD is in a healthy position and is not overleveraged.

Debt ratios are important for you to understand because T&D is expected to invest in new tools, technologies, and various other assets. Frequently, these assets are acquired through the use of some form of debt financing (including leasing arrangements) that affects the financial results not only of the department but also of the organization.

Thinking Like Management

- How leveraged is T&D?

- How are you financing the T&D assets?

- What proportion of the assets is financed by external creditors?

Marelene was somewhat perplexed by the liquidity ratios she came across. She went to see Ron, the company controller, to get a better handle on how any of these ratios would affect T&D. Ron explained that short-term liquidity is always a concern for the company, as this is the money keeping daily operations going. Any downtime for staff—especially sales, accounts receivable, and customer support staff—would affect revenue generation and collection of funds. In turn a reduction in funds would make it difficult for the company to meet its short-term obligations, such as salaries, payments to suppliers, and overhead costs. What Ron believed would be important for Marelene was the debt-to-asset ratio, as T&D often requires additional assets to conduct training effectively, especially for large initiatives. T&D assets requiring financing in the past had included additional software, training for trainer initiatives, e-learning tools, and specific tools used in one-time training activities. Marelene now had a better understanding of the financial ratios and would investigate further other impacts her decisions would have on the company and her training efforts.

Profitability ratios It is common knowledge that all companies are expected to generate a profit. This is a new concept for those who manage areas traditionally thought of as cost centers, such as T&D, and who are now required to manage such areas as profit centers. The first rule is straightforward—generate as much profit as possible. It is important to note that successful companies are more focused on maintaining or increasing their profitability than on increasing sales. This is called a bottom-line focus (whereas an emphasis on sales would be a top-line focus). Profit is equivalent to oil in an engine. Without the oil the engine would seize and not function. In business a lack of profit over a period of time will seize the company's operation. This is why profitability ratios are used often in business and asked for by management. There are several profitability ratios that you need to be aware of and to understand how to use. These ratios draw their financial data primarily from the income statement.

Net profit ratio The simplest of all of the ratios, the *net profit ratio* provides you with the amount of profit your company or department generates compared to your sales. Using the VEHD income statement figures for 2004 (see Table 1.1), the net profit ratio can be represented as follows:

Net profit ratio = Net profit / Net sales.
Net profit ratio = $34,000,000 / $167,000,000.
Net profit ratio = 0.20 (or 20% of sales).

Return on assets ratio The return on assets (ROA) ratio measures whether the organization is making effective use of its assets (what it owns). The ROA takes the company's net profit (profit before any taxes and interest charges are deducted) and divides it by the total value of its net operating assets. A low ROA number indicates that the organization is making ineffective use of its assets. Again, as with all ratios, you should compare this figure to your past performance and industry expectations. This is how we arrive at this ratio using the VEHD example (see Tables 1.1 and 1.2):

Return on assets ratio = Net profit / Total assets.
Return on assets ratio = $34,000,000 / $79,500,000.
Return on assets ratio = .43 (or a 43% return on assets).

Return on investment (ROI) The term ROI, or *return on investment,* is relatively new to T&D professionals and has become a T&D industry buzzword, but it is not a new term for management, which uses it on a regular basis. ROI can be the common ground for communication between T&D and senior management, because training is expected to deliver tangible results, or *returns* (hence, return on investment). The return on investment formula used in the business world reflects the net profit (income) the company earns in relation to its invested capital. Think about a personal investment that you might hold, such as a mutual fund, government bond, or certificate of deposit. You were told that if you invested say $1,000, you would receive a 5 percent return on that investment. The 5 percent, or $50, would be your ROI. We arrive at the ROI by dividing the net profit ($50) by the initial invested capital ($1,000)—in this example, the ROI is 5 percent. Let's look at VEHD's ROI (see Tables 1.1 and 1.2):

Return on investment ratio = Net profit / Shareholders' equity.
Return on investment ratio = $34,000,000 / $48,000,000.
Return on investment ratio = 0.71 (or a 71% return on the investment).

Analyzing key business ratios provides a lot of information on the performance of your business. In this section we addressed the common ratios that are relevant specifically to the needs of T&D. There are many other ratios that can give you valuable insights into your operations and initiatives. It is recommended that you create your own ratios based on areas of operation you are interested in tracking. A ratio is simply a comparison or relationship between two numbers from your financial results. Look carefully at what you are trying to accomplish and try to determine what it is that you want to know and then develop your own ratios.

The next step is to leverage the three types of financial analyses together. By combining the vertical, horizontal, and ratio analyses you can gain a complete analysis of the performance of your operation. Table 1.7 shows how the three types of analyses can work together for our example, VEHD.

You will also see that Table 1.7 expresses some analyses in terms of percentages. To explain the concepts behind these mathematical relationships, I have been discussing them all as ratios. However, in the business world some of these relationships are traditionally presented as percentages rather than ratios, and Table 1.7 reflects that customary use. So on this table you will see that the results for net profit, return on assets, and return on investment are now expressed as percentages (that is, the ratio has been multiplied by 100). You will see this method used on reports for your own company or department.

Break-even analysis

A break-even analysis lets you determine at what unit level or volume usage your department will cover the cost of developing or acquiring training solutions. Conducting a break-even analysis is a common strategy among business professionals and something you are likely to be asked to do. It is important to be aware of break-even levels as they will determine whether your department should move forward on initiatives or attempt to find other ways to ensure that it covers its costs. We will apply the break-even analysis in Chapter Two, which focuses on budgets.

Review

The role T&D must play in business is more important than ever before. Management recognizes the importance of leveraging the knowledge of employees. Managers are requiring T&D professionals to be more aware of business issues and the impact that learning solutions will have on the company.

For management, training or learning in itself is not what is important. Managers want to see results. These results take the form of improved performance, return on investment, and tangible results—things managers can see on a financial statement. They want to hear about solutions in a language they understand.

The first step in building T&D's creditability is to understand the business and financial language used in your company. Speaking that language will help you to be understood by management and to better understand management's needs. The

Table 1.7. VEHD Evaluation of Operating Results for Fiscal Years 2003 and 2004

Ratio Type	Calculation	2003	2004	% (+/−)
Net profit	$\dfrac{\text{Net profit}}{\text{Net sales}} \times 100$	$\dfrac{\$35,000}{\$185,000} \times 100 = 18.91$	$\dfrac{\$34,000}{\$167,000} \times 100 = 20.35$	+1.44
Return on assets	$\dfrac{\text{Net profit}}{\text{Total assets}} \times 100$	$\dfrac{\$35,000}{\$88,000} \times 100 = 39.77$	$\dfrac{\$34,000}{\$79,500} \times 100 = 42.76$	+2.99
Return on investment	$\dfrac{\text{Net profit}}{\text{Shareholders' equity}} \times 100$	$\dfrac{\$35,000}{\$48,000} \times 100 = 72.92$	$\dfrac{\$34,000}{\$50,000} \times 100 = 68\%$	−4.92
Current ratio (working capital)	$\dfrac{\text{Current assets}}{\text{Current liabilities}}$	$\dfrac{\$70,000}{\$25,000} = 2.80$	$\dfrac{\$60,000}{\$19,500} = 3.08$	+0.28
Debt-to-equity	$\dfrac{\text{Long-term debt}}{\text{Shareholders' equity}}$	$\dfrac{\$40,000}{\$48,000} = 0.83$	$\dfrac{\$29.500}{\$50,000} = 0.59$	−0.24
Debt-to-assets	$\dfrac{\text{Total debt}}{\text{Total assets}}$	$\dfrac{\$15,000}{\$88,000} = 0.17$	$\dfrac{\$10,000}{\$79,500} = 0.12$	−0.05

information you need to improve your company's performance is on the financial statements. Interpreting the results presented on these documents will help you and your T&D department to better identify the concerns and objectives of management. Using the financial analysis tools, you are equipped to identify areas for improvement, develop appropriate solutions, and communicate to management how you are going answer the need at hand.

Review Quiz

1. The training program and e-learning software that a company owns are considered

    _____ A liability.

    _____ Shareholders' equity.

    _____ An asset.

    _____ None of the above.

    _____ All of the above.

2. A company has $1,000,000 of shareholders' equity and $75,000 in liabilities. What are the assets of this company?

    _____ $1,000,000.

    _____ $75,000.

    _____ $900,000.

    _____ None of the above.

3. A company has cash in the bank in the amount of $850,000, inventory worth $50,000, and a building worth $100,000. These are the only assets for the company. The company has liabilities that amount to $925,000. How much is the owners' (shareholders') equity in this company?

    _____ $75,000.

    _____ $1,000,000.

    _____ $925,000.

    _____ None of the above.

4. Which of the following is not an asset?

   ____   A desk.

   ____   A truck.

   ____   Retained earnings.

   ____   None of the above.

   ____   All of the above.

5. Accounts receivable are considered

   ____   A liability.

   ____   A current asset.

   ____   A long-term asset.

   ____   A fixed asset.

6. Common equity includes

   ____   Retained earnings.

   ____   Shareholders' equity.

   ____   Capital surplus.

   ____   All of the above.

7. Long-term liabilities are those that

   ____   Are due in 1 year or more.

   ____   Are due in 5 years or more.

   ____   Are due less than 1 year.

   ____   None of the above.

8. A vertical analysis allows you to

   ____   Analyze the value of the company.

   ____   Determine the company's profitability.

   ____   Compare an item on the income statement with a common base.

   ____   All of the above.

9. Ratio analysis allows you to analyze company performance by

_____ Comparing two or more items from a financial statement.

_____ Determining the variance of results from one period to another.

_____ Determining the cost of goods sold.

_____ None of the above.

10. The purpose of your analyzing the financial data of your company is to

_____ Build credibility for T&D.

_____ Identify problem areas that T&D can address.

_____ Make more effective use of resources.

_____ Determine the impact T&D has made on the company.

_____ All of the above.

Answer Key for Chapter One Review Quiz

1. An asset.

2. None of the above, 1,075,000 (Assets = Liabilities + Shareholders' equity).

3. $75,000 (Assets – Liabilities = Shareholders' equity).

4. Retained earnings.

5. A current asset.

6. All of the above.

7. Are due in 1 year or more.

8. Compare an item on the income statement with a common base.

9. Comparing two or more items from a financial statement.

10. All of the above.

(2)

Understanding
Budgets and Forecasts

IN CHAPTER ONE you learned about the importance of financial components for making better business decisions and communicating with the decision makers in the organization. At VEHD Inc., the hypothetical company we are using as an example, Marelene realized that if training were to be taken seriously she would need to align it with business and strategic considerations and ensure accountability for the eventual results. The problem was that she was always looking at past financial performance and needed to find a way to develop realistic scenarios reflecting where the company was going. If this were possible, she would then be able to apply her newly acquired business analysis skills to the scenarios to view various outcomes before they actually occurred. In this chapter you will learn to develop budgets and forecasts that frame situations and set boundaries around what is required in order to see where your company and department are going.

Budgets and forecasts are essential requirements many businesspeople would like to avoid; however, they play a significant role in helping a company meet its obligations and objectives. Budgeting sets specific boundaries yet is flexible enough to adapt to new opportunities. Forecasting allows management to create a variety of scenarios without having to be tied to rigid boundaries. Successful forecasting is about flexibility.

Businesses learn early that creating effective budgets and forecasts helps them predict how they will perform financially and react to future situations. A properly developed budget and forecasting process provides an estimate of how a company, department, or project will perform financially in the future and the boundaries to be followed to attain that goal. A budget and a forecast should be seen as valued tools and not as a chore. A properly structured budget will help you determine what resources are required, such as people, money, equipment, and time. Your budget will also help you to allocate these resources effectively and deploy them appropriately.

This chapter will help you to overcome the challenges facing today's training professionals. It will provide you with the knowledge to put together useful budgets that meet your specific organizational objectives. This chapter will also explain how to create a variety of scenarios through forecasting and financial analysis techniques to answer the what-if questions asked by management. By the end of this chapter you will have learned about

- The difference between a budget and a forecast
- The types of budgets
- Conducting a variance analysis
- Preparing the budget (bringing it all together)
- Preparing a financial forecast
- Conducting a break-even analysis
- Pricing training courses

The presentation of the budgeting process in this chapter takes the perspective that the T&D department is a profit center. This shift in thinking toward a performance-based approach for T&D is essential if T&D is to gain credibility in performance-based organizations. Even though many organizations still treat their T&D departments as cost centers, senior managers expect all departments to demonstrate performance outcomes in some form. Their primary measures are financial results, preferably profitability. Increasingly, traditional cost-center activities, usually seen as functional responsibilities, are being aligned with operational functions. Accountability for T&D then takes the form of tangible measures acceptable to senior stakeholders in the organization, whether profitability or other tangible performance measures, as discussed in Chapter Three.

The Difference Between a Budget and Forecast

Business professionals often use the terms *budget* and *forecast* interchangeably, and it is easy to see why. People make the assumption that budgets and forecasts are the same because both refer to looking at expected results and resources required for a future period. However, they are independent financial documents that serve managers with related information but in different ways. Every budget tells management, in dollar terms, exactly what resources the company will require and the planned objectives for the upcoming future. A budget represents a realistic scenario allowing for limited changes. As the future period becomes reality the actual results can be compared to the budgeted figures.

A forecast, however, allows managers to develop a variety of scenarios and of possible outcomes for the same budget period. The forecast is flexible in its approach and not dependent on a fixed scenario, as a budget is. You may ask then, why doesn't management always use forecasts rather than budgets? That's because budgets are a commitment on the part of managers to resources and objectives. A forecast is not viewed as a commitment but assists in the development of the budget. It provides managers with a complementary tool in the budgeting process, allowing them to check financial possibilities, and forecasting is also especially useful when unexpected issues arise during a budgeted period.

Traditionally, forecast scenarios include optimistic, pessimistic, and realistic outlooks. This threefold view is usually sufficient for you to come to a proper conclusion about an outcome you would like to see occur. Forecasting helps you to think outside expected results and create hypothetical scenarios. Once you create situations that are realistic possibilities that could affect your budget significantly then you can begin asking the what-if questions. What-ifs are often used to look at negative possibilities. For example, what if one of your department's clients decides to postpone its employee development initiative until the next fiscal period? If this is a significant part of your revenue, then you would see a dramatic impact on your budget. This will cascade down to other costs and expenses that you have planned and committed to, which will lead to a decrease in your overall profitability.

In Chapter One we examined financial statements by following Marelene through her challenges at VEHD. In this chapter, we will continue to follow Marelene and also other learning professionals at VEHD, to learn from the way they grapple with their budget challenges. Some of these challenges involve determining the budget effects of changes that might happen under certain circumstances:

Teresa, VEHD's CEO, asked Marelene, the learning and performance director, to conduct a critical analysis to determine likely scenarios that might negatively affect the next quarter's budget. During their meeting Teresa said, "Marelene, our budgets are based on last year's results, and you know VEHD's clients well. What do you believe is the worst issue that can happen?"

"Well, I do have some reservations about a couple of situations," Marlene replied. "With the introduction of our new products to the market next year, production is under a lot of pressure to deliver the final working product."

"Will these pressures affect T&D?" Teresa asked.

"It is very possible," Marelene answered. "John [the production manager] has already advised us that he may have to push back the equipment and process training program for his department to the next quarter, since the production staff have their hands full trying to resolve other production issues. John said that the schedule change is a 40 percent possibility at this time, but he wanted to let us to know."

Teresa reflected for a moment. Then she said, "Well, that does present a problem since the production department's training requirements amount to $85,000 of the revenues for your department in the next fiscal quarter."

"That's right," agreed Marelene, "and if the program is pushed back that will also affect the purchases we make and have already made to prepare and conduct the training."

Teresa then asked Marelene to create both a forecast and a revised budget for T&D based on the information provided by the production department and to deliver copies to Teresa in the next few days.

Types of Budgets

A budget is often thought of as a document that encompasses all of the organization's financial requirements for at least the near future. Budgets can be completed for as many business activities and in as much detail as you want to see. I won't list all the budgets that you can create but will provide you with an overview of the main areas where budgets are used, how budgets are compiled, and more important, how to use and control budgets. Learning about the budgets presented here will prepare you to compile other budgets as well.

It is important that you understand that budgeting is a widely used process but also that budgets are specific and unique to each company. You should use the following to get an understanding of the budgeting process but obtain further advice from within your planning group about specific company or department approaches.

This chapter describes the following budgets:

- Revenue budget

- Materials cost budget

- Staff budget

- Capital expenditure budget

- Cash flow budget

- Master budget

The first four of these budgets will become parts of the last one, the master budget. Let's look at these various budgets so you can better understand how the T&D budget fits into a company's budgeting process.

Revenue Budget

The revenue budget is the first budget a department will develop. The revenue budget is the basis and the primary driver for all the other budgets. Without revenue (also called *earnings* or *sales*), the company will not have the capacity to operate and fund future growth.

The revenue budget is developed by

- Compiling specific assumptions about expected unit sales of each product for each period

- Determining the expected sales price for each product

- Multiplying the unit expectations by the price (Price × Units [per product]).

The unit sales amount is determined through careful research of market conditions and expected demand from current and potential customers (Table 2.1 shows a sample compilation of expected prices and revenue). As a T&D professional you have close contact with many of your internal customers. Now that your department is a profit center, you will need to forecast the expected demand from these clients for specific learning and performance needs. Contact them to find out how much they are expecting to buy from T&D in the forthcoming budget period.

Table 2.1. Sample Compilation of Expected Prices and Revenue

Item	Price	January Units	February Units	March Units	April Units
Product 1	$300	1,000	1,200	1,500	1,250
Product 2	$250	1,100	1,400	1,400	1,000
Product 3	$400	800	1,000	1,100	1,250

Revenue	January	February	March	April
Product 1	$300,000	$360,000	$450,000	$375,000
Product 2	$275,000	$350,000	$350,000	$250,000
Product 3	$320,000	$400,000	$440,000	$500,000
Total revenue	$895,000	$1,110,000	$1,240,000	$1,125,000

Marelene began to work on her revised budget for next quarter in anticipation of not conducting the production training. She asked George, her training coordinator, to assist her in this effort, as he acquired some informal experience in the budgeting process in his last job. The first thing they look at is T&D's current revenue budget, shown in Table 2.2.

Table 2.2. T&D Current Revenue Budget

Item	January	February	March
No. of participants	300	350	350
Production training	$60	$60	$60
Course development and prep	$25	$25	$25
No. of participants	425	300	325
Marketing training	$50	$50	$50
Course development and prep	$25	$25	$25

Table 2.2. T&D Current Revenue Budget, Cont'd

Item	January	February	March
No. of participants	100	175	125
Finance training	$45	$45	$45
Course development and prep	$20	$20	$20

Total Revenues	January	February	March
Production training	$25,500	$29,750	$29,750
Marketing training	$31,875	$22,500	$24,375
Finance training	$6,500	$11,375	$8,125
Total	$63,875	$63,625	$62,250

George began to revise the budget based on the worst-case scenario as stated by John—that T&D would have to put off the production training to the end of this quarter (March); he made changes to reflect the new reality of having no production department training in the first two months of the year, as shown in Table 2.3.

Table 2.3. T&D Revised Revenue Budget

Item	January	February	March
No. of participants	—	—	300
Production training	$—	$—	$60
Course development and prep	$—	$—	$25
No. of participants	425	300	325
Marketing training	$50	$50	$50
Course development and prep	$25	$25	$25
No. of participants	100	175	125
Finance training	$45	$45	$45
Course development and prep	$20	$20	$20

Continued

Table 2.3. T&D Revised Revenue Budget, Cont'd

Total revenues	January	February	March
Production training	$—	$—	$25,500
Marketing training	$31,875	$22,500	$24,375
Finance training	$6,500	$11,375	$8,125
Total	$38,375	$33,875	$58,000

Creating a revenue budget can be easy.

CD-ROM RESOURCE

Open the "Master Budget Templates" file on your CD, and then click on the "Revenue Budget" tab. Any changes you make to prices or units on this worksheet will change the budget projection so you can test your own figures in easy steps.

Materials Cost Budget

The materials cost budget is a normal part of the sourcing external materials requirements for the deployment of a training initiative. T&D may need such items as course materials, a rented location, software, and examination materials, and it may need to purchase items from external vendors. Once you have your T&D revenue projections, you can proceed to determine your materials requirements to meet the forecast demand.

At this point you will want to research and speak with suppliers and potential training vendors to determine that the quality of the materials supplied and services to be provided will meet your budget requirements and to determine what you will be paying. You will construct a budget similar to the one George constructs in the following case example.

George realized that the possible change in plans will affect the department materials budget. He sat back for the moment and decided that he would need to look first at the current materials budget for the production training initiative (Table 2.4).

Table 2.4. T&D Materials Cost Budget if Training Begins as Originally Planned

	January	February	March
No. of participants	300	350	350
No. of days	15	18	18
No. of facilitators	3	6	6
Training material @ $25 per participant	$7,500 (300 × $25)	$8,750 (350 × $25)	$8,750 (350 × $25)
Assessment costs	$4,000	$5,000	$5,000
Delivery costs @ $600 per day	$9,000 (15 × $600)	$10,800 (18 × $600)	$10,800 (18 × $600)
Total	$20,500	$24,550	$24,550

After analyzing this materials budget he decided to be cautious. He would revise it, but he would maintain some of the costs in the event the production training takes place. There was still a 60 percent chance that the training would happen as first scheduled, and it would not be wise on his part to reduce all of the costs. Also, he was facing some fixed expenses that would be incurred anyway, as shown in Table 2.5.

Table 2.5. T&D Materials Cost Budget if Training Begins at End of Quarter

	January	February	March
No. of participants	—	—	300
No. of days	15	18	15
No. of facilitators	—	—	3
Training material @ $25 per participant	—	—	$7,500 (300 × $25)
Assessment costs	$—	$5,000	$4,000
Delivery costs @ $600 per day	$9,000 (15 × $600)	$10,800 (18 × $600)	$9,000 (15 × $600)
Total	$9,000	$15,800	$13,000

CD-ROM RESOURCE

Open the "Master Budget Templates" file on your CD, and then click on the "Materials Cost Budget" tab. Any change you make to price or units on this worksheet will change the projection in one easy step. (A red dot in the upper right-hand corner of a cell indicates an attached comment. Place your cursor on the dot to read this helpful tip, or use the View > Comments function to see all comments at once.)

Staff Budget

A staff budget reflects the compensation required to staff the T&D department and to meet the needs of the clients as forecast in the revenue budget. Once you determine how many people are needed to operate efficiently, you can then budget the staff costs.

George realized that if the production training was postponed until the next quarter he would need to review the department staff budget. He worked diligently on this review and came to realize that the excess capacity of the trainers who were to be used in the production training could be allocated to other training areas. As a result, the budget did not have to be revised but remained as originally planned (see Table 2.6).

Table 2.6. T&D Staff Budget

	January	February	March
Salaries: administration	$7,500	$9,000	$9,000
Salaries: training	50,000	50,000	50,000
Employee benefits	1,500	1,750	1,750
Other related costs	—	—	—
Total	$59,000	$60,750	$60,750

Capital Expenditure Budget

A *capital expenditure* is defined as the purchase of a long-term asset, such as equipment or facilities the organization needs to function efficiently. Some examples of capital expenditures in training are the purchase of computer equipment for an e-learning deployment, of training software for the staff, and of office furniture.

Before you can prepare a capital expenditure budget, you will have to complete the revenue and any other related budgets. These budgets will suggest what capital assets you need to remedy any specific lack of resources to meet demand at a particular time. The capital expenditure budget will also prepare you to arrange for additional financing if required. VEHD's capital budget for training and development is shown in Table 2.7.

Table 2.7. T&D Capital Expenditure Budget

	January	February	March
Computer equipment (purchase)	$35,000	—	—
Training simulation software (purchase)	—	$15,000	—
Office equipment for staff	$15,000	—	—
Expansion of facilities	—	—	$64,000
Total capital expenditure	$50,000	$15,000	$64,000

Cash Flow Budget

The cash flow budget is a document that links the master budget to all the other budgets. As described in Chapter One, the cash flow statement looks at the actual use of the company's cash. The purpose of the cash flow budget is exactly the same, except that it looks at the expected use of cash in the future.

The cash that you expect to receive, as stated in the revenue budget, is your *cash inflow.* The expected *cash outflow* comes directly from all the expenditure budgets that are to be compiled into the master budget. Table 2.8 is an example of a cash flow budget.

Table 2.8. Sample Current Cash Flow Budget

	January	February	March
Income			
Sales	$3,000	$2,000	$3,000
Other income	1,000	500	500
Total income for the month	$4,000	$2,500	$3,500
Payments			
Creditors	$1,000	$3,000	$1,000
Other payments	500	1,000	500
Purchase/hire of fixed assets	2,000	500	—
Total payments for the month	$3,500	$4,500	$1,500
Bank accounts			
Opening balance at month's start	$1,000	$1,500	$(500)
Plus total income for the month	4,000	2,500	3,500
Less total payments for the month	3,500	4,500	1,500
Balance at month's end	$1,500	$(500)	$1,500

The importance of the cash flow budget should not be underestimated. Without the appropriate cash flow it will be impossible for your organization to attain its objectives. It is essential that you support the cash flow requirements so that

- Lack of cash does not place any stress on current operations or planned events.

- Sufficient cash is available to support upcoming needs.

- Sufficient cash is available to provide liquidity for unexpected situations.

- Financing arrangements can be made in advance if there will be insufficient cash available later.

CD-ROM RESOURCE

Open the "Master Budget Templates" file on your CD, and then click on the "Cash Flow Budget" tab. Modify this worksheet to analyze your specific needs.

Master Budget

Once you have completed the revenue and the expenditure budgets and determined your cash flow requirements the next step is to bring all your budget information together into one complete budget. This document is referred to as the *master budget*. The master budget is composed of many other budgets that address specific activities and functions within the company. This approach makes the budgeting process more manageable than it would otherwise be. Once these budgets of limited scope are created they can be compiled into the all-inclusive master budget. A projected balance sheet can also be created to show your business's financial position at the end of the budgeted period.

George was not too worried. If the production department did postpone its training until the next quarter he would be prepared with the new master budget he had created. There weren't many changes, but in the first quarter of the T&D master budget, the department did see a decrease in revenues.

CD-ROM RESOURCE

Open the "Master Budget Templates" file on your CD, and then click on the "Master Budget" tab. Once again, use this worksheet to test your own figures quickly and easily.

Conducting a Variance Analysis

Without some comparison or analysis, completed budgets are not all that useful. Once you put your budgets into practice, it is more than likely that your department's budgeted figures will not be the same as the actual figures it obtains. Conducting a *variance analysis* is one of the simplest ways of determining how a budget compares to the actual results. By comparing budgeted results against the real results you will

- Gain a good idea of how your expectations compare to reality.

- Be able to analyze the reasons why the results do not match.

- Have the opportunity to make the appropriate corrections or find the solutions required to get back on track.

Simply put, a variance analysis is a comparison of the financial estimates that you budgeted for a particular period with your department's or project's actual financial results. The difference between the budgeted and the actual amounts is the variance, and it can be a positive or negative amount or it can be zero. Variances can occur for many reasons, including changes in your plan, external factors, or simple calculation errors.

These variances are simple to calculate:

$$\text{Actual figure} - \text{Budgeted figure} = \text{Variance.}$$

Here is an example. The budgeted cost for a specific training project was $25,000. This covered all elements of the project, including the materials, staffing, and capital expenditure budgets. In the process of pulling all this together T&D had to spend an additional $5,000 to make sure the training project was of sufficient quality. This pushed the overall actual cost up to $30,000. Then T&D applied the formula given previously for calculating variances:

$$\$30,000 - \$25,000 = (\$5,000).$$

This variance analysis tells us that the project's budget was insufficient, with the result that there was a $5,000 loss for this project.

A variance analysis is powerful because it shows you the differences between amounts, no matter how small. Once a variance is identified you need to decide whether it is worth acting on. Small differences or differences in certain budgeted items may not be of any significant concern and can be overlooked. There will always be some amount of variance in all figures.

For variances that are significant and have a negative impact on your financial results, especially cash flow, a deeper analysis is needed. You may not be able to act on a past situation, but the analysis will help you to prevent that situation from occurring in the future.

For positive variances you may want to adjust the situation to reflect the new direction that the actual results portray. As a rule a favorable variance in revenue occurs when the actual revenue figure is higher than the budgeted figure and a favorable variance in expenditures occurs when the actual expenditures figure is lower than the budgeted figure. It is usually the negative variances that are investigated in great detail, but it is equally important to further investigate positive variances. If you have an outcome that is significantly more favorable than estimated by the budget then you need to determine why this is the case and what can be done to translate this opportunity into other areas for your department, project, or company.

Preparing the Budget: Bringing It All Together

Figure 2.1 is a graphic illustration of how each of the budgets incorporates into the cash flow budget and the master budget. Even though the cash flow and master budgets are the documents decision makers require, they can not be completed without inputs from the more manageable and specific budgets we have been discussing.

The budget process gives you the ability to effectively allocate the use of your available financial resources. By developing a proper budgeting and forecasting process you will realize more control over your types of investments. It will help you avoid unplanned expenses, overspending, and putting resources in less productive areas and enable you to put more effort into areas that generate proven results. Departmental budgeting processes should involve only those directly involved in the department, with additional input from the individuals responsible for the overall strategic direction of the organization. But for any learning and performance concerns directly affecting other areas of the company, you should involve not only the project leaders but also those directly affected by the outcomes.

Keep in mind that your budget should incorporate a certain amount of flexibility. It is a document that should work for you rather than preventing necessary action. A certain amount of flexibility will permit you to make changes for unforeseen events that may occur. However, this flexibility is necessarily limited as certain elements in the budget are fixed, such as future investments in capital assets

Figure 2.1. Bringing All the Budget Information Together

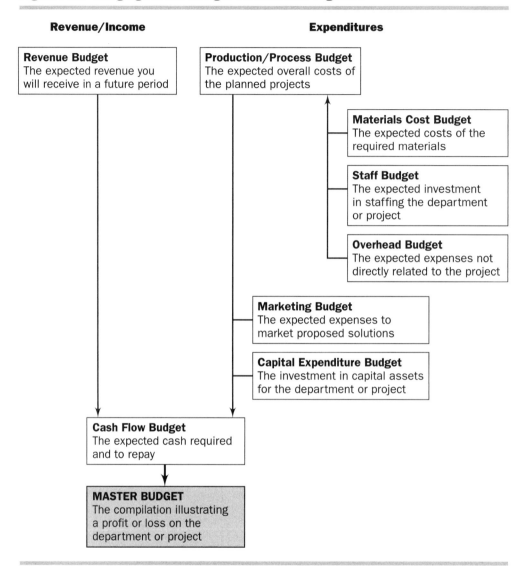

or overhead costs such as electricity and telephones. So it is important for you to, at the minimum, plan for and be able to maintain these fixed costs and expenses. This point where revenue covers fixed expenses is referred to as the *break-even point* (as I discuss in more detail later in this chapter).

Successful budgeters learn early where the limits are on specific areas in their budget that tend to place a ceiling, or an upper limit, on spending. Budgeting works best when very few exceptions are made to these upper limits. Fiscal responsibility involves forming a workable budget and sticking to it as best as possible.

Budgets designed for the short term tend to be relatively accurate. But for longer outlooks accuracy does come into question, and planning for more than one year into the future may require some thought and adjustments as you approach the period in question. For example, let say your company's chief operating officer (COO) approaches you to begin planning a major training program he would like to see implemented in the next twelve to eighteen months. It is possible to develop a budget for this program, but unexpected issues may occur, such as a decline in market conditions and thus of sales ten months from now. This will affect the number of employees to be trained as well as other training costs and expenses.

There will always be unexpected events that can drastically change the priorities of a company or an individual. Without having some flexibility in your budgeting process you will not be able to react to these events and reallocate financial resources as needed to other areas.

Preparing a Financial Forecast

Financial forecasting is one of the more intimidating tasks that all business professionals face, but it is especially overwhelming for those who have not experienced it before. A set of financial forecasts based on a set of possible scenarios helps you to foresee what could happen in a future period of time under various circumstance. As I stated earlier in this chapter, a forecast is more flexible than a budget, and the sets of scenarios managers create generally represent pessimistic, realistic, and optimistic outlooks.

Inexperienced business professionals do not believe that you can forecast business outcomes. They argue that you cannot predict what will happen because business is constantly changing and you cannot predict unforeseen situations. It is exactly for these reasons that financial forecasting is necessary and relevant, however. Because business is evolving rapidly and because changes occur frequently, forecasting provides a basis for some control and for anticipating what might happen.

A forecast allows you to preview possible specific outcomes through the scenarios you create or expect to occur. Naturally, once a forecast is implemented (as a budget) there will still be some unforeseen issues and circumstances arising, but for the most part you will be sufficiently prepared to minimize them.

Here is an analogy to forecasting. Let's say you wanted to travel across the United States. You know your starting point (New York City) and your destination

(Los Angeles). What you do not know right away is the path you will take to arrive at this destination. So you plan your trip and determine the best path to take. You plan the mode of transportation (your car), how long it will take you to arrive at your destination (this depends on the distance you drive in a day and the stops you will make along the way), what you will require for the trip (food, clothing, money, and so forth), and possible problems that may occur (travel delays, traffic, a flat tire, mechanical issues, and so forth). As a smart traveler, you may even plan for a worst-case scenario. Once you arrive at the destination, you pat yourself on the back for the excellent planning process. There may have been some unforeseen issues during the trip, but your planning (forecast) allowed you to arrive safely and within the parameters you set initially.

Savvy business professionals make every attempt to anticipate, predict, and forecast change before it occurs. Forecasting will also help you to build sound justifications for training efforts, to answer the critical questions that will be asked by management, and to establish numbers that you can use as a benchmark when examining results during and at the completion of the project. Financial forecasting is a proactive management practice. Ask questions like these to prepare accurate financial forecasts:

- What are the critical issues facing our organization for the year we are planning for?
- What are management's expectations and direction for improvement for the period in question?
- How many people will require training this year?
- How many new people will be hired or will require on-the-job training?
- What role does management expect learning and performance to play in the organization's growth?
- What amount does management expect T&D to contribute to the organization's growth?
- What amount is budgeted to T&D, and how will it be allocated across organizational requirements?

These are just some of the questions you will need to ask. You may identify many others that are relevant to your specific requirements. It will also be helpful if you answer some of the questions on the minds of senior management and others who need to ensure that the organization meets its financial and growth expectations.

In Chapter One you learned about the financial statements reflecting actual—that is, past—performance. It is through these financial statements that you can compare the expected performance—set forth in your forecasts and budgets—to the actual results. This variance analysis, as mentioned earlier in the chapter, clearly reveals any deviation, positive or negative, from your initial plans. Chapter One showed you how to calculate financial measures based on the past results, and you can conduct identical analyses using the financial forecasts you develop. You can compare the forecasts to the actual results as they happen, and you can then be prepared to present a more complete picture to those who require the information for making effective decisions.

There are two kinds of financial forecasts and projections: short-term and long-term.

Short-Term Forecasts

Forecasts that cover one year or less are considered short-term. A short-term financial forecast is useful when you are managing daily operations. A variety of financial forecasts are used, but the following are the most common:

- Cash flow
- Revenue
- Profitability
- Balance sheet

These forecasts, among many others, are important tools in overseeing the company's near-term financial requirements. If any of the forecasts carries the most importance it would be cash flow. In the short term the financial position of an organization can place it in a favorable or precarious position. It is important for you to understand the cash flow impact of training initiatives in two ways:

- The impact on the operational issues and demands of the organization
- The impact on the T&D department's budget

Although the short-term cash flow forecast shown in Table 2.9 is simple compared to others you may have come across, it clearly demonstrates the importance of monitoring the short-term liquidity of your T&D department in order to manage your funds well in the coming months. As you can see, this forecast shows an increase in the cash balance over the first four months. Then in month 5 T&D sees a dramatic drop in its cash reserves, but it still has a comfortable cushion.

Table 2.9. Sample Short-Term Cash Flow Forecast

Forecast Cash Flows	Month 1	Month 2	Month 3	Month 4	Month 5
Cash inflow (training budget or other funds) for current year (divided over 12 months)	$90,000	$90,000	$90,000	$90,000	$90,000
Cash outflow (payroll and administration)	45,000	60,000	75,000	75,000	150,000
Cash surplus (need) for current month	45,000	30,000	15,000	15,000	(60,000)
Cash surplus (need) from last month	0	45,000	85,000	115,000	125,000
Revenue earned from internal sales	0	10,000	15,000	10,000	0
Cumulative cash flow	$45,000	$85,000	$115,000	$125,000	$65,000

This T&D department can continue to forecast for the remainder of the year, creating different scenarios—preferably including optimistic, realistic, and pessimistic perspectives. In the short-term cash flow forecast displayed in Table 2.10, the organization determines not only when it will require additional funds to cover what it will pay out but also determines the impact of various investments, in this case forecasting that training will increase productivity by 5 percent. This means that the initial investment of $30,000 will be paid back within six months (with a productivity increase of $31,750 over that period) and that the organization will continue to realize a gain for the remaining six months.

Table 2.10. Sample Short-Term Cash Flow Forecast with Investment Impact Calculation

Forecast Cash Flows	Month 1	Month 2	Month 3	Month 4	Month 5	Month 6
Allocated cash budget for depart-ment for current year (divided over 12 months)	$100,000	$100,000	$100,000	$100,000	$100,000	$100,000
Cash outflow (payroll and administration)	125,000	125,000	100,000	115,000	120,000	160,000
Cash surplus (need) for current month	(25,000)	(25,000)	0	(15,000)	(20,000)	(60,000)
Cash surplus (need) from last month	0	122,500	207,000	307,250	376,250	461,250
Revenue earned from client sales (paid in full)	150,000	90,000	105,000	80,000	100,000	110,000
Productivity increase in terms of cash flow through learning solutions (projected increase of 5% of client sales)	7,500	4,500	5,250	4,000	5,000	5,500
Cost for training solutions (30,000 spread over 3 months)	10,000	10,000	10,000	0	0	0
Cumulative cash flow	$122,500	$207,000	$307,250	$376,250	$461,250	$516,750

Forecasting can be done for every financial statement your organization uses. I recommend that you focus your short-term forecasting on the financial statements that will provide you with the greatest opportunity to develop appropriate scenarios that affect your initiatives.

Long-Term Financial Forecasts

The argument inexperienced businesspeople make about the impossibility of forecasting is often magnified when long-term forecasts are mentioned. They state that if it is difficult to forecast for a period of one year how can you expect to predict for multiple years? Although this argument has gained some momentum in recent years, long-term forecasting helps an organization to gain some stability in the face of constant change and provides it with a clearer business focus and direction.

T&D departments face demands from senior management and organizational stakeholders to deliver more resources to improve performance, develop strategic learning solutions, manage human intellectual property, and account for significant T&D investments. This makes it important for learning professionals to deliver proper long-term financial forecasts answering these critical business questions.

You can create various kinds of long-term financial forecasts with a reasonable degree of accuracy. The more common forecasts that are amenable to a long-term outlook cover the same areas as the short-term forecasts we just looked at:

- Cash flow

- Revenue

- Profitability

- Balance sheet

Long-term forecasts often get a bad rap as a result of the poor information used by those who prepare them. Long-term forecasts are based on certain assumptions and specific research, so if the data you use are flawed, inaccurate, or simply false, then your long-term outlook will also have those faults. It can be only as reliable as the information on which it is based. That said, it is only natural to experience a decline in dependability the further out you forecast, and so you should expect this. The accuracy of your financial forecasts will also largely depend on your organization's industry. For example, a high-technology firm may find that forecasting more than one to two years out is unlikely to be of use. But a company that produces a traditional product may be able to forecast as far as five years into the future. This has several implications for T&D and how you need to forecast to help your organization attain its future direction. Answering questions like these will get you started:

- What is the long-term strategic direction of your organization?
- What are the challenges your organization will have to address in the coming years?
- What skills, abilities, and intellectual capacity does your organization possess to prepare itself to meet these challenges head-on?
- What is your organization lacking to prepare for these challenges?
- What is your organization prepared to invest to develop what it requires to answer these challenges?

Long-term financial forecasts are created in pretty much the same way as short-term forecasts. The difference is that their increased time horizons require greater attention to trends and the other internal and external factors that can greatly influence the accuracy of the projected results. To help make your long-term T&D forecasts accurate, look at

- Historical trends in your organization and its past T&D efforts. Learn from the past failures, and determine what made other efforts a success.
- Internal trends. Interview management colleagues and senior management to identify these trends. Determine what organizational role T&D is expected to play in the coming years.
- External trends and the best learning and performance practices among other organizations and in your industry.

CD-ROM RESOURCE

Open the "Budget Forecast Templates" file on your CD. Using these templates, you can be creative, seeing how your various scenarios are likely to affect your financial outcomes.

Conducting a Break-Even Analysis

The *break-even analysis* is an essential part of a proper profitability analysis, but it is also an analysis that is not always clearly understood. For every project, business, or financial investment, it is important for you to be able to predict what unit volume level you will have to achieve to reach the break-even point (for example, how many participants must be enrolled in a training session to cover its costs). When conducted during the forecasting period, the break-even analysis provides a prediction of where you need to be to make your financial investment viable and whether you are on track to make the profits you need. A break-even analysis also encourages you be critical of costs and expenses, pushing you to find ways to lower expenditures and increase profits.

Break-even is the volume at which all fixed and variable expenses are covered.

A break-even analysis starts with establishing all your fixed (overhead) expenses. To do this right you need to account for all of your direct costs and expenses, even the ones you believe are not directly related to your initiative. Your budgets, when completed properly, will encompass all the upcoming expenses you require to conduct an analysis.

Why is a break-even analysis important for you to understand? Most businesspeople understand this calculation to be fundamental and the minimum achievement needed for any endeavor to be successful. You can be assured that those seeking T&D's accountability will ask about this important measurement.

Defining Break-Even for T&D

In T&D break-even analysis answers the question, How many individuals will need to participate in our initiative in order for our financial investment to begin to pay off?

Let's look at a simple scenario. The T&D department at a company I'll call Euphoria Inc. is planning to design and develop a customer service training program for the company's internal sales and customer support staff. The company is expecting to put all 1,250 of the sales and customer service staff across North America through the training in the next twelve months.

- The *fixed costs* to design, develop, and deliver the training program total $15,000.

- The cost to carry out the training program with its supporting material is $8 per participant (this is a *variable cost*).

- The acceptable *transfer price* charged to the sales and customer service department is $25 per participant.

Determining the Break-Even Point

The first step is to determine what the *contribution margin* (CM) is. The CM is the difference between the variable cost (VC) and the transfer price (or in business terms the *selling price*). Using the Euphoria example this calculation would be as follows:

$$\text{Contribution margin} = \text{Transfer price} - \text{Variable cost.}$$
$$\text{CM} = \$25 - \$8.$$
$$\text{CM} = \$17.$$

The next step is to determine how many employees, in this case from the sales and customer service department, Euphoria's T&D department needs to train to cover the fixed costs (FC) of the training program. To find this we simply divide the fixed costs by the contribution margin, as follows:

$$\text{No. of training participants} = \text{Fixed costs} / \text{Contribution margins.}$$
$$\text{No. of participants} = \$15,000 / \$17.$$
$$\text{No. of participants} = 883.$$

This means that the T&D department requires 883 participants to cover the costs of the training program—this is the break-even point. If more people than this participate, then the T&D department will realize a profit.

If the T&D department knows that company management wants all 1,250 of the sales and customer service staff to go through the training, it can easily determine what its profit will be for the training initiative, as follows:

$$\text{Contribution margin} \times \text{No. of participants} - \text{Fixed costs.}$$
$$\$17 \times 1,250 - \$15,000 = \$6,250.$$

Even for an initiative this simple, T&D can conduct further analysis to see how it can improve this figure or it can look at some what-if scenarios. Questions to ask include these:

- Can we reduce the costs or expenses to lower our break-even point?

- Can we offer the training program to other departments or divisions or to related partners and suppliers?

- What if there is a change in plans and the program ends up with fewer participants? Will this change anything for us and the training program?

Along the way, expenses tend to creep up in both the direct and indirect categories, and you may fall below the break-even participant volume because you think it is lower than it has now become. Make sure that you regularly recalculate and reevaluate your break-even target number.

The Goal Is Profitability

Increasingly, T&D is asked to shift its focus from being a cost center to being a profit center. Training and development departments are now in business to make a profit, and their managers need to understand how to determine the point where costs are covered and profits begin. Knowing your break-even point you can

- Allocate sales and marketing efforts to get your department to the sales volume it needs to have.

- Watch expenses to minimize losses, especially during slow periods. A few really bad months can wipe out much of the previous profit.

- Manage the costs to maximize the bottom line.

Once you have gotten this far in the knowledge of the elements of your business, you are well on your way to success.

Exhibit 2.1 presents a glossary of terms used by businesses when talking about the concepts involved in break-even analysis.

Exhibit 2.1. Glossary of Break-Even Terms

Fixed cost	The sum of all costs and expenses required to produce or develop your product of service
Variable unit cost	Costs that vary directly with the production of one additional unit
Expected unit sales	Number of units of the product projected to be sold over a specific period of time

Exhibit 2.1. Glossary of Break-Even Terms, Cont'd

Unit price	The amount of money charged to the customer for each unit of a product or service
Total variable cost	The product of expected unit sales and variable unit cost (Expected unit sales × Variable unit cost)
Total cost	The sum of the fixed cost and total variable cost for any given level of production (Fixed cost + Total variable cost)
Total revenue	The product of expected unit sales and unit price (Expected unit sales × Unit price)
Profit (or loss)	The monetary gain (or loss) resulting from revenues after subtracting all associated costs (Total revenue − Total costs)
Break-even	Number of units that must be sold in order to produce a profit of 0 (but that will recover all associated costs) (Break-even = Fixed cost / [Unit price − Variable unit cost])

CD-ROM RESOURCE

Open the "Break-Even Template" file on your CD. Any changes you make to price or units on this worksheet will change the projection in one easy step.

Pricing Training Courses

When you are ready to cost out your training plan, you will need to work with your training staff and the department requiring training to figure out the cost of the courses you'll develop in-house and the cost of delivery. You will also want to contact the vendors you have selected as sources of materials, a single course, or full instructional design services in order to get specific amounts for the materials and services you would like to buy from them. Here is how Diane Valenti (2004) describes the process in *Training Budgets Step-by-Step.*

Price Courses You Plan to Outsource Development of or Buy

Contact vendors and describe the course. At minimum, you'll need to be prepared to answer the following questions:

- Who is your target audience (position, size, location, and so forth)?

- What is the course?

- What is the purpose of the course?

- What is the length of the course?

- How do you plan to deliver the course (classroom, WBT, or [other])?

In order to provide you with a more accurate estimate, vendors may ask additional questions, depending on the situation.

For example, if you plan to hire a vendor to develop a three-hour, Web-based course on a proprietary system, the vendor may also need access to any system documentation your organization has. This will help the vendor assess how much additional information will have to be collected to develop the course. In this case, the more information the vendor needs to collect in addition to what's been documented, the higher the cost of the course. Once you've answered the vendor's questions, ask for a rough estimate of the cost.

Price Courses You Plan to Develop In-House

Besides salary costs for in-house training and instructional design staff, you might have additional costs associated with developing courses in-house. These costs could include any of the following:

- Travel for instructional designers to gather information

- The purchase of books or reprints of articles needed to research the course topic

- Course materials, such as binders or videotapes, that must be purchased for a course

- Reproduction of course materials

- Authoring software to build the course

Price Course Delivery

As you price the cost of delivering each course, think about the delivery method chosen, how many sessions you'll offer, and what the potential cost is per session. Costs associated with delivery could include the following:

- Travel for learners to attend the training

- Travel for instructors to deliver the training

- Outside facilitators hired to deliver the training

- Meals or snacks provided with the training

- Facilities, such as hotel rooms, needed to deliver training

- Equipment or software, such as conferencing software, flip charts and markers, to support the course delivery

- Technical support required to support course delivery

- Delivery of course materials

- Administrative costs, such as registration, arranging for facilities, tracking attendance, and so on

- Storage/warehouse space to house training materials

- Upgrade of servers to support Web-delivered training

Source: Valenti, 2004, pp. 98–100.

You will also want to want to include costs associated with the evaluation of the training course.

Review

The one thing that management is concerned with is ensuring that targets are reached, profit is maximized, and costs are accounted for and controlled. The budgeting process helps you to do this effectively for the T&D department.

The budgeting process is often perceived as difficult and time consuming. It does not have to be. When you break the master budget down into smaller, more manageable parts, as discussed here, you can then focus on the areas that require attention and be more precise in determining your department and training needs. This process will also give you a good idea of what you might have to deal with in the future, and it will help you to act appropriately even if something unexpected occurs.

The difficulty with budgets is they are relatively restricted in their flexibility, as they are your commitment, as close to reality as possible, about what will occur. To gain better control of your budget results it is important to regularly compare them to the actual results as they happen. The difference between the budgeted and actual results is called a variance, and comparing these sets of results against each other is a variance analysis. There will always be some variance, but for larger variances control is essential, helping you address critical differences as they occur.

Forecasting is the process of arriving at budgets and developing what-if scenarios for situations that may occur in the future. Forecasts are simply the manipulation of budgeted figures to see what will happen if, say, a major program is cancelled or the company encounters a major disruption in business. Conducting these exercises through a forecast helps you simulate possible situations, no matter how remote they may be.

Understanding how to cost your training will help you price your training services more effectively to other departments, as the goal for many T&D departments is to be a profit center. To come up with program pricing that meets the criterion of producing a profit, you must know the program's break-even point—the point at which T&D has covered all of its costs and any revenue earned above this point is profit.

Budgeting and forecasting do not have to be insurmountable tasks. Begin with simple and relatively small tasks and then incorporate them together. You will not only impress management but also have more control over the outcomes of your department and projects.

Review Quiz

1. A budget is defined as

   _____ A set of different scenarios and a variety of possible outcomes.

   _____ A realistic scenario for a future period allowing for limited changes.

   _____ A flexible approach to financing a company.

   _____ None of the above.

2. A forecast assists in

    ____   Developing the final budget.

    ____   Checking a budget for unexpected issues.

    ____   Creating optimistic, pessimistic, and realistic scenarios.

    ____   All of the above.

3. What budget type(s) will a company or a department develop?

    ____   Revenue budget.

    ____   Materials cost budget.

    ____   Cash flow budget.

    ____   Master budget.

    ____   All of the above.

4. A capital expenditure budget is defined as a budget for

    ____   The purchase a governmental agency plans to make.

    ____   The purchase of short-term assets necessary to function efficiently.

    ____   The purchase of long-term assets necessary to function efficiently.

    ____   Financial health and borrowing needs.

5. It is essential that managers support organizational and departmental cash flow requirements so that

    ____   These requirements do not place any stress on current operations or planned events.

    ____   There is sufficient cash available to support upcoming needs.

    ____   There is sufficient cash available to provide liquidity for unexpected situations.

    ____   Financing arrangements are made in advance if there is insufficient cash available.

    ____   All of the above.

6. The smaller budget documents are compiled into one all-inclusive document called the

_____ Super budget.

_____ Organizational budget.

_____ Financial budget.

_____ Master budget.

7. Conducting a variance analysis allows you to

_____ Compare budgeted figures to actual figures.

_____ Compare cash flow results to financing needs.

_____ Build a budget or a forecast with varied components.

_____ None of the above.

8. By comparing budgeted results to actual results you will be able to

_____ Better determine how your expectations compare to reality.

_____ Analyze the reasons why the results do not match.

_____ Make the appropriate corrections or find the appropriate solutions required to get back on track.

_____ All of the above.

9. A financial forecast differs from a budget because it

_____ Helps managers analyze a past performance by using a variety of possible scenarios.

_____ Helps managers foresee what might happen in a future period by using a variety of possible scenarios.

_____ Is less flexible than a budget.

_____ None of the above.

10. You are launching a training course for your department. If the selling price is $50 per unit, variable cost is $10 per unit, and fixed costs are $20,000, how many participants would you require to break even?

   ____ 750 participants.

   ____ 495 participants.

   ____ 500 participants.

   ____ None of the above.

Answer Key for Chapter Two Review Quiz

1. A realistic scenario for a future period allowing for limited changes.

2. All of the above.

3. All of the above.

4. The purchase of long-term assets necessary to function efficiently.

5. All of the above.

6. Master budget.

7. Compare budgeted figures to actual figures.

8. All of the above.

9. Helps managers foresee what might happen in a future period by using a variety of possible scenarios.

10. 500 participants.

3

Evaluation and Return on Investment
What It Means to Management

GIVEN THE CURRENT COMPETITIVE business environment, it is surprising how many companies still question the value of continuous workplace training. Too often the training investment companies make in their employees is neither adequately measured nor well understood. And for whatever measurements might be in place, T&D is not always held accountable.

Measuring the return on investment (ROI) of training is one way to show management the impact of the knowledge acquired by employees and the value of training investments in financial terms. Training ROI answers the question, For every dollar invested in training, how many dollars does the employer get back?

Measuring other businesses investments requires a simple calculation of total costs and total benefits. Measuring training ROI involves identifying the expected benefits and ensuring that they are in line with the organization's strategic objectives. Regardless of how training is measured, it will not deliver value if it isn't aligned with the organization's overall objectives and strategic direction. An often overlooked component of training measurement is the direct ROI impact on the organization itself.

In this chapter I will explain the fundamental aspects of conducting a training ROI analysis, the impact of training on the organization, what organization managers expect from you to help them make informed T&D decisions, and how to communicate the results of an ROI analysis in order to reinforce the need for T&D. This chapter will explain

- Management's concerns
- The primary evaluation and ROI techniques
- The principle ROI calculations expected by management
- The values that ROI does not address
- An approach to communicating results to management

Management's Concerns

With accountability at the center of all management decisions T&D professionals must clearly identify the critical questions training is to address before proposing or conducting any type of training. For a T&D department to gain real credibility in any organization it must demonstrate results and value for every learning initiative. This is the reason for management's increasingly frequent demand that T&D answer the ROI question.

Many T&D professionals believe that the only way to satisfy management's concerns is to deliver a monetary payback greater than the sum initially invested. It is true that management wants to see a payback on its investment but that payback does not always have to be in a monetary form. For T&D, showing the value of training should begin well before the training itself. And that means T&D professionals need to ask the right questions at the outset. These questions include (but are not limited to) the following:

- What ability or knowledge does the organization need to develop?
- Who needs to be trained?
- What is the objective?
- Is this development best done in-house or by an outsource service?
- Is it really needed?
- What are the critical measures of performance?
- What are the financial implications, in both the short and the long term?

- What are the implications for the organization?
- And ultimately, what results are expected?

The answers to these questions (and others directly related to your specific needs) help T&D and management attain a common understanding and provides a starting point for sound decision making for the organization.

Management is looking for one thing and that is results. Like every other operational and functional activity, T&D must be accountable for meeting the requirements of the organization and delivering solutions that answer management's concerns.

As in the previous chapters, I will use the example of VEHD, a hypothetical software company, to illustrate key concepts.

> Carol, VEHD's vice president of operations, had some concerns about new office productivity software that VEHD itself was using. The organization had invested a significant amount to purchase and customize the software to its specific needs. However, the software tool's promise of increasing productivity was being undercut by employee resistance and lack of adaptability. Carol realized that training could play a major role not only in developing employee skills but also in building acceptance from all levels of users and thus proving that the software was a wise investment.
>
> Carol called Marelene, VEHD's learning and performance director, and explained the situation. After speaking with Teresa, the CEO, about the software introduction, Marelene had been expecting Carol's call. She knew that the training provided by the vendor covered only basic use of the software and was inadequate for what VEHD expected to get out of the software. She believed that the training could succeed with some modification to the existing training modules and the support of the in-house training team. Despite her best efforts to convince the senior managers of these concerns, however, they decided to go with the vendor training module. They said they would consider the possibility of improving the training but that T&D would need to demonstrate some results. Marelene understood their decision. She realized that management did not always see the relevance of training and preferred to allocate financial resources to such direct impact investments as sales, marketing, and production.
>
> Marelene was prepared. Her goal was to focus on getting management to see training as a strategic partner to other operational areas and to the

organization. She knew that if the training demonstrated the results management wanted, the training department would be seen differently. Marelene told Carol that she would need to conduct some simple preliminary assessments to make sure that the final expectation for the training would be met. Carol agreed to meet with Marelene immediately. Marelene knew it would also be essential to speak to other people in the organization, especially those who would be affected by the training solution. She equipped herself by looking at a basic financial review of the organization's past performance and a review of current financial forecasts and learning what was important for management to focus on, especially the financial indicators monitored. She quickly put the questions to be asked together into a form.

After the meeting with Carol, Marelene went back to her office and reviewed the answers she had gathered on a *preassessment form* (Exhibit 3.1):

Exhibit 3.1. Marelene's Completed Preassessment Form

1. What does the organization need to develop?

The training required is to support the implementation and integration of the recently acquired office productivity software. This software is replacing the current archaic semiautomated process, gets all of the employees using one common platform, and helps to fully automate and electronically document the needs of the organization.

2. Who needs to be trained?

The organization expects that all employees will be knowledgeable about and capable of using the new software. This means that a total of 1,000 employees in 10 departments across the country will need to go through the training sessions. There is a particular focus on the departments that are highly dependent on the software. This includes all associated administration departments (accounting, finance, and general administration), sales and marketing, management, and customer support.

3. What is the objective?

The objective of the training program is to create consistency throughout the organization in ability to use a common software platform. People must be capable of using 70% of the tools in the software and must understand the new processes required for proper electronic documenting and archiving of all written communication in the organization.

Exhibit 3.1. Marelene's Completed Preassessment Form, Cont'd

4. Is this training best done in-house or by an outsource service?

It requires a combined effort. The software vendor provided training in the basic use and functionality of the noncustomized software. This gave users a good introduction. However, the software purchased has been modified to our company's needs, and so it is company training in the use of the customized tools along with the new processes in place that is required. We will be doing this with our in-house training staff.

5. What results are expected?

According to Carol, the organization is willing to invest in the training but expects to see tangible results. Management would like to see some evidence of the improvement in work processes and, if possible, a return on the company's training investment. Management trusts T&D's judgment on the selection of measures but these measures must be relevant to the organization. Carol did state that management monitors the effects on bottom-line financial results and nonfinancial indicators such as employee productivity (specific to each department), client satisfaction, and how these results are aligned with departmental and global objectives.

In making this assessment Carol and Marelene put themselves in the mind-set of management; they knew that their final report would have to address these potential concerns of management.

The Primary Evaluation and ROI Techniques

Measuring training's return on investment is one way to show the tangible impact of an employee's acquired knowledge on the organization and on the bottom line.

Return on investment for the learning community is a relatively new concept, because, as mentioned earlier, T&D did not have to be accountable for tangible results in the past. In recent years a number of publications on this important topic have been written by authors such as Donald Kirkpatrick, Harold Stolovich, and Jack Phillips (see the References and Suggested Reading section), to name just a few. All are very credible sources for learning about the measurement and evaluation of training and will provide you with greater detail on this topic. It is important when learning about training evaluation that you maintain an open mind on how it fits within your organization and your specific requirements. Every measurement and evaluation strategy is unique to its situation and the specific training event. Now that T&D is seeking credibility and management is being driven by results, ROI is being seen as one ways to attain both these objectives. It is important to ensure, at a minimum, that learning is applied to the job and that it has some type of impact on the business.

One problem, however, is that the term *return on investment* is being overused. First, it is not necessary to determine ROI in all training evaluations. Second, ROI also can have different meanings for those involved with T&D and for senior management. For T&D, the most important return from training initiatives is the application of learning, whereas for management ROI implies a recovery of all costs plus a monetary surplus justifying the initial investment. A T&D manager's objective is to demonstrate that an investment in training provides a type of return acceptable by the decision makers in the organization.

Before we go any further you need to understand the purpose of evaluating training both as seen by T&D and as seen by management, as these purposes differ greatly. As defined by Elaine Biech in her book *Training for Dummies* (2005), T&D evaluation focuses around "changing or modifying employee behavior, opinions, knowledge, or level of skill. The purpose of evaluation is to determine whether the objective was met and whether these changes have taken place." Management evaluations are focused on improved performance or return on investment. What is important for you to understand is that when you communicate with your management counterparts you need to do so in their language. For T&D, the acquisition and application of skills is crucial; for organizational management, performance and profitability are at the top of the list. What ROI means from management's business perspective is to show results in relation to organizational objectives. When required and possible, a conservative monetary benefit will help in proving the worth of training and also help to build T&D credibility.

In short, there are two meanings of return on investment that are important for you to know. In the T&D community ROI is most commonly used to mean the form of evaluation that allows an organization to find out if a training program has demonstrated some form of payback for the organization. The purpose of ROI in this use is to determine if the monetary value of the results exceeds the cost of the training. The second and lesser known use of an ROI measure demonstrates how an investment in training directly affects the organization's financial results. In this section we will look at both types but it is important to understand that responding to management's concerns is first and foremost. Let's look at each perspective in more detail.

Begin with the End in Mind

Training professionals understand and recognize the five-step ADDIE model; ADDIE stands for *a*nalysis (or *a*ssessment), *d*esign, *d*evelopment, *i*mplementation, and *e*valuation (Figure 3.1). In this model, evaluation is the last step in a five-step process. There are, however, two points that are not always understood about ADDIE. The first is that ADDIE is not meant to be a sequential or step-by-step process; it is a cycle, a continuous process of trying to improve on each step. The second point that is often misunderstood about ADDIE is that even though evaluation appears as the final step, achieving credibility with management requires evaluation to be integrated throughout the cycle (Figure 3.2). Evaluation is an essential process for management, and T&D must adopt the same thinking process. Waiting until the end to see if a training initiative made any type of impact is a waste of the organization's two most valuable resources—time and money. Evaluation should be used throughout, to help every training effort become a success.

Figure 3.1. ADDIE Model

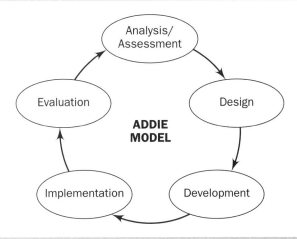

Figure 3.2. ADDIE Model with Evaluation Integrated Throughout

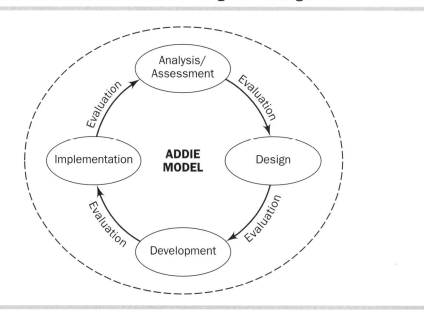

Successful evaluation is based on asking as many questions as possible up front and then focusing on the answers that will help you direct the training initiative to its objective. Asking questions provides clarity and will help you design your training program to attain business results. Some of the questions you will want to ask are these:

- What is the purpose of the training program being designed?
- What results do you plan to achieve?
- What is management expecting from the training?
- How will you know if the results are achieved?

ROI and Evaluation

Analyzing ROI is an important step in the training evaluation process. We will look at this training ROI in more detail later in the chapter. First, let's examine two prominent and widely accepted methodologies for evaluating and measuring the impact of training:

- Kirkpatrick's four levels of evaluation
- Phillips's ROI methodology

Kirkpatrick's four levels of evaluation

Over fifty years ago Donald Kirkpatrick wrote his thesis on the four levels of training evaluation. Prior to Kirkpatrick's model, training evaluations were not given second thought. Kirkpatrick's methodology helped to make them important, and half a century later Kirkpatrick's methodology is more essential than ever. This simple model is widely used in a variety of learning environments. Simply, the levels are defined as follows (also see the summary in Table 3.1).

Level 1: Reactions of the training participants Evaluation at this level measures how participants in a training program react to it. It attempts to answer questions about the participants' perceptions. According to Kirkpatrick every training program should be evaluated at at least this level to foster program improvement. In addition, the participants' reactions have important consequences for their learning (level 2).

Level 2: Evaluation of what participants learned (testing) To assess the amount of learning that has occurred due to a training program, level 2 evaluations often test participants before training (pretests) and after training (posttests). Assessment at this level moves the evaluation beyond learner satisfaction and attempts to assess how far students have advanced in skills and knowledge.

Level 3: Application or transfer of the training to participants' jobs This level measures the change in learners' behavior due to the training program. Evaluating at this level attempts to answer the question, Is the newly acquired skill, knowledge, or attitude being used in the learner's everyday environment? For many trainers this level represents the truest assessment of a program's effectiveness. However, measuring at this level is difficult as it is often impossible to predict when the change in behavior will occur, and thus trainers must make important decisions about when to evaluate, how often to evaluate, and how to evaluate.

Level 4: Measurement and impact of the training on the business Level 4 evaluation attempts to assess training in terms of business results. This is the level that is the focus of management and decision makers in your organization. Frequently thought of as the bottom line, this level measures the success of the program in terms that managers and executives can understand—increased production, improved quality, decreased costs, reduced frequency of accidents, increased sales, or even higher profits or return on investment. From a business and organizational perspective, achieving such results is the overall reason for a training program, yet level 4 results are typically not addressed in evaluations.

Table 3.1. Kirkpatrick's Four Levels of Evaluation

Level	Description
Level 1: React	Obtaining participants' evaluation of the training immediately after the session is complete (*smile sheets*).
Level 2: Learning	Testing participants to determine if they learned what was taught (pre- and posttesting).
Level 3: Application/behavior	Determining whether participants are doing things differently back on the job as a result of the training. Are they applying the knowledge gained?
Level 4: Business impact	Determining how the organization benefits from this new behavior.

The biggest challenge for T&D is overcoming the tendency to use only level 1 or level 2 evaluations. The concept of evaluating the impact of training on the organization (level 4) is seen as unattainable. This perception suggests that the T&D department either is not sufficiently knowledgeable about how to conduct a level 4 evaluation or is uncertain about the true results its solutions offer to the organization. Whatever the case, resolving it is important so that T&D can learn how to evaluate at level 4 and instill confidence in management about T&D's capability.

Overcoming these challenges requires, first, addressing the common misconceptions T&D has about the evaluation process. It is these preconceived notions that limit the impact of the training process, resulting in programs that demonstrate few or no results. Let's address some of these notions:

- *Evaluation is conducted after training is complete.* As mentioned earlier, in fact evaluations must begin before the training is delivered. Identifying business issues the training needs to address, benchmarking, and pretesting are some of the many tools at your disposal to conduct a proper evaluation at this early stage.

- *Level 4 evaluations must show a direct financial impact.* Although financial measures are important (see the later discussion of Phillips's ROI methodology), many other tangible, nonfinancial measures are equally important for demonstrating how well training has affected the organization.

- *Proving training has an impact is about evidence of change.* It is sufficient to show evidence of training results. It is often time consuming and expensive to provide undeniable proof for anything in business.

- *It is all right to have only a general idea of the training need.* T&D must focus on defining the exact problem to address and then develop an appropriate solution. This will lead to sustainable results.

Five concepts for developing effective evaluation

A comprehensive business thinking process is required if T&D is to gain respect and credibility from management. Understanding and integrating the five points that follow will assist you in developing an effective evaluation process and improving training's role in your organization:

Evaluate based on corporate values Your organization has a culture, philosophy, and entrenched values. Do you know what the values are? Have you made attempts to determine what they are? How are you building them into your training solutions? Effective evaluation is based largely on what the organization values. The organization's values are based on its people and strategic objectives. So by incorporating these values into your training solutions you will be helping T&D to develop more focused evaluations.

Business values are very different from T&D's values. T&D evaluates its worth according to feedback from participants, whereas business values relate to performance and tangible results. To determine exactly what is of value to your organization conduct a business needs assessment. Speak to a cross section of people in the organization. Set time aside to learn what is important to other departments, to employees, and to senior management. Doing this will help you to develop solutions that are practical and relevant to the organization.

ROI and results are not created equal Today's decision makers are placing tremendous pressure on T&D to deliver level 4 results. In reality, level 4 evaluation is not necessary for every training effort and the results do not always have to be in financial terms. Even when there is pressure to demonstrate level 4 results, factors other than the organization's financial results can measure success at this level.

Evaluations deliver the best results when the process is kept as simple as possible and when the measures are directly related and relevant to the training proposed. The more complex the process becomes, the less relevant it will be to the individuals and stakeholders involved. Evaluations also deliver the best results when the measures used are related directly to the results desired. Management tends to measures results against traditional financial contexts such as profitability or revenues. But when it is explained that the measures T&D proposes are more specific and will show the immediate results of the training program, you are assured of getting management buy-in.

Condition your organization to think past the common understanding that business impact is defined by financial results. Demonstrate that specifically identifying how and what you measure will deliver more precise outcomes. Here are some examples of measures that will resonate well with senior management and decision makers (more are discussed in the explanation of the Phillips methodology):

- Inventory levels
- Order-processing efficiency
- Employee injury levels
- Client satisfaction
- Product defect rates
- Equipment utilization

Another benefit of more precise indicators is that you can use data that your organization is already collecting for reasons other than measuring training outcomes. Using these data as your level 4 indicators will reduce the cost of the evaluation process and directly affect what needs to be improved. Using what is important, readily available, and tangible to the organization will help to make T&D a more strategically aligned business partner.

You need evidence, not proof Many training evaluation experts have not been able to deliver undeniable proof that any training solution has actually contributed to the improvement desired. It is also difficult to isolate how a training effort contributes to business results because the training is often an integrated part of a larger solution. So how do you go about proving that training delivered on what was promised? You don't. You look for evidence that supports this achievement.

Don't get caught up in how critical T&D is to the organization's efforts. T&D is an important part of how an organization fares, but it is not the sole contributor to organizational success. T&D is one part of a complex, interrelated system. Isolating training's impact is at best difficult and often impossible. So proving results from a training effort is not crucial. Most decision makers will be relatively satisfied with tangible evidence that training has performed as needed. As I stated before, management is concerned with results, not necessarily the means.

Understand organizational interactions Management often expects to hear of a direct link between the training effort and its organizational impact. This expectation is so pervasive that T&D is conditioned to try to find this link, but that effort is largely in vain. Finding a direct link between the results and training is usually like searching for a needle in a haystack. The reason for this is, again, that training is only one of many other intervening factors contributing to improving operational issues. It is also unfair to expect T&D to bear all the responsibility for organizational improvement given that it is not in control of these other factors.

Delivering reliable evaluations requires that you determine in advance the relationships and interactions of other issues involved in reaching the desired outcome. Project managers recognize this process as finding the *critical path* to an objective. For example, a training program directed to improving the financial reporting process would be difficult to link directly to an increase in organizational profitability without identifying the other relationships and interactions involved. Establishing such indirect links is not as difficult as it might first appear. Many factors can affect an organization's profitability. Depending on the structure of the organization making an indirect link might be as simple as creating efficiencies in the reporting process, or training might provide the staff with new skills for identifying areas where profitability is being negatively affected. By improving staff skills and abilities in one area, T&D might set changes in motion that will eventually improve the organization's profitability.

Although this is a brief example, it may help you to think differently about how T&D affects the results of the organization. Thinking in this manner is important as it can help you do a better job of

- Understanding the interactions involved in your organization
- Designing training programs to maximize impact on the critical links in organizational profitability chain
- Evaluating training outcomes and impacts throughout the T&D process

Become a strategic partner As mentioned earlier, training is not the sole contributor to improving the organization's performance. If your T&D department is going to be successful and make a real difference, then it must become a real partner to other departments and levels of management in your organization.

The Kirkpatrick evaluation process remains a fundamentally sound process for determining the success of training efforts. This model produces results that may seem more relevant to T&D than they are to management. Evaluations at all levels are important, but level 4 provides the most essential information required by management. The key is to explain that financial results are not the only or most precise measure of business impact. By developing a better understanding of the business issues and relationships and by selecting specific measures in light of this understanding, T&D and its evaluation process will quickly be seen as a strategic partner.

Measuring level 5 ROI (Phillips's ROI methodology)

A recent measurement practice is to use Phillips's ROI methodology. This method takes level 4 of the Kirkpatrick model and converts it to an ROI measure (level 5). It also identifies nontangible results at a sixth level.

At times T&D managers lack the understanding needed to adequately evaluate training ROI. As a result they tend to evaluate ROI as a level 1 (assessment of the training or trainer) or level 2 evaluation (testing of what the employees learned). This leaves the T&D department and the organization with the impression, at least initially, that the training initiatives were successful because the participants gave the course a good evaluation and tested well. Only later do managers realize that having positive training evaluations and employees with more knowledge does not automatically translate into organizational benefit and into the return or results expected by management.

At the same time, it is not essential to measure every training effort at the ROI level. If the training result needed is not critical to the organization's strategic direction or there is no significant investment in getting it, then it is not wise to evaluate it at level 4 or level 5. The sales example mentioned earlier would meet both these criteria and hence require a level 5 evaluation. But when you are assessing an employee orientation program, then a level 2 or level 3 evaluation is more than sufficient.

Most of your training efforts should be evaluated at level 3—how does the participant applies what he or she learned to the job? This is where most training evaluations fall apart. Yet this is also the minimum you need to do to prove some type of business impact to management. The process should be simple and help you justify the need for training. For example, if you sent your staff on a word-processing course you would first determine what they know before the training by conducting a preevaluation to identify their weak areas and what they require to do their jobs more effectively. Now you are in a better position to select the training courses that are most appropriate and that meet their specific needs. Once the training is complete, ensure that participants are using the new skills acquired. This can be done through postevaluation, coaching, productivity output measures, and actual tasks that require the use of the skills. This is level 3.

Conducting training ROI analysis is not in itself a difficult process. The problem occurs when decision makers want to see immediate results through standard and obvious measures such as revenue or profitability—essentially linking the organization's ROI measure directly to the training effort. Integrating a benchmark can help you to measure the improvement. ROI measurement requires you to identify specifically what to improve, determine the expected output, and be able to quantify the results in monetary terms. If the objective is to improve product quality, for example, the outcome to measure would be a reduction in production defects, in customer complaints, or in product returns as a result of training effectiveness.

Getting Proven Results and Returns from Training

Financial measurement is important but should not be the only measure of training's impact on the organization. ROI data alone do not address other key business impacts (level 6), such as increased employee morale, better communication, or increased customer satisfaction. Nor will ROI data alone improve training efforts so that they yield a higher ROI. And demonstrating a positive ROI does not necessarily mean that the organization is actually getting the right results or going in the right direction. These issues are equally important to management and indirectly affect the organization's business and financial results.

Training and employee development must be accountable in terms of business results and strategically aligned. Providing training and expecting it to be the whole solution to a business problem will certainly result in failure. The same business rules apply to training as apply to any other business investment. A systematic approach to researching, developing, and integrating a true learning strategy will provide measurable and proven results far beyond the standard measure of ROI.

Keep in mind of course that training is not appropriate for all situations. If it's decided that some type of learning initiative is required, then the questions to answer are, Who will require training? and, What is the most effective way to transfer the needed learning? Always challenge preconceptions and groupthink. Don't be misled by what people may assume is needed but focus on what is actually needed. This will help you build credibility for T&D and provide the results management expects. If you cannot do these things, all your effort will go to waste.

> Marelene recognized the importance to her organization of its software training needs. She realized that she would have to develop a proper evaluation process to account for the results and outcomes. Even though the four levels of evaluation are essential, Marelene knew that the only thing that would get the attention of senior management was the impact the training would have on the business. This would require a level 4 evaluation for certain and, considering the expected investment, a return on investment measure. Rarely, however, had T&D ever been able to get to these levels, except with simpler training projects. Marelene understood that this would require a better understanding of business impact and ROI calculations.
>
> Reviewing the preassessment form completed with Carol, Marelene began the process of compiling the information required to calculate the ROI. The costs involved would require the training of 1,000 employees across ten departments. Marelene realized that her department staff had their work cut out for them.

Thinking Like Management

- Do we need to evaluate a financial return on investment?
- What other impact can we have directly on the business?
- What is the value of the training to the business?
- How do we effectively evaluate that training has met its objectives?
- How do we correct the situation if we're not meeting the objective of the training program?
- How do we see if the training provided a return on investment?

The ROI Calculations Expected by Management

Here are the basics of making return on investment calculations, including some essential formulas.

What Is Involved in Calculating Training ROI?

Before looking at the various ROI formulas, you must understand what is involved in the calculations. To properly calculate training ROI you should establish estimates or ascertain the costs and benefits associated with the training program for which ROI is to be determined. The calculation of ROI is a relatively simple process once you understand what is involved. Some of the costs required are

- Design and development costs
- Participant costs
- Training material costs
- Delivery costs
- Administration costs
- Promotional costs
- Location costs
- Evaluation costs

As you can see, to arrive at an ROI result that is credible and justifiable you must take into account all the costs required to bring training to realization. The mistake made by many T&D managers is not including all the factors relevant to the level 5 evaluation. An ROI figure that is inclusive of all factors, of both direct and indirect costs, is one that will build the credibility and worth of T&D. Let's look at what each cost factor covers and what is required to properly calculate training ROI.

Design and development costs

The design and development costs of a training program include the costs of instructor-led sessions, e-learning activities, self-study materials, and coaching sessions or possibly a combination of training events. To compile a complete cost figure for design and development you need to consider:

- The number of internal staff days needed for the design and development of training
- The costs of external designers, developers, and consultants
- Any other direct design and development costs (purchase of copyrights, travel, expenses, and so forth)
- The purchase of off-the-shelf materials and other training tools for effective delivery

Participant costs

Participant costs are usually of primary concern to the management team because they represent a significant contribution to the investment in training and are opportunity costs to the organization. While employees are in a training session they are not doing their jobs, resulting in a short-term decrease in productivity. When employees go through a training program during work time, the organization is not only paying them to be in the training but is also losing the opportunity for these people to add value to the organization in a productive capacity. For example, when a salesperson is on a course, she is not bringing in new business. Similarly, a production line worker is not creating products, a researcher is not developing new ideas, and an accountant is not finding ways to save money.

Participant costs are charged to the training program if the session is conducted during time that would otherwise be productive for the trainees' primary role, time that one way or another the trainees have to be paid for. These relevant costs include the costs of lost opportunities, those that are foregone because employees are in the training session. A lost opportunity is often referred to by management as an *opportunity cost.* For example, the salesperson mentioned earlier may lose a certain amount of sales because she is in the training session. Realistically estimating these opportunity costs in dollars is essential as it will produce a more conservative and relevant ROI figure for management. However, arriving at an agreeable amount for opportunity costs is not simple and can be highly subjective. The subjectivity arises because opportunity costs, apart from the hard cost like wages, are based on suppositions about productivity. The estimate for opportunity costs will require close collaboration and discussions with those directly involved in the trainees' area of responsibility.

Theoretically, one can avoid opportunity costs by replacing the employee in training with another employee. Then there is no lost opportunity—the only costs are simply the hard costs of the participant, such as wages. In practice, however, using a replacement employee is inadequate as a short-term replacement, lacking the original employee's specific job experience, can never be as productive as the original employee. Add to this the time required to bring the replacement person up to speed on the job requirements, and the direct costs of replacing an employee often turn out to be equivalent to the lost opportunity costs incurred when the employee is not replaced.

It is important that you factor in only the chargeable work time and not unproductive work time, such as coffee breaks and lunches. Also include any other relevant participant costs and expenses, like travel, accommodation, and food.

Training materials cost

Every training session requires some supporting materials. The cost of these materials may be minimal or substantial. Materials required for training have been traditionally thought of as participant workbooks and trainer manuals. But they include much more than this. Accounting for all the materials used is essential, and so you need to calculate the cost per participant for such items as

- Training materials, such as workbooks, manuals, and so forth
- Writing needs, such as pens, pencils, markers, pads of paper, and so forth
- Consumables, such as flipcharts, acetates, place cards, exercise tools, and so forth
- License fees, for use of off-the-shelf materials
- E-learning requirements, such as software licenses, supporting documentation, leasing of equipment, and so forth
- Experiential items for task training, such as raw materials, organization products, and so forth

Delivery costs

Often overlooked by T&D is the estimation of delivery costs. Delivery not only plays a significant role in training but has costs associated with it. Delivery costs are incurred in both instructor-led (instructors, facilitators, or coaches) and self-administered approaches (workbooks, e-learning modules, correspondence, and so on). Let's start with the information needed to calculate delivery costs for a program:

- Number of students
- Hours of group training (whether classroom-based or delivered in real time online)
- Hours of one-to-one training (typically face-to-face but also conducted by telephone, through video conferencing link, or in real time online)
- Hours of self-study training
- Hours of preparation time (reviewing the material)
- Hours of assessment time (grading and reviewing submitted participant work, corresponding with participants)
- Instructor and delivery expenses (travel, accommodation, food, and so on)
- Instructor wages for this program

Administration costs

Every activity in an organization requires administration support, and training activities are no exception. With training playing an increasing role in companies today and with many business solutions incorporating blended learning activities, administration is the necessary backbone for training's overall success. An allowance of time and financial resources must be made to administration. Your training team must be aware of what is involved in properly administering the training initiative. Keep in mind that as a training program grows so do the administration requirements. The costs involved in administering training include the following:

- Hours of administration required per student

- Registration support per student

- Scheduling of training sessions for both participants and facilitators

- Support of training activities included in the session

- Sourcing of such logistical items as location, food, and transportation

- Sending supporting materials to participants

- Following up with participants after the training

Promotional costs

Promotional efforts are important for any training initiative if it is to be successful and especially for programs involving large investments. This is another cost factor that is not always seen as relevant to the ROI process, but accounting for these costs is required because they can greatly influence the ROI outcome. Chapter Five will demonstrate the techniques you will need to promote, or sell, your training to various organizational stakeholders. Here I outline the promotional costs to include when compiling your T&D costs. You need to consider the cost of the

- Development and distribution of promotional material such as brochures, posters, e-mails, Web-sites, and letters

- Preparation and delivery of presentations to management and affected employees

- Time required for conducting the promotional activity

- Support needed from other departments and management

- External support from such sources as a marketing consultant, a printer, and so forth

Location costs

Location is a critical component in the effective delivery of the training program. You will want to seriously consider your location needs. You may have the location readily available in your organization, or you may have to source external facilities that are more accommodating and conducive to meeting the session needs. In either case the location and related resources must be budgeted as this cost will affect the ROI result. Even when you are an using internal facility you still need to allow for the cost as if it were an external location. When calculating rental or internal location costs, make sure to include the following:

- Number of training rooms and pieces of equipment required
- Number of open learning or self-study rooms required
- Cost of rental or use of training rooms
- Cost of rental or use of equipment
- Cost of preparation, maintenance, and clean up of the location

Evaluation costs

Also frequently left out of T&D's calculations is the cost of evaluating the training. An evaluation process takes a significant investment in resources, specifically time and effort. There are costs for documenting, tracking, and benchmarking and also for the compiling of T&D costs and benefits. For any evaluation process, you must make an allowance for the time spent evaluating the training. Converting this time and effort to a dollar figure will affect the return on investment you will show to the management team.

T&D will be under a great deal of scrutiny as to the reliability of its return on investment calculations and projected outcome, so it is critical that you completely account for all the data and costs required to arrive at a credible result.

CD-ROM RESOURCE

Open the "ROI Analysis Templates" file on your CD, and: select the "12-Month ROI Analysis" tab to see a list of costs and benefits. Use this template and also the "Summary" and "Assumptions" templates in the "ROI Calculator" file, modifying labels if necessary, to account for the costs and benefits of your

own training programs. (A red dot in the upper right-hand corner of a cell indicates an attached comment. Place your cursor on the dot to read this helpful
tip, or use the View > Comments function to see all comments at once.)

The ROI Formulas

T&D professionals are learning the importance of providing evidence of training's
impact in a language that managers understand. There are three widely accepted
return on investment formulas for determining the success of a training investment
and the impact on the organization's financial results. These ROI and ROI-related
calculations are seen as "hard results" for the organization and include

- ROI percentage
- Benefit-cost ratio
- Payback period

ROI percentage

The ROI percentage formula provides the percentage return made over a specified
period as a result of investing in a training program. On the assumption that benefits will continue to accrue for some time after the training, then the period that
you specify is critical to the ROI figure you will obtain. It is important that you specify a period that fits within your organization's planning cycle.

Although the Kirkpatrick model of evaluation is effective for measuring impact
on business, managers regularly measure ROI using a standard formula of business investment and expenditures similar to Phillips's level 5. The formula is net
benefits (realized monetary benefits minus total direct and indirect costs) divided
by the total direct and indirect costs. The result is expressed as a percentage. It is
relatively simple to calculate return on investment in this way:

$$\text{ROI \%} = \frac{\text{Realized monetary benefits} - (\text{Total direct costs} + \text{Total indirect costs})}{\text{Total direct costs} + \text{Total indirect costs}} \times 100.$$

Benefit-cost ratio

The benefit-cost ratio (BCR) is determined simply by dividing the total benefits the
training program delivered by the total costs of bringing the training to reality. It

is equivalent to the traditional cost-benefit calculation an organization might conduct for any other business investment. The BCR is useful because calculating an expected BCR (before the training takes place) and comparing it to a post-BCR (actual result) can show another form of return on investment. BCR is represented as follows:

BCR = Total training benefits / Total training costs.

Payback period

Another way to look at ROI is to determine how long it would take a training initiative to break even, to pay back the amount initially invested. This *payback period* formula calculates how many weeks, months, or years will pass before the benefits of the training match the costs and the training pays for itself. The payback period for training is the total training cost divided by the total monthly benefits.

Payback period = Total training cost / Total monthly benefits.
Note: Total monthly benefits is calculated as follows: Total training benefits / 12.

For example, if a sales training program results in an increase of $60,000 in realized monetary benefit and the total program cost was $10,000, the ROI would be 500 percent. In other words, for every $1 invested in this training, the net benefit realized would be $5 in increased revenue from additional sales. The BCR would be $6, and the payback period would be two months.

Payback period is a powerful measure. If the figure is relatively low—perhaps only a few months—then management will be encouraged to make the training investment. As a measure, it also has the advantage of not requiring evaluators to specify an arbitrary benefit period.

Sample of ROI analysis final results

Here's an example of the final results for an ROI analysis.

The T&D manager of XYZ Inc. designed and implemented a comprehensive training program to develop the skills and the abilities of 750 XYZ employees. Table 3.2 summarizes the results. The detailed calculations made by the XYZ training and development manager, using the costs and benefits data in Table 3.2, are as follows:

Table 3.2. XYZ Training Costs, Benefits, and ROI

Duration of training	33 hrs
Estimated no. of students	750
Period over which benefits are calculated	12 months
Costs	
Design and development	$40,930
Promotion	$4,744
Administration	$12,713
Delivery	$86,250
Materials	$15,000
Facilities	$40,500
Students	$553,156
Evaluation	$872
Total cost	$754,165
Benefits	
Labor savings	$241,071
Productivity increases	$675,000
Other cost savings	$161,250
Other income generation	$0
Total benefits	$1,077,321
Return on investment	43%
Payback period	8 months
BCR	1.43:1

$$\text{ROI \% } = \frac{\$1,077,321 - \$754,165}{\$754,165} \times 100.$$

$$\text{ROI} = 43\%.$$

$$\text{Payback period} = \frac{\$754,165}{\$89,777}.$$

$$\text{Payback period} = 8 \text{ months.}$$

Note: $1,077,321 (total training benefits) / 12 = $89,777 (total monthly benefits).

$$\text{BCR} = \frac{\$1,077,321}{\$754,165}.$$

$$\text{BCR} = 1.43.$$

And here is how the VEHD T&D department began to focus on ROI:

Marelene decided to change things at VEHD so that the evaluation process would play an integrated role in the ADDIE model. Evaluation of the training program would include a benchmark and a preassessment to determine how the employees were using the current process and to identify areas of needed development. Marelene figured that because the T&D department was developing the staff to work with a new tool, it should also evaluate improvement of their abilities, that is, their performance improvement.

Marelene worked hard to identify and compile all the costs involved in rolling out the office productivity software training course. Finally, she had the preliminary data to begin conducting an ROI evaluation (Table 3.3).

Table 3.3. VEHD Initial ROI Analysis

	Preassessment	Postassessment
Duration of training	35 hrs	35 hrs
Estimated no. of students	1,000	1,000
Period over which benefits are calculated	12 months	12 months

Continued

Table 3.3. VEHD Initial ROI Analysis, Cont'd

	Preassessment	Postassessment
Costs		
Design and development	$40,000	—
Promotion	$5,000	—
Administration	$10,000	—
Delivery	$70,000	—
Materials	$15,000	—
Facilities	$30,000	—
Students	$700,000	—
Evaluation	$1,500	—
Total cost	$871,500	—
Benefits		
Labor savings	$250,000	—
Productivity increases	$600,000	—
Other cost savings	$125,000	—
Other income generation	$0	$0
Total benefits	$975,000	—
Return on investment	12%	—
Payback period	11 months	—
BCR	1.12	—

CD-ROM RESOURCE

Open the "ROI Analysis Templates" file on your CD, and click on the "ROI Analysis" tab. Use this template to conduct your own ROI analyses, following the discussion and examples in this chapter.

Thinking Like Management

- Show us the costs involved in developing and delivering the training program.

- How does the ROI of the training program proposed compare to other alternatives?

- What are the expected and the actual ROI results for the training program?

- How long will it be before we break even on our investment in the training program and begin to show a profit on it?

- What is the benefit of the training versus the cost of it?

- Is an ROI measure required, and how will T&D measure it?

Values Not Demonstrated Through ROI Analysis

For management, ROI is probably the single most important measure for any business investment and that includes T&D investments. But ROI is not the sole indicator of tangible returns on training investment, and demonstrating a positive ROI does not necessarily mean that the training is actually getting the right results or going in the right direction. As mentioned earlier in this chapter, there are many intangible measures of training success that cannot be measured through ROI (Phillips's level 6).

Most, if not all, training programs produce some type of intangible benefit. These benefits cannot be measured through financial results. Intangible results are varied and completely dependent on the training delivered. Some of the more common intangible benefits are shown in Exhibit 3.2.

Exhibit 3.2. Common Intangible Benefits of Training

· Increased job satisfaction	· Decreased customer dissatisfaction
· Increased organizational commitment	· Enhanced community image
· Improved work climate	· Enhanced investor image
· Fewer employee complaints	· Fewer customer complaints

Continued

Exhibit 3.2. Common Intangible Benefits of Training, Cont'd

- Fewer employee grievances
- Reduction of employee stress
- Increased employee tenure
- Reduced employee lateness
- Reduced absenteeism
- Reduced employee turnover
- Increased innovation
- Increased customer satisfaction

- Faster customer response time
- Increased customer loyalty
- Improved teamwork
- Increased cooperation
- Reduction in conflict
- Improved decisiveness
- Improved communication

Source: Phillips and Stone, 2002.

Whether you are measuring training in terms of ROI or any other measure, your goal is to find some type of value from the investment. Measuring the value of training is difficult at the best of times. Traditionally, the term *value* is associated with monetary worth, but value has many other implications for the training activity, management, and the organization. It is safe to say that value is directly related to the expectations of the project (expectations of the kinds of benefits shown in Exhibit 3.2, for example) and the measure of value selected. A project would have a high value if all its expectations were met and a low value if they were not.

Sometimes there is too much focus on the bottom line or payback period of a training project. Usually, the decision to implement a training solution is treated as a simple choice rather than the complex choice it probably is. Usually an assumption is made that training is required for a particular issue, and the training is then conducted with little evidence of its effectiveness. T&D allocates a budget and is told to spend it. Seldom is any analysis conducted to determine the value the training has brought to the organization.

Thinking Like Management

- What other benefits can we expect from the training program?

- How will the intangible benefits provide value to the participant or the organization?

- Can the value of the intangible benefits provide any monetary or financial returns?

- How will we know if the intangible benefits are realized or are genuine?

Communicating Results to Management

The purpose of conducting an ROI measurement or finding a direct impact on the business (level 4) is to prove that training is worth the investment required. No one will argue that the evaluation of training is not inherently a good thing. But the biggest challenge for T&D and the primary concern of management is achieving shorter-term objectives rather than meeting the goals of a longer-term outlook.

For those not working directly with T&D, training is not a priority, only a support mechanism. When any attempt is made to evaluate training's effectiveness it is usually at the lowest levels—the measurement of participant reactions to the training program through evaluation forms completed immediately after training (level 1) or measurement of what people have learned (level 2). Participant feedback about reactions and about what participants retain is important and serves a purpose but does not support T&D's efforts when further investment in training is required, major changes are made in strategic direction, or there is competition for scarce resources.

The real question is, What do you need to communicate to management? or rather, What does management expect to hear from T&D? The answer is dependent on each organization's concerns. Many issues fall into one of these two categories:

- Business benefits
- Employee benefits

Business Benefits

By now you understand that management's concerns revolve around benefits to the business. When communicating your evaluation and ROI results, don't just regurgitate numbers to managers and stakeholders. If they want numbers they will read your report. Also, financial results alone do not provide management with the full significance of your training. Communicate the results in a manner that demonstrates the meaning behind the numbers and that adds significant value to T&D efforts. Successful training is focused on supporting your business objectives.

There are many ways to communicate evaluation results, and it is up to you to determine the best way to illustrate value results to stakeholders. Here are some of the more common benefits that are emphasized.

Improved quality and productivity

High on the list of priorities for every manager are quality and productivity. When evaluating any training effort these are the two areas likely to gain the most attention. When training meets the needs of both employees and employer it can increase the quality and flexibility of an organization's offerings by fostering

- Accuracy and efficiency
- Good work safety practices
- Higher levels of skill leading to faster work
- Higher levels of motivation leading to increased effort

The cascading effect

The effects of a well-developed and executed training effort are rarely restricted to the issues the effort is attempting to solve. Often the benefits of training in one area will cascade to other parts of the organization. Over time, training can boost the bottom line and reduce costs by decreasing

- Wasted time and materials
- Maintenance costs of machinery and equipment
- Workplace accidents (leading to lower insurance premiums)
- Recruitment costs (through the internal promotion of skilled staff)

Maintaining a competitive edge

The business environment is highly dynamic. To maintain market position, satisfy clients, and keep pace with competitors, an organization must continually change the way it does things and be adaptive to fluctuating conditions.

T&D's role is more than reacting to the needs of the organization and goes beyond the traditional skills training. This functional T&D role is quickly decreasing in importance. To address the competitive challenges, T&D must get involved and work in an operational context rather than in a functional one. This means that it must partner with operational departments whose needs are continuously changing and whose results directly affect the bottom line. In this capacity training can improve

- Staff morale and satisfaction

- Soft skills, such as communication and leadership

- Time management

- Customer satisfaction

- Many other competitive issues

Labor savings

Business is about efficiency, and when T&D evaluations demonstrate any type of savings management will be listening. Labor is one of the more costly aspects of an organization, and reduced effort means a direct financial savings for the organization. Savings translate to increased profit, without having to increase product price, because it costs less to produce the product. Examples of labor savings that might arise from training include

- Reduced duplication of effort

- Less time spent correcting defects or mistakes

- Increased knowledge about production requirements

- Better workflow processes

- Faster access to information

New business opportunities

Evaluation measures at times miss obvious areas that demonstrate benefits indirectly related to a training effort. No longer are products, quality, or price the competitive advantage of a successful organization—that advantage is the organization's employees. Well-trained and motivated employees who possess a thorough understanding of your operations are indispensable. These individuals can give a business a competitive edge by

- Increasing productivity, quality, and production standards, resulting in a better reputation for their organization

- Helping the organization to open new markets through their ability to undertake a greater variety of work

- Allowing the organization to obtain specialized, high-value contracts

- Achieving the organization's objectives

- Making it possible for the organization to capitalize on new opportunities or acquire other companies

Employee Benefits

When you are communicating the benefits of training, remember that management likes to hear how well employees are doing. Most managers recognize that a productive and profitable organization is the result of well-developed, well-skilled, and of course well-managed employees. Such employees reflect favorably on managers' abilities, and increasingly, managers are seeking ways to maintain this level of efficiency.

An evaluation that looks at how employees contribute to business and professional growth is a win-win opportunity for both the employees and the organization. Continuous learning opportunities are an investment that allows employees to prosper and develop their careers while it also gives the organization a highly skilled workforce and a competitive advantage in the market. Some examples of these evaluative measures follow.

Staff turnover and recruitment

There is evidence showing that companies with low employee turnover budget more money on employee development and welfare. Employee retention is important to a organization because there is fierce competition for talent and the cost to hire and retrain employees is significant. Companies also don't want proprietary information walking out of their doors and into the hands of a competitor.

Employees who receive continuous development and support are more loyal to their employer because

- They see this training effort as part of their professional development.
- Training empowers them to take on greater responsibility and leads to promotions and increased financial rewards.

Measuring potential candidates against competencies delivered in your training programs also streamlines the recruitment process and reduces the induction period.

Improved attitude and morale

Training leads to often-ignored but beneficial by-products. When successful a course can lead to better communication, increased synergy, and positive attitudes.

Generally, people will become more involved in and accepting of training when it is relevant to their needs and contributes to helping them be more effective in their jobs. This also increases the probability that participants will apply their new skills and knowledge in practical situations.

Well-trained and well-developed employees are usually more satisfied in their roles than employees with less effective training are. Higher job satisfaction reduces workplace stress and conflicts, leading to a work environment that is more conducive to employee productivity and more positive. When the organization invests in their training, employees feel that

- The organization has confidence in their abilities to do the job.
- Management values them and is giving something back over and above wages.

As a result, employees†will become more independent in their jobs and interdependent with others. Training is an excellent opportunity for†employers to discover new leaders and to better understand the dynamics and culture in the workplace.

> Marelene was happy with the results of the training program. They exceeded what she had initially forecast in her preassessment of the project. In reality, Marelene knew management was not expecting to see any tangible results from the training strategy, but she felt she had made a good decision in choosing to evaluate the effort. She compiled the final, hard results in a table (Table 3.4).

Table 3.4. VEHD Final ROI Analysis Results for Software Training

	Preassessment	Postassessment	Variance
Duration of training	35 hrs	30 hrs	5
Estimated no. of students	1,000	1,250	250
Period over which benefits are calculated	12 months	12 months	—

Continued

Table 3.4. VEHD Final ROI Analysis Results for Software Training, Cont'd

	Preassessment	Postassessment	Variance
Costs			
Design and development	$40,000	$45,000	$(5,000)
Promotion	$5,000	$4,800	$200
Administration	$10,000	$13,700	$(3,700)
Delivery	$70,000	$89,000	$(19,000)
Materials	$15,000	$17,000	$(2,000)
Facilities	$30,000	$42,500	$(12,500)
Students	$700,000	$740,000	$(40,000)
Evaluation	$1,500	$1,000	$500
Total cost	$871,500	$953,000	$(81,500)
Benefits			
Labor savings	$250,000	$283,000	$33,000
Productivity increases	$600,000	$840,000	$240,000
Other cost savings	$125,000	$180,250	$55,250
Other income generation	$0	$0	$0
Total benefits	$975,000	$1,303,250	$328,250
Return on investment	12%	36.75%	24.75%
Payback period	11 months	9 months	2 months
BCR	1.12	1.37	0.25

Some of the intangible benefits Marelene's training program realized were

- Increased efficiencies in document processing
- Reduction in hours worked by the staff in documenting paperwork
- Reduction in time spent searching for required documents
- Reduction in the space required for archiving physical documents

- Increased employee productivity as a result of not having to handle physical documents

- Faster response to internal and external clients

- Fewer employee complaints

- Reduction of employee stress

What You Need to Know

The topic of training's return on investment can be complicated. It is important to keep in mind the following points:

- ROI often has different meanings to management and to you as a T&D professional. Understand what is expected from you, and be clear about what T&D will deliver, in terms understood by management.

- Often management is not concerned with the means you have used to demonstrate outcomes. They want to see the results and do not really care how you achieved them. More specifically, management wants to see results and outcomes that contribute directly to the objectives of the organization.

- A return on investment for management is more than monetary results. It is relevant to ensure that the costs of implementing a particular training solution do not exceed the benefits, real or perceived. However, returns can also address the impact your solution will have on business operations: for example, increased sales, reductions in defects, more efficient resource allocation, cost reductions, increased customer or employee satisfaction, and so forth.

- When it comes to making decisions on what is essential and what can be sacrificed, management looks at the direct contribution of every operational activity in the company. It is critical that you change the way management perceives T&D, repositioning T&D as having a critical role in the company. This requires reducing T&D's functional role and ensuring that T&D becomes a strategic business partner to other operational areas. It also requires that you speak the language of business and understand how T&D solutions directly affect the company and its ability to help attain objectives.

- Credibility takes some time to gain. T&D will need to demonstrate accountability for the solutions it proposes to the organization. This is not to say T&D was not accountable in the past; but this is a new accountability for learning and its impact on the business, rather than accountability only for the learning itself.

Thinking Like Management

- How will the organization tangibly benefit from the training, beyond what you have presented?

- Can you further justify the required investment in the training program?

- How will employees benefit in the long term from the training program?

- What makes this training program any better than what our competitors do?

Review

In dynamic business environments accountability, performance, and results are drivers to success. No business responsibility in a organization has the luxury of not delivering tangible results. If T&D is to gain credibility and be seen as a strategic partner, then it must provide answers to the same questions and meet the same criteria. But T&D must do more than simply report participant satisfaction and measures of acquired knowledge.

Measuring training results must not occur as an afterthought or as the last step of the training process—it must become a fully integrated component of the training development process. Evaluations must answer the questions that management requires. That means the measurement of any training program with a significant investment must take place at level 4, business impact, or at level 5, financial return on investment.

T&D professionals must begin thinking in business and strategic terms. Although return on investment is an important measure, many training initiatives should be evaluated at level 4, with specific and tangible nonfinancial results. Management wants to see some type of business results. T&D professionals can easily leverage the existing measures and resources of their organizations to determine how their training solutions have positively affected the business operations. Proving that training has produced unquestionable results is difficult, but delivering evidence of improvement in terms that management understands will establish training and development departments as true business partners.

Review Quiz

1. Which question helps T&D address the concerns of senior management:

    ____ What is the objective of the organization?

    ____ Who requires training?

    ____ What does the organization need to resolve or develop?

    ____ What are the expected results?

    ____ All of the above.

2. Benchmarking is the process that provides T&D and management with a

    ____ Comparison of the situations before and after training.

    ____ Method to properly seat large groups of people.

    ____ Financial tool that shows the profitability of a training program.

    ____ None of the above.

3. The training ROI answers the question:

    ____ How much training will be conducted in relation to a certain quantity of payback?

    ____ For every dollar invested in training, how many dollars does the organization get back?

    ____ For every dollar spent, how much training is delivered?

    ____ None of the above.

4. For management, the most important level of Kirkpatrick's evaluation model is

    ____ Level 1.

    ____ Level 2.

    ____ Level 3.

    ____ Level 4.

    ____ All of the above.

5. Evaluation adds the most value to the training process when it is used as

    _____   The final step.

    _____   The first step.

    _____   A fully integrated process.

    _____   All of the above.

6. If a training program generates $500,000 in tangible benefits, and the total direct costs amount to $167,000, what is the ROI of the effort?

    _____   246%.

    _____   199%.

    _____   399%.

    _____   None of the above.

7. What is the benefit-cost ratio (BCR) of the program described in question 6?

    _____   2.99.

    _____   4.99.

    _____   1.99.

    _____   None of the above.

8. What is the payback period of the training program described in question 6?

    _____   9 months.

    _____   13 months.

    _____   4 months.

    _____   6 months.

9. Evaluation of training programs should demonstrate

    _____   Value to the organization.

    _____   Financial business impact.

    _____   Intangible benefits important to the organization.

    _____   All of the above.

10. Communicating training evaluation results to management should focus on

____ Business benefits.

____ Employee benefits.

____ All of the above.

Answer Key for Chapter Three Review Quiz

1. All of the above.

2. Comparison of the situations before and after training.

3. For every dollar invested in training, how many dollars does the organization get back?

4. Level 4.

5. A fully integrated process.

6. 199%.

7. 1.99.

8. 4 months.

9. All of the above.

10. All of the above.

4

Outsourcing and Vendor Management

THE FIRST THREE CHAPTERS demonstrated how a trainer can use basic business knowledge to help learning and performance initiatives have more impact on the organization and to build credibility for training within the organization. Business acumen, however, entails not only building training around results and managing budgets but also effectively making decisions about whether to make or to buy training and development resources and products. As described in the previous chapter in our ongoing case study, this is the kind of decision Marelene, VEHD's director of learning and performance, faced as she sought to supplement a vendor's product with her own training staff.

All companies today are facing fierce competition in the market, placing a tremendous amount of pressure on them to be more efficient and focused on their core competencies. This is a mixed blessing for T&D departments. The focus on core issues requires solid employee training and support. As a result, training plays an increasingly important role in companies' overall strategy. But at the same time, companies are doing more with less and scaling back budgets on noncore activities such as T&D.

The pressure is now on T&D to find a balance between eliminating nonessential training activities and producing the essential training required to adequately support the core activities of the company, having this essential training available when needed.

This chapter will help you to understand how to attain this balance and satisfy management's need to better manage the essential and noncore training requirements. By the end of this chapter you will be able to

- Understand outsourcing and its role in T&D
- Decide between hiring and outsourcing
- Write a request for proposal (RFP)
- Select vendors for your project

Understanding Outsourcing and Its Role in T&D

Outsourcing occurs when one company hires or contracts with another company to provide services; these may be either services the hiring company has never done for itself or services usually performed internally by the hiring company's employees. Companies of all sizes and in various industries are now outsourcing what they consider to be noncore activities. Some examples include human resource functions such as payroll and hiring, sales responsibilities, technology issues, and now some training and development. These roles are now handled by external companies specializing in the respective services they are contracted to do.

Outsourcing is not unfamiliar territory for T&D. It is one of the few business responsibilities that routinely outsources certain components. It is commonplace for a small group of training professionals to compose a corporate T&D department. These learning professionals are expected to be experts in a wide variety of functional issues, skills, and procedures. Another of their strengths is expected to be the capacity to acquire essential training needs for the company from outside when necessary, including a wide variety of learning programs and management and executive development programs, books, other training materials, and multimedia. They may buy these items off the shelf or arrange to have them produced.

There are many reasons that companies outsource various jobs, but the most prominent advantages are

- To gain additional expertise and experience
- To reduce fixed overhead costs for one-time or infrequent needs

- To better allocate valuable resources
- To increase business impact (level 4, as discussed in Chapter Three)
- To save money

Gaining Additional Expertise and Experience

Many in management look to outsourcing as a quick and easy way to save money and allow the company to focus on critical business issues while having the details taken care of by outside experts. But for some functions, such as T&D, saving money is not necessarily a major issue when outsourcing.

Training and development has evolved a great deal in the last ten to fifteen years, and it is virtually impossible for even the largest company to possess all the expertise required to build an effective learning environment let alone be able to afford to acquire all the knowledge, technology, and resources required to support a totally self-sufficient T&D department. And why should it? Not all learning solutions are required or effective for the needs of each company and each training situation. Also, internal T&D professionals, who once had many of the day-to-day T&D responsibilities fall on their shoulders, can now be used to handle broader and more management oriented issues in the company.

By outsourcing to organizations that specialize in a desired activity and allowing them to meet the specific need, companies gain extended capabilities that normally would not be accessible or affordable to them.

Reducing Fixed Overhead Costs for One-Time or Infrequent Needs

T&D is an area of business that often must produce specialized solutions for the various demands of other operational areas. Many times training requirements are unique to an operational area's needs. This means that the training developed for these needs is used only once. If it is used for other purposes it is usually modified, if not redeveloped altogether to meet the new needs. This results in the company investing significant resources and money in training solutions for a single purpose. Outsourcing the more specialized training activities helps T&D maximize its capabilities in areas that are truly important to the broader company and allows it to focus on issues where it can leverage its skills and internal expertise. When T&D outsources training in specialized topics and one-time training that cannot deliver economies of scale, management has an opportunity to see T&D as a strategic partner—reducing overhead and large investments.

Reallocating Valuable Resources

A few years ago Bersin & Associates conducted a study to examine the economics of outsourcing training. Here are some key findings from that work.

> The research shows that companies that outsource spend, on average, 31 percent less per learner and have a 26 percent lower staff-per-learner ratio. They also have 30 percent to 40 percent smaller program staffs and 25 percent smaller administrative staffs. In addition to [having more efficient operations], companies that outsource often have the option of offloading administration, help-desk support and reporting functions.
>
> One of the most interesting aspects of the study compared the differences in staff allocations between companies that outsourced and those that did not. In addition to having smaller administrative, technical and support staffs, companies that outsource devoted 28 percent of their training staff to content development, compared to 17 percent in non-outsourcing companies. This means that these outsourcers can focus on more strategic activities: building and delivering the right content to meet their immediate business need. . . .
>
> When training managers and other executives were asked how they spend time saved in outsourcing, they responded:
>
> • Focus more on strategic planning with line managers.
> • Spend more time on measurements and analytics.
> • Spend more time planning and budgeting.
> • Work with line managers to better understand training needs.
> • Evaluate new technologies and approaches for greater efficiency and effectiveness.
>
> Notice that all of these areas are strategic and put the learning organization closer to the business. The more back-office functions that can be offloaded, the more effective the learning organization can be [Bersin, 2005].

Increasing Business Impact

Leveraging internal strengths and bringing in the appropriate outsourced expertise helps the company have a greater impact on business. As mentioned in Chapter Three, management wants to see the relevance of training to the company and this is witnessed by attaining Kirkpatrick's level 4. Companies that outsource some of their training activities quickly see synergies between the training efforts and business objectives through this tactic of leveraging the capacities of an outside resource—usually strengths and abilities unavailable internally.

Saving Money

There are many economic benefits to outsourcing parts of T&D. Operationally, many of the administrative and repetitive tasks that often slow down T&D and prevent it from focusing on strategic and operational solutions are reduced. Development costs are also reduced by leveraging the expertise and efficiencies of the outsourced training provider. Other areas of savings include a reduction in certain payroll costs, such as costs for technical and specialized training staff.

Understanding the Drawbacks of Outsourcing

There are, however, also some disadvantages to outsourcing any function of a company, for example:

- The outside provider may not always understand the internal needs of the company.
- You lack total control over the outsourced activities.
- Communication and project implementation may be delayed.
- Your training is not a priority for the contractor who is managing multiple clients.
- You lack control over proprietary knowledge and rights.
- You run the risk that the contractor may not complete the project or may back away from it.
- You may develop a dependency on the external provider.

So even though outsourcing may prove highly beneficial for many companies, it also has many drawbacks. It is important that each individual company accurately assess its needs to determine if outsourcing is a viable option. Answering the questions in Exhibit 4.1 is also a useful preliminary step.

Thinking Like Management

- What resources are we lacking?

- Why are we lacking these resources?

- What are our options for obtaining these resources?

- How will these resources affect the business?

Exhibit 4.1. Preventing an Outsourcing Disaster: Ten Questions to Answer Before Turning to an External Vendor

1. How does your outsourcing strategy fit with your organization's objectives?

2. Have you determined what results to expect?

3. Have you defined performance standards to measure the success of your project?

4. Have you objectively evaluated the capacity and capability of your internal resources (employees and workload) before outsourcing to external providers?

5. Does the outsourced provider have access to expertise or technology unavailable or inaccessible to you?

6. Is the outsourced provider more efficient or effective (will outsourcing liberate internal resources for more important issues)?

7. Will the decision to outsource be financially beneficial to the organization?

8. Can the outsourced solution be easily integrated into the existing environment or within the organization?

9. Will your employees be able to leverage the outcomes from the outsourced activities provided by the external resource?

10. Will the outsourcing decision negatively impact your efforts or the objectives of the organization in any way?

> Marelene had just returned from meeting with Carol, VEHD's vice president of operations. Carol had confidence in Marelene's abilities as the company training director and wanted to get her involved in a new operations initiative to restructure the workflow process of the production staff. Marelene understood that what was required was well beyond what her team could accomplish internally and that she would need to make a decision on outsourcing the training project or bringing in additional staff. The budget was set, and the senior team was expecting to see a quick impact on the business. Marelene's concern was how to allocate the resources she had at her disposal without placing any additional strain or stress on her T&D team.

Deciding Between Hiring and Outsourcing

The flip side of outsourcing training needs to a vendor is hiring additional employees. The hiring versus outsourcing question is one of the more difficult questions managers have to address. Answering this question properly comes down to your budget, people, and need.

Every company operates based on a budget (see Chapter Two). But it seems that the budget is always insufficient to support any added requirements or to really accomplish the tasks you want to do. Companies also face the problem of doing too much with too few employees. Employee workloads continue to increase, and customers expect more for less. The pressure on management to increase profitability pulls in one direction and trying to increase organizational performance pulls in another. This leads to a growing frustration at not having enough people to meet the company's needs.

The last thing you want to do is to go through a time-consuming process of screening, interviewing, hiring, and training additional employees. The quicker decision is simply to meet the need yourself through outsourcing rather than go through this hassle. Bringing on an external consultant appears to be the easier option. But let's look at the pros and cons of each choice. Tables 4.1 and 4.2 summarize the findings.

Hire Employees

Hiring employees rather than using external contractors is a worthy option in many ways, but it also presents many challenges. Finding the right employees requires

Table 4.1. Pros and Cons of Hiring Employees

Pros	Cons
Able to hire the right people	Pay for downtime
Have more control	Cope with employees distracted with other tasks
Able to set the priorities	Deal with a longer learning curve
Pay lower wages or hourly rate	Must retain the right skills
Integrate employees into team	Always start from scratch
Begin the project work immediately	Must do the work involved in hiring
Train skills your way	Have to train skills your way

Table 4.2. Pros and Cons of Outsourcing to External Contractors

Pros	Cons
Get work based on performance	Not able to get supplier's complete attention
Get experienced people	Pay higher wages and project fees
Get faster turnaround	Not able to start immediately
Get the right skills	Have your project be just one project among other projects

considerable investment in time and money to ensure you hire the right people. Too many companies simply place an ad, receive a bunch of résumés, interview a few people, and hire the first few people they meet. Finding and hiring the right people requires attention to detail and a thorough selection process. You will minimize your risk by screening out unqualified candidates but there is no guarantee you will hire the right person.

There are other challenges to hiring new employees for a project, including dealing with the extended learning curve employees go through to do their work properly, paying employees even during extended periods of downtime if there is a delay in the project chain, being overwhelmed with too many priorities and distracted from the project focus, and using employees for tasks unrelated to the project. These are considered unaccountable soft costs by many, but the results are quickly apparent in missed project milestones, low quality of work, and exceeded budget targets.

There are also many advantages of hiring compared to bringing on an external contractor. First, you are able to hire the right people required for the project. You are also in complete control of the project, the tasks employees perform, and setting the priorities for the project. The wages you pay are often less than an external contractor would charge, and the employees are part of your team, not someone else's.

Exhibit 4.2 helps you to think about some of the important questions to answer before you decide whether or not to hire employees. Please add any questions that are relevant to your situation and company culture.

Exhibit 4.2. Questions to Ask About Hiring Employees

	Yes	No
1. Do you require complete control over the project?		
2. Are you able to use the employees after project completion?		
3. Do you have an effective hiring process?		
4. Do you have the resources to train the employees?		
5. Are the skills required for the project available through hiring?		
6. Does your budget support the addition of employees?		
7. Are management's objective met by hiring employees?		
8. Will the project objectives be met by hiring employees?		

If you answered yes to most or all of the questions in Exhibit 4.2, then it is recommended that you consider hiring additional employees.

Outsource Project Needs

Outsourcing is an advantageous alternative to hiring employees for many valid reasons. Outsourcing helps you to quickly gain the knowledge, expertise, and experience for a project. The responsibility rests on the shoulders of the external contractor, including the responsibility to respect the project budget, meet milestones and deadlines, and acquire the resources required for the project. A contractor's success is highly dependent on its team's performance and the successful completion of the project.

There are, however, challenges in using an external contractor. Unlike the situation in which you have employees, you do not have complete control over the project. Even though workers' performance is directly linked to the project's performance, you are usually completely dependent on the contractor's efforts. Also, your team and the contractor's team may have communication differences that affect the direction and vision management wants to achieve.

The contractor may have more than one project to complete and may not devote the attention and time to your project that it deserves. Having access to the contractor's experience and expertise also means that you are paying a higher wage and possibly more project management fees.

Most important, external contractors do not always understand your business and what you may want to accomplish in the long term. Their objective is to win the contract, complete it as fast as possible, and then move on to the next project.

Exhibit 4.3 can help you think about some of the important questions to answer before deciding to outsource your project. Please add any questions that are relevant to your situation and company culture.

Exhibit 4.3. Questions to Ask About Outsourcing

	Yes	No
1. Is the project a one-time concern?		
2. Are the skills and expertise required held by the contractor?		
3. Do you need to see a quick turnaround on the project?		
4. Are your employees overwhelmed with other responsibilities?		
5. Are the skills required for the project highly specialized?		
6. Does your budget support outsourcing of the project?		
7. Are management's objectives met by outsourcing?		
8. Will the project objectives be met by outsourcing?		

If you answered yes to most or all of the questions in Exhibit 4.3, then it is recommended that you consider outsourcing your project requirements. The Outsourcing Institute's *Outsourcing Index 2000* finds that there are many reasons why companies outsource. Exhibit 4.4 displays nine of the top reasons.

Exhibit 4.4. Nine Primary Reasons to Outsource

1. **Reduce and control operating costs.** When you outsource, you eliminate the costs associated with hiring an employee, such as management oversight, training, health insurance, employment taxes, retirement plans, etc.

2. **Improve company focus.** It is neither practical, nor possible, to be a jack of all trades. Outsourcing lets you focus on your core competencies while another company focuses on theirs.

3. **Gain access to exceptional capabilities.** Your return on investment is so much greater when you outsource to a firm that specializes in the areas you need. Instead of just the knowledge of one person, you benefit from the collective experience of a team of professionals.

4. **Free internal resources for other purposes.** You may have someone in your office that is pretty good in a certain area, but most likely these were not the jobs he or she was hired to do. If they are spending time taking care of other issues, who is doing what they were hired to do? Outsourcing allows you to retain employees for their highest and best use, rather than wasting their time on things that may take them longer than someone who is trained in these specific areas.

5. **Resources are not available internally.** On the flip side, maybe you don't have anyone in your company who can manage your needs, and hiring a new employee is not in the budget. Outsourcing can be a feasible alternative, both for the interim and for the long term.

6. **Maximize restructuring benefits.** When you are restructuring your company to improve costs, quality, service, or speed, your non-core business functions may get pushed aside. They still need to be handled, however, and outsourcing is an optimal way to do this. Don't sabotage your restructuring efforts by failing to keep up with non-core needs.

7. **Function difficult to manage or out of control.** This is definitely a scenario when outsourcing to experts can make a big difference. But don't make the mistake of

Continued

Exhibit 4.4. Nine Primary Reasons to Outsource, Cont'd

thinking you can forget about the problem now that it's being "handled." You still need to be involved even after control is regained.

8. **Make capital funds available.** By outsourcing non-core business functions, you can spend your capital funds on items that are directly related to your product or your customers.

9. **Reduce risk.** Keeping up with changing needs can be expensive and time consuming. Because outsourced professionals work with multiple clients and need to keep up on industry best practices, they typically know what is right and what is not. This kind of knowledge and experience dramatically reduces your risk of implementing a costly wrong decision.

Source: The Outsourcing Institute, 2000.

The decision to outsource or hire additional employees is not always clear. The final decision will have a direct impact on your project and company. It will also affect how management views the T&D function and its ability to function as a strategic partner. Be systematic, thorough, and objective in making your decision. Conduct a complete analysis on the costs, the impact on employees and workload, the scope of the work involved, and the intangible factors that will directly affect the project. If your decision is to outsource, then cost should not be the only factor in your selection. Make sure that you choose a trustworthy, experienced, and reputable contractor that is willing to commit to the project and build a lasting relationship with you.

Often the best solution is to have a mix of external contractors and internal employees, in order to leverage the best of both groups and build lasting synergies. In the end this solution will be about building strategic partners in both your internal and external teams that will contribute to the overall success of the company.

Thinking Like Management

- Have we objectively and equally evaluated both outsourcing and hiring?

- What are some of the expected challenges of bringing on additional employees?

- What is the financial impact of hiring additional employees?

- Will we be able to leverage the employees for other purposes?

- What stress is placed on existing employees if we do not hire?

- What impact will not hiring additional employees have on clients and other parts of the company?

- Are we seeing hiring as an additional cost or as an investment?

Writing a Request for Proposal

If you decide you want to outsource, you have options; depending on your needs you may outsource to a company vendor or to an individual contractor. Let's look first at outsourcing to vendors. If you are outsourcing to a vendor you may ask potential vendors to submit proposals. Let's explore.

A request for proposal, or RFP, is a document prepared by a company that is seeking bids from potential vendors on a specific project. Every project, especially training-related ones, requires clear definition of the company's objectives so that potential vendors understand and accurately respond to the RFP. The nature and scope of the training project is defined by the request for proposal. The RFP gives prospective training vendors the information, the training project requirements, they will need to prepare a bid. The contents of the bid submitted in response to the RFP depend on the requirements but usually include the services to be offered along with details of other relevant items needed to fully complete the project.

Writing an RFP is an involved and at times tedious task. A well-prepared RFP, however, will save you both time and money and prevent future problems and confusion about what is required from the project and the vendor. Writing an RFP forces you to think through in detail what is required before you commit to moving forward with the vendor. It puts forward your ideas and allows others involved, such as other company operations or management, an opportunity to provide their input and respond to your plans.

Define the Scope of the Project

Writing an RFP is more than just itemizing the components that you require for the project and from vendors—it is a process. The most effective RFPs are researched and structured.

The first step in preparing a well-developed RFP is to define the scope of the training project. Decide exactly what the objective of the project is, in clear, precise and concise terms. For example, if the project is to implement an e-learning solution, then research the content requirements, content development, technology requirements, equipment, and any other issue that will need to be addressed to put the e-learning course into place successfully. Address as many issues in detail as necessary to ensure that the project is clearly outlined in the RFP.

While scoping the project you will want to identify company policies that T&D must adhere to and that potential vendors will have to address in their bid. Include your procurement or purchasing department in this phase of the RFP so as not to overlook any policies, procedures, governmental, or tax regulations in the final document.

Deciding how to distribute the RFP is the next step in the process. The first question is whether you are conducting an open bid or a closed one. In an *open bidding* process, any vendor has access to the RFP and is allowed to bid on the project without restrictions. In a *closed bidding* process, the opportunity to respond to the RFP is restricted to certain vendors or to certain conditions. Your answer to this questions will depend in part on whether your organization is public or private. Public organizations must usually meet specific regulations and public policies on the issuance of RFPs or tenders. It is extremely important that you determine these restrictions and policies if your department is part of a public group. Private companies have the liberty of selecting the vendors they will distribute the RFP to, but they may also have internal policies and even industry regulations that all companies in that industry must abide by. In either case be sure to research what is required when issuing an RFP in your organization and industry.

If you are able to restrict the bidding process to specific vendors, you must decide whether you actually want to do so. If you do choose to be restrictive, then create a list of the potential vendors prior to issuing the RFP. You can also restrict the distribution of the RFP by fully defining your requirements. By defining criteria specific to those vendors with whom you want to work, you will limit the vendor selection process to them. Others that do not meet these criteria are quickly disqualified because they do not have the requirements specified in the RFP. Don't be too restrictive, however, because then you may not receive the best representation of the solutions available to your company, or even worse, there may be accusations of favoritism. An adequate response to an RFP is probably a minimum of three to five proposals, allowing you to compare the various offers. Always consult with legal counsel during the RFP process.

The scope of the project will include budget constraints. But don't limit yourself by the budget outlined in the RFP when reviewing the bids. You may realize that some of the overbudget solutions proposed by the vendors have validity, and this might result in expanding the project scope. For example, the e-learning project mentioned earlier might have been planned as a stand-alone project. But in reviewing one bid you might realize that adding other learning aspects would create more impact and result in a faster return on investment. Another bidder might be outside the budget constraints in one area but might demonstrate cost savings in other areas.

Let's look at essential components and what you need to know to write an RFP for a training project. Keep in mind that the content of your own proposals will vary from these descriptions and examples depending on your training needs and other criteria and restrictions that you need to tell potential training vendors. Although more information can be added to the document, the components that follow represent the basic set of information that an RFP should contain (also see Exhibit 4.5).

Exhibit 4.5. Top Ten Tips for an Effective RFP Process

1. Identify your needs prior to working on the RFP.
2. Plan out the work to create the RFP.
3. Identify company resources to assist in your efforts.
4. Gain the commitment of others in your company to work on the RFP.
5. Provide sufficient time for the RFP process (creating the RFP).
6. Provide sufficient time for bidders to prepare and submit a proposal.
7. Implement a transparent evaluation and selection process.
8. Advise bidders of the outcomes and close the RFP.
9. Thank all the bidders for their proposals.
10. Debrief the completed process with your RFP team.

Marelene sat with Samantha, her workforce planning assistant at VEHD, and began scoping the new training project. The company's primary objective was to have all the production staff adopt the more efficient workflow process recently piloted with great success in one of the company's production facilities. The project would require deploying a blended learning program across five production facilities and 1,000 employees. The project would require eight months to complete, a team of ten to fifteen facilitators, and an e-learning course to support the effort.

As mentioned earlier Marelene had already suspected that this new project would require hiring an external vendor, and she and Samantha now confirmed that the demands on the T&D team members would be too great, as they were already involved in supporting other company needs. This project would require sourcing an external training provider that could complement existing team members work and support new needs. Samantha went back to Carol and stated that they would need to put together a request for proposal to solicit bids from training vendors. Carol agreed and authorized her to begin the RFP process.

Select RFP Components

How your request for proposal is organized depends largely on its scope and involvement. The general structure and organization of all RFPs is basically the same, but structure is important for consistency of response from the bidding vendors. Depending on your needs you may want to change the following outline by removing, modifying, or adding sections. For involved and complex RFPs, creating subsections will help you develop a useful and understandable document. An RFP should include the following sections:

- Executive summary
- General information
- Administrative issues
- Proposal structure
- Technical issues
- Contractual obligation

Let's look at each section in greater detail.

Executive summary

Like all business documents and proposals the RFP has an executive summary. The executive summary provides a quick review of the project and the company's expectations. This brief summary is usually written once the rest of the RFP is completed. It provides readers with an overview so they don't have to delve into the details of the project. If they do want more detail they will read the RFP. There is no standard length for the executive summary but keep in mind that it is a summary. Usually, it is no longer than two to four pages, depending on the complexity of the project, but it should be brief and concise.

General information

This section generally takes the form of a general introduction that provides information to help the reader understand what the RFP is about and what is covered in the following pages of the document.†If your RFP is complex this introduction should give the reader an indication of how to proceed through it and explain the important parts to address. Describe more than the project at hand. Explain the business and any other relevant objectives that will help the bidder formulate a proper proposal. Describe the type of business that your company is in and any issues that bidders, not being directly involved in your industry, may not be aware of but that may influence the outcome of the project.

Administrative issues

An RFP must include two schedules—one for the administration of the bidding process and a second for the project. The project schedule is included under the contractual issues and is discussed later.

The administrative aspects of the RFP dictate the boundaries and deadlines that bidders must adhere to to respect the conditions of the proposal. This section outlines the administrative issues and steps that all bidding vendors must take to have their proposals accepted.

The administration schedule is usually included in the general information section or it can stand alone as a separate section. This schedule includes

- The release date of the RFP
- The bidder's proposal submission date
- The date the decision will be announced
- The number of copies to submit
- When supplemental information is required
- When bidders will be contacted
- Whether a vendor presentation is required

The administration section of the RFP also tells potential bidders how to submit their proposal, including how many copies are required, whose attention to address it to, and where to submit it. Always include an administrative contact whom bidders can speak with should they require additional information. The administrative process also answers such bidder questions as these:

- How will bidders' questions be addressed?
- Will all bidders have access to the questions and answers?
- Will the submitted proposals be published?
- What is the official process for communicating during the RFP process?
- How will the proposals be evaluated?

There may be other issues that are not addressed here but that are relevant to your RFP. The administrative aspects of the RFP process are often very useful for vendors preparing their proposals for bid. But be careful not to place too many constraints on yourself, as the bidders will hold you to the conditions outlined in the RFP.

Proposal structure

The objective of your request for proposals is to obtain as many submissions from vendors as possible. However, receiving a large number of proposals can be overwhelming, especially if each is structured differently and does not provide the same information. It is also unfair to the bidders if they are not compared on an equal and fair basis. It is your responsibility to state clearly in the RFP how you want to see submitted information organized. This also demonstrates to the bidder the thought process and thorough organization of the project.

Each RFP you produce may differ in some ways from others, but it should have the following proposal sections for the bidders to adhere to.

Vendor authorization Each vendor must include a letter with the proposal that legally binds the vendor or consultant to the proposal if it is accepted. This is to prevent vendors from backing away from their commitment and holds them accountable for what they promise to deliver in the proposed solution. A legally binding document can be as simple as a letter of transmittal signed by an officer of the company. The letter of transmittal is usually the cover letter to the proposal.

Budget outline A central component of all RFPs is the budget. You may or may not disclose the expected range for the project but you will want to structure vendors' budget presentations in one format. A standardized budget structure will provide a common format for all bidders to follow and facilitate your reviewing process. Essentially, it helps you compare proposed investments equitably. Make sure that you include any details that are important to you and develop a standardized budget structure for your project. Each project may require a different budgeting structure.

Project scheduling It is wise to develop a project schedule and to include it in the RFP. A project schedule outline provides boundaries for the bidders and demonstrates your expectations and standards. If you do propose a project schedule, state clearly that all proposals must adhere to it as a condition of bid acceptance. Alternatively, you may ask the bidders to include their proposed schedules. If this is your choice, be explicit about the level and kinds of detail you expect from them and state that they will be held to this schedule if their bid is accepted. Be certain to include specific milestones you want to see, evaluative processes you want conducted, and the consequences of not adhering to the schedule.

Company information Every bidder must include complete information about itself (company or individual). This is especially important for vendors that are not well known or with which you have had little experience. The information required includes

- Description of the company and its history
- References (for example, from previous clients for similar projects)
- References and résumés for the individuals who will be involved in the project
- Complete address and contact information
- Any other relevant information or documents

Technical issues

Technical issues are becoming a growing area for T&D. A technical section is included if you anticipate or require that some form of technology will be a part of the overall project. With new technology often becoming an integrated part of delivering and supporting training initiatives, the technical section of the RFP can be important. Let's say you are developing a training program for your administrative staff. You may want to have a blended learning approach that includes classroom work, coaching, and an e-learning support mechanism after the training is complete. The e-learning component would constitute the project's technology requirements. Moreover, your IT department members will tell you when you consult them that you also need to think about the technical infrastructure to support the e-learning. These issues should be listed in the RFP if you expect the selected vendor to support these requirements.

If your project has technical needs and requires technical support, work with your IT department to review the specific requirements. Begin by giving an overview of the technical goals. This should be followed by a detailed description of the technical requirements and the current configurations. Explain any technical constraints you are placing on the project and itemize the equipment you will need. This can include computer hardware and software, technician time, peripherals and accessories, communication equipment, and presentation equipment (television, projector, DVD or video player, and so forth). If you expect the bidder to support these needs then you will want to include other details that will help vendors to budget appropriately. The items may include some of the following:

- Number of participants and users
- Locations of training, and whether these locations are geographically dispersed
- Your current technical configuration and specifications
- Equipment available for vendors' use
- The liberty vendors have to integrate their own technology needs

If you expect the vendor to implement new software or a learning solution that requires some type of software support then you will want to provide the vendor with information about your network (without providing critical information that may place your company network security at risk). Some items you will want to identify include the

- Current operating system
- Hardware configuration and communication
- Security software
- Supporting software for the new application

It is also critical to consider the installation and support of the required training technology. Does your company have staff capable of supporting the new application, or would you rather have the vendor support it? Are there any upgrades or revisions required? What happens if the technology fails or adversely affects the company's infrastructure? All these questions and many more must be asked and your resulting needs outlined in your RFP. If your RFP does not include this information then the bid you receive will be misleading and incomplete and the responsibility will rest with you.

Contractual obligation

The RFP is a contractual process that commits the chosen provider to completing the project as defined in the RFP. The RFP is basically your outline for the contract that the vendor will sign. For this reason it is important that you work closely with legal counsel to include any standard terms and conditions expected from all your suppliers and to protect your interests. The RFP must disclose all your conditions so potential bidders are clear about the type of contract they will be entering.

Evaluation of Proposals

The evaluation process for received bids must be fair and objective. To ensure the integrity and fairness of the proposal evaluation it is crucial that you put together a cross-functional group of people from your company to perform the evaluation task. This will help you to

- Not assume full responsibility for the final decision
- Delegate the evaluation of complex proposals
- Delegate the evaluation of specialized areas to company experts
- Gain the input of those affected by or investing in the project
- Reduce subjectivity and bias
- Ensure that bidders feel they are treated fairly
- Simplify and accelerate the proposal process

The objective of this evaluation process is to select the best vendors to participate in the final round in the selection process. It is important that the evaluation be transparent so bidders will respect the final decision and bid again in the future. You may want to include the evaluation method in the RFP.

As you can see, the RFP process can be involved, especially as projects become more complex. The points presented here provide you with a solid foundation to help you put together your next RFP. Whether this is your first RFP or you have done one previously, these quick tips will ease your efforts:

- Put together a cross-functional team from your company.
- Gather other successful RFPs and compare yours against them.

- Delegate the areas of the RFP in which you are weak (for example, technical issues).

- Focus on the details.

- Review the RFP with management and legal counsel.

Thinking Like Management

- Is tendering an RFP our only alternative?

- Who needs to be involved in developing the RFP?

- What is the objective of the RFP?

- What challenges will we face in creating the RFP?

Samantha began the RFP process and put together a cross-functional team to assist. Her team was made up of Edward, the production director of the pilot facility; Joshua, the operations manager; Ron, the company controller; and herself. They discussed the requirements for the RFP and began working to put it together. (Their RFP is displayed in Exhibit 4.6.)

Exhibit 4.6. Request for Proposal Used by VEHD Inc.

Executive Summary

VEHD Inc. is a leading North American software manufacturer. The products are sold worldwide and produced in five production facilities in the United States.

VEHD is in the process of developing and implementing a work process production training program. The program has been implemented in a pilot manufacturing facility with success and positive feedback from the production employees.

VEHD is moving forward to deploy this unique training program across all its facilities in the United States. The company's primary objective is to have all the production staff adopt the more efficient workflow process. The training program will be a blended learning approach, comprising classroom and e-learning solutions. The training provider interested in participating in this project would need to commit a qualified work team along with 10 to 15 facilitators and collaborate closely with the VEHD training and production department. The selected company will have experience and demonstrate results in both e-learning and class-based training delivery.

Exhibit 4.6. Request for Proposal Used by VEHD Inc., Cont'd

General Information

All proposing training vendors must complete the enclosed request for proposal in full. All components must be completed. Any information left out will immediately disqualify the vendor's RFP.

VEHD Inc. has been in business for 12 years and has grown into one of the leading manufacturers of software. The company has 5 facilities across the United States with over 1,000 employees. The company is ISO 9000 certified and currently has a comprehensive production training program for all of its employees.

The current training project will entail training all of the 1,000 employees over an 8-month time frame. The project would require a minimum of 10 to 15 facilitators and a supporting e-learning course.

Administrative Issues

RFP release date:	February 1, 2006
Proposal submission date:	April 1, 2006
Decision date:	June 1, 2006
Number of copies required:	5 complete copies
Date limit for additional info:	July 1, 2006
Presentation date:	July 20, 2006
Submit to:	VEHD Inc.
	c/o Samantha Hague, Director of Training
Address:	1234 Anywhere Street, Suite #400
	City, State, Zip

Questions and Additional Information

All questions and inquiries regarding this request must be directed to Samantha Hague, c/o the RFP Production Training Committee. A maximum of 5 inquiries is permitted. If there are more inquiries the submission will be disqualified.

Additional information is available directly through the VEHD Inc. Web site at www.vehdinc.com/rfp. Please do not contact VEHD or any of its employees or representatives. The RFP committee will contact you should further information or clarification be required.

Continued

Exhibit 4.6. Request for Proposal Used by VEHD Inc., Cont'd

Communication Process

The RFP committee and VEHD Inc.'s management are permitted to communicate with prospective bidders. Unless stated otherwise, the RFP committee will communicate directly with the bidding vendors. Only the vendors' bids that move to the next round of selections will be notified. All postings and selections will be posted on the VEHD Web site.

Evaluation Process

All proposals received by the submission date will be evaluated. The evaluation process will use a weighted average process, measuring the following criteria on a scale of 1 to 4, with 4 representing that the bid meets the condition completely. The criteria are

- Reputation
- Experience
- Technical capacity
- Delivery experience
- Quality of training
- Cost in relation to value

Vendor Authorization

All proposals must include a letter of transmittal signed by officers of the company. This will verify the vendor's commitment to the information disclosed and proposed in its proposal. The letter of transmittal will constitute a legal and binding bid on the part of the vendor.

Budget Details

The project budget is not disclosed in this RFP. The budget will not be disclosed at any time during the bidding process. A proposal will be selected based on the weighted scores and the estimated budget proposed by the vendor in its proposal.

Project Schedule

The project schedule listed below is not modifiable. Vendors unable to comply with this schedule will be disqualified. The vendor selected not adhering to the schedule will face penalties.

Exhibit 4.6. Request for Proposal Used by VEHD Inc., Cont'd

Acceptance date:	August 1, 2006
Project start date:	August 20, 2006
Project completion date:	April 1, 2007
Needs analysis review:	Aug 21, 2006 to Aug 31, 2006
E-learning development:	Aug 21, 2006 to Oct 1, 2006
Training delivery:	Sept 15, 2006 to April 1, 2007
Plant 1:	Sept 15, 2006 to Oct 30, 2006
Plant 2:	Oct 1, 2006 to Nov 30, 2006
Plant 3:	Nov 1, 2006 to Jan 1, 2007
Plant 4:	Jan 1, 2007 to Feb 1, 2007
Plant 5:	Jan 20, 2007 to Mar 1, 2007
Completion details and review	Mar 1, 2007 to April 1, 2007

About Your Company

Every bidder must include complete information about itself. Please provide as much detail as you believe is relevant to this project and for VEHD to get to know your company. The information required includes

- Description of the company and its history
- References (such as previous clients for similar projects)
- References and résumés of those involved in the project
- Complete address and contact information
- Any other relevant information or documents

Technical Considerations

As this project involves an e-learning support course for all members of the production team, the selected vendor must demonstrate skills and experience with technical and computer-related issues. The following information will assist you in completing the RFP:

VEHD computing platform:	Windows NT Professional
Number of terminals:	900
Connection:	Wide and local area networks

Continued

Exhibit 4.6. Request for Proposal Used by VEHD Inc., Cont'd

Internet and Web:	Available or connected
Number of participants and users:	1,000
Location of terminals	
Plant 1:	Montreal, Canada
Plant 2:	Ithaca, New York
Plant 3:	Atlanta, Georgia
Plants 4 and 5:	Monterey, California
Equipment available for use:	IT test center, Monterey, California
IT staff available:	5 IT MS Certified professionals
Security:	Firewalls, antivirus programs
Integration of your technology:	Limited to the IT test center
Learning management system:	Learn LMS

Contractual Obligation

This RFP will constitute the basis of the final contract. All information presented in the vendor proposal and obtained from the RFP will be regarded as legally binding. The signed agreement and contract will include all the promised deliverables and specifications of the RFP.

CD-ROM RESOURCE

Open the "Request for Proposal Template" file on your CD for a blank template that you can use as a framework when structuring your own RFPs.

Selecting the Right Vendor

Today's T&D departments are realizing the important role that external vendors and suppliers of learning solutions play in improving learning productivity. With increasing demands placed on T&D and new and innovative tools and techniques available, selecting and developing long-term relationships with suppliers is critical. Given the importance of selecting the right vendor, the selection and evaluation process must be objective and thorough.

There are many ways to evaluate potential vendors and suppliers, but implementing a recognized and systematic process used among industry peers is your best choice. The selection process can be delicate and is best served by an unbiased approach. There are two widely used selection methodologies that are relatively simple to use and implement:

- Categorical approach
- Weighted average approach

Each method offers flexibility, simplicity, and adaptability to any size or complexity of vendor selection process.

Categorical Approach

The categorical approach is a simple and informal process of vendor selection. You have probably used it or something similar to it for your needs already, perhaps without knowing its name. This approach works best when more than one person or a cross-functional team is involved.

Each process participant lists his or her preferred selection criteria. For example, management's selection criteria might include price, implementation time, and ongoing support. The list of criteria should be focused on the needs of the project and on the concerns of the process team members.

The next step is to establish a simple scale for measuring how well each vendor meets the selection criteria. The scale could use verbal descriptions of quality, such as "poor," "fair," "good," and "excellent," or numerical descriptions, such as a 1 to 5 scale in which the numbers represent ascending levels of quality. The choice is up to you and the requirements of the selection process. Independently, each member uses the scale to grade each vendor on the member's selection criteria. The group then meets to agree on the primary selection criteria that will decide final selection. They then state their independent findings and discuss their differences, finally selecting an appropriate vendor.

The categorical approach is convenient and more objective than simply having one or two people make a subjective decision. The approach is not perfect but its greatest strength is avoiding personal biases and relationships with bidders that may affect the outcome of vendor selection. The approach is simple and very adaptable to a variety of selection scenarios. The problem with this approach is its informality and its potential for producing a biased outcome if some team members are particularly influential or if groupthink starts operating. There is no real way to formally track which criteria have the most impact on the decision and to determine what influences led to a particular decision.

Weighted Average Approach

The weighted average approach uses elements similar to those used in the categorical approach. There is a list of selection criteria and a quality scale to measure how well the criteria are met. The selection criteria, however, are decided by the group prior to reviewing any vendor proposals. The criteria are usually derived from the RFP and from knowledge of what is important to successful project completion. Some of the criteria may address items related to the vendors, such as warranties, reputation, and support. The criteria chosen are at the discretion of the selection team. The main difference from the categorical approach lies in the weighting of each criterion.

Each criterion is assigned a numerical factor, which is called a *weight.* A criterion's weight is directly correlated to its importance in relation to the other criteria. For example, the criterion of technical support for e-learning software may be more important, and hence assigned more weight, than the criterion of a vendor warranty. The range of the weighting scale is usually 0 percent to 100 percent. For example, vendor location might have a weight of 5 percent whereas vendor experience might carry a weight of 40 percent.

For each vendor you are evaluating, a table of ratings and weights is completed. In Table 4.3, for example, we see that Vendor A has received a total score of 2.65 on a scale running from 1 to 4. This result on its own does not mean anything of course; it must be compared to the results for the other vendors evaluated. Use a separate table to score each vendor. Once this part of the evaluation is complete, the next step is to compile the results into one table (see Table 4.4), so all the vendors can be compared side-by-side.

Table 4.3. Weighted Average Score for Vendor A (Vendor Evaluation)

Vendor Name: Vendor A

Selection Criteria	Excellent	Good	Fair	Poor	N/A	Weight	Total
	4	3	2	1	0		
Knowledge	X					0.15	0.6
Reputation		X				0.10	0.3
Quality			X			0.20	0.4
Customization					X	0.20	0.2
Support		X				0.15	0.45
Experience	X					0.10	0.4
Cost/value		X				0.10	0.3
						1.00	2.65

Table 4.4. Weighted Average Scores for Comparing Vendors A, B, C, and D (Vendor Selection)

Selection Criteria	Vendors			
	A	B	C	D
Knowledge	0.6	0.4	0.5	0.45
Reputation	0.3	0.5	0.4	0.4
Quality	0.4	0.2	0.6	0.4
Customization	0.2	0.1	0.4	0.2
Support	0.45	0.3	0.45	0.3
Experience	0.4	0.1	0.3	0.2
Cost/value	0.3	0.2	0.4	0.1
Weighted total	2.65	1.80	3.05	2.05

The average scores in Table 4.4 provide a clear overview of how the vendors compare with each other overall and on each of the selection criteria. As mentioned earlier, some selection criteria will have priority over others, and if a vendor does not meet your minimum score for the criterion in question then that company is automatically eliminated from the selection process. The minimum number for qualification is totally up to you, but it is important to set a minimum, to set a base for your evaluation and judgment. What you need to be careful about is subjectivity in selecting a minimum score and bias in the scores themselves. Let's say, for example, that customization is a priority for your project and your team has determined that the minimum score a vendor must receive in this area is 2.0. If Table 4.4 represented your vendors' scores, then Vendor B would be automatically eliminated from your selection process.

When you are responsible for the selection process, be sure to watch for discrepancies and large variations in the evaluators' scores. Large gaps and swings in score results may indicate that evaluators do not all have the same information or that some bias is involved in the process. The weighted average approach is a dependable process for selecting vendors. It is important that team members agree on the

- Selection criteria
- Measurement scale
- Weighting of each criterion

The weighted average approach is more dependable and objective than the categorical approach and is adaptable to a variety of selection processes. The bias that can occur is in the decisions about the selection criteria along with the weight attributed to each criterion. However, you can minimize this bias by developing measures around your team's and organization's requirements and by seeking input from other functions and external resources.

CD-ROM RESOURCE

Open the "Vendor Evaluation and Selection" file on your CD. Click on the "Vendor Evaluation" tab for a template that you can use to rate how well a vendor meets your criteria. Click on the "Vendor Selection" tab for a template that you can use to select from among your top-rated vendors.

A total of ten vendor proposals were received by VEHD, of which four were disqualified for violating strict RFP conditions. Samantha gathered the evaluation team together and presented the six remaining proposals. She asked that team members go through the six proposals independently to screen out the remaining vendors that did not meet the most important criteria of the RFP, such as having experience in e-learning development, being able to dedicate ten to fifteen facilitators, and having previous experience or references.

When the team reassembled after one week, three vendors remained to be considered. Samantha and the team used the weighted average process to evaluate the three vendors based on the criteria stated in the RFP. Their findings are shown in Table 4.5.

Table 4.5. Weighted Averages for Proposed VEHD Vendors A, B, and C

	Vendors		
Selection Criteria	**A**	**B**	**C**
Knowledge	0.4	0.6	0.6
Reputation	0.15	0.5	0.5
Quality	0.4	0.2	0.6
Customization	0.2	0.1	0.4
Support	0.3	0.45	0.6
Experience	0.2	0.4	0.3
Cost/value	0.3	0.2	0.2
Weighted total	1.95	2.45	3.20

The Importance of Selecting the Right Vendor

Selecting a vendor can be a short process. But if you want to select the right vendor then it will require an investment of time and effort. Taking shortcuts will likely result in your eventually regretting your initial quick decision, and most of the time it will be too late to make any changes. The saying, "If you want something to last do it right the first time," applies here. A vendor today, especially in T&D, is more than just a supplier of products or services—it is a partner to your company in achieving long-term success and growth. To find the right vendor will take time. Not investing the needed time and effort in the vendor selection process will lead to certain challenges to overcome, including

- *Lack of continuity leading to a lack of direction and focus.* Not having the right vendors leads to constant change that does not leverage any type of synergy or consistency.

- *Exhausting available vendors and not being able to turn to others.* If you are using one vendor after another, you will come to be seen as lacking loyalty to your suppliers. This leads to a lack of trust and vendors who do not want to do business with your company.

- *Having too many vendors involved in the company and projects.* Using the services of many different vendors leads to inconsistencies and wastes time and money. It is costly to have new vendors constantly taking over from previous ones because each vendor has its own way of working and these changeovers can lead to mistakes.

- Selecting the right vendor right from the beginning is important, not only for the T&D department itself but also for building management's confidence in T&D's value in the long term.

Here is some further advice on selecting vendors.

Look for an established reputation

When seeking vendors, much depends on two things: (1) the quality of the vendor and (2) the relationship you build with the vendor. Both are directly related to the vendor's reputation. This is not to say that more recently formed vendors are worse than established ones, or smaller ones worse than larger ones, but established vendors with good reputations understand how to develop result-oriented solutions and build quality relationships. This applies to large and small vendors alike. Size has nothing to do with the result—it is reputation and references that create long-term value. Even if takes more time to find the right vendor and more money to pay for this vendor's solution, that is outweighed by knowing that this company will be not just your vendor but also a partner.

Get what you contract for

The biggest challenge many companies face when bringing on a new vendor for a project is not obtaining the people who were promised in the initial bid. This places you in a difficult position that you should not be in. At times this is not intentional and at other times vendors do this to convince you of their abilities. Whatever the reason for it, you need to ensure that you have the right people on the project. There are a few ways to accomplish this. First, during the negotiation stage of the contract ask the vendor for a contractual commitment that the people presented to work on the project will be available and will be directly involved. There are terms, conditions, and exception clauses that can ensure that this contractual obligation is respected. You can, for example, stipulate that if for some unexpected reason the people presented are unavailable during the project, you will have the right to approve the résumés of the replacements.

This is a good first step if you are in the negotiation stage, but what if last-minute changes happen during the project itself? As mentioned earlier, it is important to verify the vendor's background and references. But often the vendor will provide you with only the best references to impress you. Take the verification a step further, and conduct your own informal background checks of the vendor and of the people who will be involved in the project, especially individuals who are being parachuted in as last-minute replacements. Another option is to find people who have had experience with your company before or on similar projects who can work through the vendor. If the vendor really wants to make you happy, it will hire some of the people you recommend. This will also take some of the pressure off the vendor as these people are your recommendations.

Select a vendor strategically

Let's go back to a point I briefly discussed earlier. Selecting a vendor is more than simply finding a supplier to do a job. Your project is too important to leave to the lowest bidder. The goal is to build credibility for T&D and position it as a strategic partner to management. You have come too far to shortcut the vendor selection process. There is a considerable time and resource commitment in selecting the right vendor, accompanied with the risk of making a wrong decision. This is why it is important to find a vendor that will be involved for the long term and act more as a partner than just a supplier.

Building relationships with vendors is a challenge. On the one hand you want to involve them as much as possible, but on the other hand you do not want to be completely dependent on their services. Vendors who are serious will understand that they have a vested interest in building a relationship. If you spread a project out among several vendors and don't develop any repeatable pattern of work, these vendors won't be partners in helping you reach your goals because you're not helping them reach theirs.

It is important to rcfcr to vendors as partners. But being partners means working together for one successful outcome, not one party working for the other. Building a vendor into a strategic partner requires that both parties

- Have open and forthright communication
- Work collaboratively
- Focus on common objectives
- Challenge preconceptions
- Contribute their different points of view

The true test to determine if your relationship with your vendor is growing into a strategic partnership is to ask the difficult questions: Are you keeping any information from the vendor? Are you limiting access to budgets and resources constraints? Are you questioning the vendor's ability to fulfill certain aspects of the project? If you are holding back on any information relevant to the success of the project, then it is possible that you may not have a strong partnership with the vendor.

> The members of the vendor selection team were happy with the process and were confident that the right choice had been made when they selected Vendor C. However, there was one more thing on Samantha's mind. She knew that the process they put in place was solid, but she wanted to make certain that the vendor selected met some additional criteria. She realized the importance this project had in the eyes of senior management and wanted to ensure that the vendor would become a strategic partner with the training department and the company. She and the team moved forward to review the vendor's reputation and references. They decided to do some informal research on Vendor C and to ensure that the formal reference provided was not biased in the vendor's favor.

The research discovered that the vendor had a solid reputation but also one failed project. The vendor had made a concerted effort to correct the problem, however, even though that effort was unsuccessful. This demonstrated the vendor's commitment to the project. The team also discovered that some of the projects the vendor worked on showed significant returns on investment within twelve months of implementation. This pleased the team members, and they moved forward to contact the vendor to announce the news that it was selected for the project.

Thinking Like Management

- Have we found the top vendors?
- Is our process fair and objective—immune to attacks from external sources?
- Did we verify the backgrounds and references of the top vendors?
- Do we have a secondary vendor in the event the first does not work out?
- What is the cost in relation to the value we will receive by using a vendor?

It's important to know how to negotiate a contract with a vendor. Exhibit 4.7 offers some key points to keep in mind.

Exhibit 4.7. Seven Negotiating Tips

1. Clearly define your specific requirements, including goals and objectives.
2. Put into place a request for proposal (RFP) process with the essential details.
3. Define vendor responsibilities.
4. Outline clear and specific performance measures.
5. Never utilize the vendor's contract, as it presents a bias to their needs.
6. Set up a reporting mechanism that measures the outcomes of the contract.
7. Ensure you account for the vendor's position and understand their motives.

Review

As the demands on business grow and become increasing specialized, there will always be a need for additional resources to fill the gap. The choice for businesses is either to hire additional staff or to outsource their requirements to external vendors and consultants. T&D departments are certain to face both situations, and what you decide and how you handle the situation will determine how T&D is seen among managers and decision makers.

Outsourcing external help is often seen as a viable option as it delivers the expertise required, reduces the demands on internal resources, and is an excellent option for highly specialized, noncore, and nonrecurring projects. It is also a way to demonstrate to management an impact on business and a potentially positive return on investment.

Your ability to select the right external resource is highly dependent on how you develop and structure the vendor request for proposal (RFP). Successful RFPs present a clear scope of the project and include all relevant project information. The RFP states the requirements of the project in clear and definable terms and should include as much detail as possible. The RFP is the basis for the contractual obligations to which the winning vendor must adhere.

Once you received proposals from potential vendors, the next step is to pick the right one. The selection process should be taken seriously. Using a systematic process such as the categorical or weighted average approach will assist you in making the best decision for your project. Although the evaluation score is based on predetermined criteria, it is always important to consider other factors, including strategic alignment and the vendor's reputation.

There is much to consider when deciding to source and select an external resource. The other alternative is to hire additional employees. When done properly this option presents its own benefits and challenges. Whether you choose to outsource or hire internally, one thing is certain—you must know how to manage successful working relationships. This process is about building strategic partners and relationships. Here are some tips:

- Clearly form and communicate the goals and objectives of your project or business relationship.
- Have a strategic vision and plan for your project or relationship.

- Select the right vendor or new employee through research and references.
- Insist on a contract or plan that includes all the expectations of the relationship, especially the financial aspect.
- Keep communications open with all affected individuals and groups.
- Rally support and involvement from all decision makers involved.

Review Quiz

1. Outsourcing is defined as

   _____ One company hiring or contracting with its employees to provide services usually performed by external companies.

   _____ Management contracting with shareholders to provide services to the public usually performed by the company's employees.

   _____ One company hiring or contracting with another company to provide services usually performed internally by the first company's employees.

   _____ None of the above.

2. Advantages of outsourcing include

   _____ Gaining additional expertise and experience.

   _____ Reducing fixed overhead for one-time or infrequent needs.

   _____ Increasing business impact (level 4).

   _____ Saving money.

   _____ All of the above.

3. Disadvantages of outsourcing include

   _____ Lack of total control over the outsourced activities.

   _____ Delayed communication and project implementation.

   _____ Lack of control over proprietary knowledge and rights.

   _____ All of the above.

4. RFP is an abbreviation for

   ____ Request for profitability.

   ____ Requesting formal purchases.

   ____ Request for partner.

   ____ Request for proposal.

   ____ None of the above.

5. The first step in preparing a well-developed RFP is

   ____ Preparing the project budget.

   ____ Defining the scope of the training project.

   ____ Determining who will be involved.

   ____ Deciding how much food to order.

6. One component of an RFP is

   ____ A budget outline.

   ____ Administrative issues.

   ____ Contractual issues.

   ____ A project schedule.

   ____ All of the above.

7. For all RFPs it is important to

   ____ Put together a cross-functional team from your company.

   ____ Delegate the areas of the RFP in which you are weak (for example, technical issues).

   ____ Review the RFP with management and legal counsel.

   ____ Focus on the details.

   ____ All of the above.

8. The process of assigning scores to select potential vendors is called

    ____   Categorical approach.

    ____   Numbered benefit approach.

    ____   Cost-benefit approach.

    ____   Weighted average approach.

9. Not selecting the right vendor leads to

    ____   A lack of continuity.

    ____   Having too many vendors involved.

    ____   Exhausting the available vendors.

    ____   All of the above.

10. Hiring employees rather than outsourcing provides the company with

    ____   More control over the project.

    ____   Higher wages.

    ____   Delays in the project.

    ____   A shorter learning curve.

Answer Key for Chapter Four Review Quiz

1. One company hiring or contracting with another company to provide services usually performed internally by the first company's employees.

2. All of the above.

3. All of the above.

4. Request for proposal.

5. Defining the scope of the training project.

6. All of the above.

7. All of the above.

8. Weighted average approach.

9. All of the above.

10. More control over the project.

Section 2
Partnering Skills

5

Building Institutional Support

LARRY CLOSED HIS COMPUTER BAG in disgust. This was the third senior-level meeting he had attended in the last two weeks where he had not been given an opportunity to speak. Each time he had been on the meeting's official agenda, but somehow there never seemed to be enough time to discuss his topic. There was little doubt in Larry's mind that people were simply paying him lip service. He had had such high hopes. Two and half weeks ago, Dana, the new CEO of Perfect Plastics, had sent a company-wide memo emphasizing the central role training and development would play in the company's new strategy. Her vision called for the company to grow its product line, diversify its market, and develop a new service arm of the business. Every area of the company would be affected by the changes. Overall the climate at Perfect Plastics was good. Whatever fear and uncertainty people were feeling was counterbalanced by excitement. People were ready to roll up their sleeves and get to work.

Prior to articulating her vision, Dana had asked each department head to develop a list of key recommendations of what he or she felt the company needed to do to successfully execute its new set of goals and objectives. Larry spent two months and many late nights developing his recommendations. This was the opportunity Larry had always dreamed about. He and his team were sick of the random, careless training requests thrown over the wall to the training department. Maybe at last training and development could become a proactive player as opposed to a reactive player. Last year's annual training survey indicated that the organization's level of satisfaction with training was low. Larry faced another obstacle. The department's recent implementation of a learning management system (LMS) was viewed by many of the other functional areas in the organization as an unnecessary expenditure in tight times. In fact, Larry's success in getting the project funded had created a few new political animosities.

During Larry's five-year tenure as director of training and development, his quiet, attentive, purposeful demeanor had helped him earn the respect and trust of his employees. However, things were different outside his department. Larry's sphere of influence within the company was weak at best. What did it matter if he was on Dana's radar screen when no one else would give him the time of day? Larry walked into his office, put his laptop down on the conference table, and pulled out a yellow pad from his desk. What he needed was a plan for winning the trust and support of the organization. He had lots of great ideas about how his department could make a difference; now he had to find a way of getting the word out.

The first four chapters of this book gave you an overview of the financial mechanics that are essential to increasing business acumen. In this chapter we turn our attention to the subtleties of building relationships. Our value as professionals will never be realized unless we form strong strategic relationships throughout our organizations. None of us want to find ourselves in Larry's predicament. I start the chapter by discussing how we can go beyond the charter of our functional silo to become key strategic contributors to our organizations' success. Next I look at how to be more effective at selling T&D's services throughout the organization, including detailed instructions for conducting a stakeholder analysis that examines perceptions of T&D. Two case studies are then offered. One concerns TDS Telecom and the second one is fictitious, but both will get you thinking about the chapter's theme. Instead of a review quiz, the four chapters in this section of the book end with some questions for reflection.

Beyond Functional Silos

Gone are the days of functional silos operating independently of one another. The success of today's organization rests in its ability to integrate all its differentiated parts. Work is not done in isolation. We are dependent upon everyone's unique talents and experiences. Organizations are challenged to respond quickly to competitive changes. This necessitates information moving across functional silos. For example, the marketing department needs to share its information with sales, product development, and other functional areas. Unless functions have almost real-time access to each other's information and can develop complex business processes, they and their larger organizations lack agility. T&D faces these same challenges. We must learn how to reach beyond the comforts of our well-established practices, processes, and procedures and continually discover new ways to bring value to the organization.

Building institutional support for T&D's work requires us to reach out to our organizations. The way we define T&D's role and the activities we are engaged in are going to be driven by the organization and its goals. Because an organization's goals are constantly shifting, T&D needs to continually reinvent itself. We cannot develop or execute T&D's charter in a vacuum. Our challenge lies in positioning T&D as a flexible resource capable of optimizing itself to facilitate the delivery of key organizational objectives. We must also provide a clear core mission and stable environment for the people who work in T&D. Serving as the organization's "heart of learning" requires that we tear down many of the preconceived notions we have about the walls of our own silo.

Selling T&D in the Organization

Listening is an essential skill for selling T&D in an organization. Listening demonstrates T&D's ability and willingness to adapt to the needs of an organization. We must go out of our way to understand our customers in order to determine how to help them achieve their objectives. We cannot expect people to come to us. Only after we build strong inroads with people and establish our credibility will people proactively seek our help. Until then we need to reach out. When we listen to people and observe the work they are engaged in, we will discover opportunities where we can make a difference. They may not be what we expect. Going in with an open mind and attentive eyes is what is necessary. We also need to be careful not to jump to conclusions or take what we hear from people at face value. What people ask for and what people need may be very different. Working together we can explore solutions.

The ability to think from other people's organizational and personal perspectives is central to building institutional support and selling T&D. Each area of an organization represents a frame of reference. Because T&D serves all areas of the business we have to become skilled at moving in and out of various perspectives. Our perspective becomes secondary to understanding, appreciating, and thinking from other perspectives. Pacing with people, meeting them on their turf, and making an effort to speak the language inherent to their functional area is our greatest challenge. When we succeed in temporarily abandoning our perspective and immersing ourselves in other people's organizational worldviews, tremendous results become possible. It's a simple truism; when people feel that you have listened to them, they are more inclined to listen to you.

We have to be careful to avoid the temptation to immediately fit a functional area's needs into our collection of prefabricated solutions. That flies in the face of listening. People need to feel that their unique needs have been understood and that we haven't rushed to offer them a cookie-cutter solution. Selling T&D as a strategic asset demands that we help our customers feel unique even when we may realistically slot them into tried-and-true interventions. We stand to learn a lot in the process. Our customers offer us wonderful opportunities to continuously develop, grow, and stretch in new directions. Learning is dynamic, so it should come as no surprise that we need to model these principles in the way we do our work.

As we become more skilled at listening, we also become better at anticipating what our customers will need. We start viewing our customers' new projects and initiatives as opportunities for T&D. We come to the table with ideas and recommendations. Our customers begin viewing T&D as a strategic partner. Powerful things happen when our customers realize we are looking at the world from their organizational perspective. In the beginning it will be impossible for you to reach out to all the areas of your organization, so start with a small win. Small wins add up to bigger ones. As you build momentum and institutional support other areas will hear your T&D success stories and begin coming to you.

Focusing on building strong relationships is critical to the success of selling T&D. We need to allot greater amounts of time to cultivating relationships. How people perceive us is directly related to the amount of time and effort we spend in reaching out to others and taking an active interest in them. Achieving results is only one part of the equation. Broadcasting our achievements and accomplishments in the form of hard facts is not convincing enough to engender trust and widespread support of our activities. We have to reach out and make an emotional connection with people. One of the best ways to do this is to share a story (see *The Strategic Use of Stories in Organizational Communication and Learning* [Gargiulo, 2005], and *Stories at Work: Using Stories to Improve Communications and Build Relationships* [Gargiulo, 2006]). Our customers need to realize we have their best interests at stake.

There is an interesting paradox in people's perceptions of T&D. People require ongoing learning to succeed. Learning implies that the learners are missing some information or experience. However, most people avoid parading their deficiencies in front of others. No one is accustomed to exhibiting personal vulnerabilities and people often fail to see their blind spots. So on the one hand people have a built-in resistance to T&D's generic charter of promoting learning, yet on the other hand people possess an intrinsic desire for receiving learning help and support. Our T&D customers need to believe we can help them and be willing to trust us. When we become too focused on the formalities of T&D we are apt to weaken our relationships with those customers. Marching people through our procedures, processes, and standard course offerings may hinder rather than aid our cause. Not that these things should be eliminated—it's just that they are not enough to build new relationships and nurture existing ones.

In order to build long-term institutional support and sell the benefits of T&D, we need to leverage every person of our team as an ambassador of goodwill. It takes a critical mass of people working together to effectively reach out to all areas of an organization. The foundation for promoting T&D stewardship is the culture we develop within our own teams. We must endeavor to create an ethos for our T&D team that exudes warmth, fascination, and tireless interest in others' well-being and development. These are qualities that generate excitement, commitment, and ownership. There is nothing soft and fuzzy here. Beyond the obvious humanistic merits of such an approach, this advice is couched in utilitarian benefits. Our customers and employees alike will embrace and respond to the positive energy we create. Encouraging our team members to be ambassadors and building a positive working environment for the team will help T&D to become an indispensable partner at the organization's strategic table. We want people to seek our participation and ideas when planning key organizational initiatives. In fact, we will know we have really succeeded in selling the potential of T&D when we begin to help the organization uncover new opportunities, when we are not just responding to support it in achieving the goals and objectives it has already set.

Stakeholder Analysis

The quickest way to build institutional support for T&D in your organization is to accurately assess how the various functional areas and individuals within them perceive the value of T&D's work. Use the "Assessment of Perceptions of T&D" form (on the CD accompanying this book) to evaluate where you stand. You will seldom have enough time or energy to address all the opportunities to build stronger institutional support, so you will want to develop an action plan that prioritizes the areas and people with the lowest assessment scores first. Keep in mind that it might also be prudent to attend to functional areas and people where you can score a *quick win.* These quick wins amount to simple actions that you can take quickly and that will yield visible positive results to T&D, to the functional area or person targeted, and to others in a position to notice the impact of your actions.

CD-ROM RESOURCE

Open the "Assessment of Perceptions of T&D" file on your CD for a form and instructions for evaluating and thinking about T&D's relationship with other organizational functions.

A Framework for Selling T&D in an Organization

The following article provides an excellent framework for selling T&D in an organization.

Selling Training

by Teresa Kirkwood and Ajay Pangarkar

. . . Selling training internally is all about being prepared, involving the appropriate individuals, and clearly understanding what executive management wants to hear. The focus must be on the benefits of the proposed training, not the features. For example, if you are proposing a customer service program for front line workers one feature would be resolving client problems. But the

Reprinted from an article that appeared in the March 2004 issue of *CMA Management* magazine by Ajay Pangarkar and Teresa Kirkwood, with permission of Certified Management Accountants of Canada.

benefit would be an increase in customer satisfaction or an increase in repeat sales. Applying the feature/benefit principle will help you sell your program to the biggest critics.

Know Your Audience

When seeking buy-in for training-related projects, training managers often focus on getting support from the high-level decision makers, executive management. But there are only two possible outcomes to this—either management approves or rejects the project. If it's approved, then only one level of decision makers is sold on the idea. The training, more often than not, rarely succeeds because those directly affected were not consulted. Resistance from that group can destroy the project.

Successful training managers recognize early who they need to approach to get a training program off the ground. Essentially, there are three groups to address: the training participants, mid-level managers, and executive management.

Training participants will accept any training if it provides them with value-added resources and doesn't take time away from their immediate responsibilities. The training must be easy for them to absorb and incorporate into their daily activities if it's to change behavior. It's important to balance the needs of the participant with the need for performance improvement. Effectively doing this aligns their goals with the needs of business managers and broadens the scope of training.

When dealing with mid-level managers, it's important to recognize their requirements. They need to leverage their employees' ability to achieve specific departmental or production objectives. At this level, managers are involved in budget planning and the allocation of funds directly affecting their environment. Being directly on the front lines of business, they are accountable for pre-set performance benchmarks on many levels, which places high demands on resources. Taking these concerns into account, business managers have little patience for training solutions that don't produce immediate results and take employees away from their daily responsibilities.

Decision making at the executive level focuses on maximizing profitability and minimizing expenses. These managers want to create an environment that increases sales through improving product quality and customer and employee satisfaction. Their objective is to optimize the return on their investment in every business-related activity, especially when investing in employees. In the knowledge economy, ideas, innovation, and synergy are critical to long-term success. Every training investment must ensure that the performance of the organization improves by developing a knowledgeable team of employees to effectively serve clients and to capitalize on new opportunities. It's at this level that many training managers and consultants pitch their proposal, ignoring the other participants involved in a program's execution.

Success depends on how a manager addresses the concerns of each decision maker and how the decision makers are involved in developing the training solution. Knowing your audience is essential to gain support and the first step to selling training solutions internally.

Essential Questions to Answer

It's easy to find critics for any training solution. Even if you justify the need for training there will always be individuals at every level of management challenging your reasons. As an athlete prepares for an important event, you should do the same to sell your solution. The following are common questions you'll be faced with when proposing a training solution. Understanding the questions will help you defend your position and will help you better understand how training can be effective within the organization. . . .

Do All Employees Need Training?

Management believes that every person must pass through training if they are to maximize their investment. This is a myth. Training is most effective only when the right individuals are involved. Focus your training efforts on the people with the need and those who will benefit most. For example, if you are introducing a new product, then the production team may require training in quality procedures whereas customer service employees would require training on the use of the product.

What Are the Expected Outcomes?

This is one question that management will surely ask. Training professionals often misdiagnose the problem that the required training is attempting to solve. Training's primary goal is to improve on existing processes and outcomes. This leads back to the benefits mentioned earlier. When attempting to build a case for training you must ensure that the benefits answer the needs of your audience and the investment delivers on the actual expected returns.

How Will the Training Move Us Closer to Our Goals?

Executive managers expect that every business decision should move them closer to a desired goal. Human capital investment is no exception to this rule. Managers recognize that their people are the key to their success or failure. Even more important, they also recognize that the investment they make in people is also unpredictable and volatile. Your responsibility is to assure and show management that the proposed training solution will lead them one step closer to their goals.

What Are Management's Expectations?

Each level of management has certain expectations from their investment. Clearly understanding what they are will help you in marketing training internally. At the top level, managers expect to see links between productivity and profitability. Setting up clear benchmarks against both internal and industry measures will certainly improve your case for training. Mid-managers want to see immediate outcomes and short-term results. Work closely with them to develop an implementation plan that minimizes workplace disruption and provides the necessary skills to move them closer to their immediate objectives.

What Resources Will the Training Require?

All organizations are constrained by limited resources. Many managers also believe that there are more critical issues to resolve with these resources before they will commit to training. To avoid this objection, you need to know what resources are required. Without underestimating your needs, prepare to justify your position. Then present this case to the decision makers and those that are affected by the training. . . .

The perception of training is changing and the need is growing. If real change is to take hold, training professionals, both managers and consultants, need to find effective ways to ensure true learning leads to results. Training is about developing abilities and knowledge that translate into sustained performance. Building organizational requirements and employee needs into the proposed training solutions is essential to gain acceptance.

Any effort to increase T&D's perceived value in an organization requires patience, diligence, and thoughtfulness. Although it's a truism, nothing could be more important to our work than "knowing our audience." We all try to live this adage and we preach its merits when we are delivering learning, but it's so easy to forget when we are caught in the day-to-day challenges of working inside our own organization. Without taking the time to become acquainted with our organization's needs, its people, and its goals, we will never succeed in selling T&D.

Article authors Teresa Kirkwood and Ajay Pangarkar also make an important point regarding our natural reflex to fit everything into a training solution. After all, it's what we know best and it's what we do so well, but it's not always what the organization needs. (If you are looking for a fuller discussion of how T&D departments can be more sensitive to learning and performance alternatives to training, see Harold D. Stolovitch and Erica J. Keeps's 2004 book, *Training Ain't Performance.*)

Let's reconsider Larry's predicament, as described at the beginning of the chapter, by asking the essential questions presented in Kirkwood and Pangarkar's article and seeing if answering them might help Larry in his work at Perfect Plastics.

Do All Employees Need Training?

One of the quickest ways Larry could break down some of the natural resentment and distrust he is experiencing for a variety of reasons would be to assure his stakeholders that they will not need to participate in any unnecessary or mandatory training. Of course there are times when mandatory training programs are necessary, but people are apt to be suspicious of any training recommendations as infringements on their time, as veiled excuses for justifying T&D's existence, or as eaters of scarce capital resources. Larry's stakeholders will be more willing to engage in a dialogue to identify their unique needs if they are convinced they are the drivers, and not Larry.

What Are the Expected Outcomes?

Larry needs to align his training initiatives with two or more levels of goals. The new CEO, Dana, has articulated organizational objectives. Each functional area or process area will determine a set of goals and strategic directives to support the organizational objectives. Larry must facilitate discussion with the leaders of these areas to understand their tactical plans for executing against these goals. Only then can Larry assess learning needs and put forth a set of expected outcomes created in partnership with the people whose performance will be most impacted by them.

For example, consider Dana's new organizational objectives. Recall that "her vision called for the company to grow its product line, diversify its market, and develop a new service arm of the business."

These three areas of growth identified by Dana could easily expand into a collection of cross-functional goals, each with its own learning needs that can be linked to expected outcomes. Growing the company's product line might require the research and development arm of the organization to develop new competencies in working with certain types of plastics. The manufacturing group will then need to alter some of its fabrication processes to develop the new products. The testing and engineering group will need to develop metrics and statistical quality assurance tests to ensure the integrity of the new products. The marketing group will have to better familiarize itself with competitors' products and pricing and develop new marketing initiatives and so on. Within each one of these functional areas will be a whole slew of learning needs, identified as individual roles and responsibilities are assessed. Then Larry and the director of research and development will be able to determine a set of expected outcomes. They may decide that ten of the scientists working on new products will need to spend three days with researchers at MIT who have been working with a type of plastic material that is new to the scientists working at Perfect Plastics.

How Will the Training Move Us Closer to Our Goals?

Inevitably, Larry and his organizational partners will uncover opportunities for formal training interventions. For example, staff running the new service arm of the business will need to be trained on new business processes and develop stronger customer relationship skills. At this early juncture Perfect Plastics may not have a solid understanding of the competencies required to succeed in its new business. Larry can help the organization research and benchmark itself against others to develop a stronger understanding of how employees need to be developed. Working in this fashion will ensure that any training conducted will be perceived as playing an essential role in moving the organization closer to its goals. As more is learned about running the new service arm, Larry and his team can modify and change the training to better help the organization realize its goals.

What Are Management's Expectations?

Larry and the rest of the organization know what their CEO's expectations are. The difficulty for Larry lies in how differently each of T&D's internal customers wants to pursue realizing these expectations. Some may see no place for Larry and his team, and others may be unsure of what they are doing and eager to assume training will be the magic cure-all leading to success. Either extreme is sure to be bad news for Larry. Wherever possible Larry must find ways to guide and mold the expectations of his customers. When he gets pushback from his customers, Larry will have to exercise patience and look for innovative ways to support these customers without having them feel that he is meddling in their affairs. These ways will amount to small proactive gestures aimed at softening the resistance and paving the way for more substantive interaction in the future. For those customers eager to dive into an arsenal of training solutions Larry will have to exercise caution, ask a lot of questions, and attempt to refocus their expectations.

What Resources Will the Training Require?

Whatever training Larry delivers will need to realistically identify all the resources, hidden costs, and even risks associated with it. Given the tremendous rate of change at Perfect Plastics, it's doubtful that all of the training initiatives implemented will hit their marks. Developing the trust and respect of our organizations demands we be forthright about potential failures. Training will not always equate to improvements in performance or easily measured attainment of organizational objectives. If Larry helps his customers go into a training initiative with open eyes, then all parties will be well prepared to make whatever changes are needed and dedicate the necessary resources to make the training more effective.

Case Studies in Building Institutional Support

Here are two case studies showing approaches to gaining organizational support for training and development. The first one offers the actual experience of a senior trainer at TDS Telecom.

▶ TDS TELECOM: CUSTOMER SALES AND SERVICE GROUP

The Customer Sales and Service Group (CSSG) is the heart of TDS Telecom. The group numbers over 1,000 frontline employees (outside salespeople, technicians, and residential service representatives), and it accounts for over 60 percent of the TDS Telecom training team's work. Renee Stoll, currently manager of Training, Education, and Employee Development at TDS Telecom, recounts her early experiences as a senior trainer in that team, working with an initially unenthusiastic client and bringing about change.

> When I started with the Training Team our relationship with CSSG was rocky at best. At that time 80 percent of our work was for CSSG. I was hired as Senior Trainer to do a road show of new technical training and change management.
>
> During the project I met many of CSSG's key players. Along the way I did everything I could to develop huge levels of trust. In the past CSSG saw training doing what training wanted to do and not what they needed. I was frustrated because I could see that we were not doing a good enough job of listening and understanding their needs. We were not viewed as credible. I heard from CSSG employees things like, "You might as well do it yourself; the Training Team doesn't understand us and there's no way they will hit the mark." As a team we became determined to turn around this attitude.
>
> Selling skills and product training was a complete mess. A lot of CSSG's training was happening all over the place and not being centrally funneled through our team. We made the case for more resources.
>
> I spent more and more time in the field cultivating relationships. I rolled up my sleeves and got right in there and learned as many of CSSG's systems, processes, and roles as I could. Things started to change and the pendulum swung in a new direction. Before too long the Training Team had so many training requests we couldn't handle them. We felt completely overwhelmed. I was putting in sixty to seventy hours a week in my new position as a Training Manager and I was barely treading water. I knew we needed to start prioritizing our work.
>
> I realized we were not doing a good job of communicating what we were doing. Once we received a training request from CSSG we were not keeping them informed of our progress. We started conducting quarterly meetings and then went to a monthly meeting. We began with a huge Excel spreadsheet. It became a collaborative prioritization process. The stakeholders began vying with each other. I learned how to speak in business results terms. Taking a current project and kicking it up a notch. We started evaluating what training initiatives could help generate revenues, versus efficiencies. It was not an easy process. In fact it was incredibly painful but

really worth it. Now meetings rarely last more than half an hour. I wouldn't call our Training Team proactive but we are aiming to be proactive. We are poised and ready to jump into action once CSSG begins a new business initiative. Furthermore we don't have to say no to a training request. CSSG understands what we work on and why because we are working together as partners. ◄

The next case study requires your participation, putting to use what you have learned so far. Read about the situation at the hypothetical company named Productive Industries, and then answer the questions at the end of the example.

► PRODUCTIVE INDUSTRIES

Ellen glared at her calendar. The last two months had been tough. How could her fifteen years as a successful director of training and development at Productive Industries be unraveling right before her eyes? Last year she had been honored with the company's coveted Performer of the Year award. Ellen had put training on the map by cultivating strong relationships with all the functional areas. The contributions of her team were seen as a key factor in the company's ability to achieve its business objectives.

As far as Ellen could tell, the troubles had begun at the start of the fiscal year, when a planned merger with one of Productive Industries' main competitors failed. Wall Street's earning expectations had been based on the successful completion of the merger. The stock price had soared and tensions had run high in an otherwise calm and stable company.

The $350 million a year, 1,200-employee company had been the market leader. However, in the last few years Productive Industries had lost ground to its competitors because the other companies had been more successful in diversifying their products. If Productive Industries was going to hit analysts' forecasts it would need to introduce a new product line and grow gross revenues by more than 15 percent in under a year.

The CEO decided to jump-start the development of the new product line by hiring Jennifer as vice president of product development. Jennifer, who had defected from the company Productive Industries had planned to merge with, turned out to be a bull in a china shop. She capitalized on the latitude that had been granted to her by introducing rapid change, regardless of its impact on other areas of the company. Among other things, Jennifer had hired Brad as sales and customer service training manager for the new product line. Jennifer insisted that Brad report directly to her, with a perfunctory, dotted-line relationship to Ellen.

Ellen had tried several times to set up meetings with Jennifer to learn more about the new product line and to explore how T&D could play a supporting role. Despite Ellen's attempts, Jennifer kept brushing her off and assuring her that when the time was right she would let Ellen know what role T&D could play. Ellen knew that at Jennifer's previous company T&D was not valued and was viewed more as a hindrance than a help.

The two areas of Productive Industries hit the hardest by all the activities leading up to the launch of the new product were the information technology group (ITG) and the call center. Jennifer quickly gained the political support to change ITG's priorities. ITG staff were instructed to halt work on other development projects and to reallocate funding from these projects in order to implement a new warranty application. Jerry, the director of technology, complained ad nauseam to Ellen about the new system. Ellen was shocked to learn that none of the customer service representatives (CSRs) had been involved in the user requirement meetings. The new warranty system was a commercial off-the-shelf package that Jennifer had used at her previous company. Many customizations would be necessary in order to integrate the software package with Productive Industries' other systems. Jennifer swore by the software package and was quick to point out that its Web user interface would be easier for CSRs to use than the current system.

Meanwhile Theresa, the director of the call center, was pulling her hair out. Her fifty employees had come to trust her. She had the lowest CSR turnover rate in the industry, and she attributed this to two things. First, Theresa had partnered with Ellen and human resources to design thorough training for new hires, provide ongoing training for CSRs, offer opportunities for cross-training, and identify career paths for CSRs. Second, Theresa had worked with Jerry to develop systems and tools to streamline CSR's challenging job.

Yesterday, HR had informed Theresa and Ellen that Productive Industries would need to hire twenty additional CSRs and reassign ten current CSRs; their exclusive task would be to support the new product line. Brad, the new sales and customer service training manager, recommended that training for new hires be limited to a one-day, instructor-led session to cover the company's customer service and warranty policies. All seventy CSRs would be responsible for using the company's intranet to acquaint themselves with information on over one hundred of the company's new products. Lastly, Brad had decided that no training would be required for the new Web-based warranty system. Job aids, in the form of laminated checklists, would be used, and two roaming coaches would be on site at the call center for the first three days. ◄

Questions

1. Whom do you think the new sales and customer service training manager (Brad) should report to?

2. If you were Ellen, how would you handle Jennifer's resistance to meet with you?

3. If you were Ellen, how would you respond to the immediate issues?

4. After responding to the immediate issues, if you were Ellen, what would you do to build strong relationships and institutional support for the future?

Suggested Answers

Now that you have thought about your own answers, check how thorough you were by reading through the suggested answers that follow.

1. Whom do you think the new sales and customer service training manager (Brad) should report to?

Ellen seems the best option here. Although the new sales and customer service training manager will be tightly coupled with the new product, it makes the most sense to keep training under one roof. Alternatively, Brad could report to the director of the call center. In large organizations various functional areas may have their own trainers, but it becomes challenging to manage the organization's overall learning strategy and maintain solid lines of communication.

2. If you were Ellen, how would you handle Jennifer's resistance to meet with you?

There are two principal ways to deal with Jennifer's resistance. Depending on the situation, Ellen could insist that Jennifer articulate her training and performance strategy to her, or she could express concern to senior decision makers. It's always better to work directly with the person involved, but this is neither always possible nor feasible. Stepping aside and respecting Jennifer's request is not a good option in this case. Ellen has a responsibility to the business and her department to understand any potential detrimental impacts of Jennifer's behavior and to do everything in her power to help everyone succeed.

According to the competency model of the American Society for Training and Development (ASTD) (also referenced on Table 8.1), two of the most important actions associated with business acumen are

- Understanding the business
- Understanding business operations

Ellen brings both of these attributes to the table. Jennifer may have a solid understanding of the new business processes and operational capabilities that will need to be developed, but she doesn't know or understand Productive Industries. Ultimately, a successful launch of a new product line hinges on everyone's ability to partner; not just Ellen's and Jennifer's.

3. If you were Ellen, how would you respond to the immediate issues?

There are several possible approaches:

- Get everyone together in the same room and push for collaboration.
- Make the situation work and do everything to help it succeed.
- Leverage your own rank and stature.

4. After responding to the immediate issues, if you were Ellen, what would you do to build strong relationships and institutional support for the future?

There is a set of new players in the organization. T&D's work needs to be tireless. Ellen has done an excellent job of developing strong relationships in the past. However, the addition of even one or two key new players in an organization, as in this case study, can radically alter the interpersonal dynamics. As difficult as the situation may be, Ellen does not have the luxury of taking sides. Ellen must help Jerry and Theresa develop cooperative, collaborative ties with Jennifer and Brad. This is the quickest way to ensure an ongoing, solid commitment from all involved to keep their eyes focused on the organizational target of success and not just the preservation of their own fiefdoms. Regardless of how she may feel and how difficult Jennifer is to work with, Ellen cannot let her feelings contribute to any of the negative perceptions her colleagues are forming. It's one thing to acknowledge and respect the frustration Theresa and Jerry are feeling toward Jennifer, Brad, and the situation, but it's another thing to add emotional steam to that frustration. Ellen can let Jennifer's performance speak for itself. If she continues to be a negative force in the organization there will be plenty of opportunities to address them and bring them to the attention of the appropriate decision makers.

Once the smoke clears from the frenzy of activities around the new product launch, Ellen can look for proactive opportunities to offer ad hoc training, coaching, and performance aid for the CSRs. Brad should be the first quick win. Ellen should prove to him that she wants him to be successful and that T&D is willing to share whatever resources it can. She can help Theresa and Jerry foster a strong working relationship with Brad. If Jennifer is going to be difficult to reach due to whatever past attitudes she has about T&D and perhaps some insecurity and pressure she feels in her new role, then Ellen can leverage Brad as a way of eventually reaching her. Brad will become a strong advocate for T&D if Ellen helps him succeed. He is her quickest path to Jennifer and developing institutional support. Ellen must be sure she listens carefully and understands what will help Brad succeed. Theresa will be very useful in understanding Brad's challenges and the kinds of proactive tools and strategies that T&D can provide because she has the pulse of the CSRs.

Key Points

- Building institutional support requires a focus on relationships.
- Positioning T&D as a flexible resource capable of optimizing itself to facilitate the delivery of key organizational objectives will increase T&D's importance.
- Listening is an essential skill for selling T&D in an organization because it demonstrates a willingness to adapt to the needs of the organization.
- The ability to think from other people's organizational and personal perspectives is central to building institutional support and selling T&D.
- Answer at least these essential questions when trying to sell T&D:
  1. Do employees need the training?
  2. What are the expected outcomes?
  3. How will the training move us closer to the goal?
  4. What are management's expectations?
  5. What resources will the training require?

Questions for Reflection

1. Reread the opening scenario featuring Larry. If you were Larry, what would your next steps be?

2. Think about a communication plan for Larry. Whom should he speak with? What should his message be?

3. How can Larry mitigate some of the negative perceptions people have of him and his team?

6

Partnering
with Your Customers

LILLY **PACED BACK AND FORTH** in front of the door. The class-room was full and there was no instructor. With thirty-five people waiting and the clock showing fifteen minutes past the designated start time, Lilly wasn't sure what she should do. Where was the instructor? If no one showed up in a few minutes she would be forced to teach the class, and she had neither the time nor experience to do so. "Isn't this why I hire out-side vendors?" Lilly thought to herself.

Lilly had been in her T&D position for less than six months, and she had inherited from her predecessor a whole cadre of approved vendors—most of whom she had never even met. As far as Lilly was concerned she had no interest in meeting them. The vendors were accountable for very detailed statements of work and elaborate service-level agreements. Thanks to the corporate disciplines enacted by purchasing, all training ven-dors and contractors had to adhere to standardized work agreements, work processes for interfacing with the company, and general service-level agreements. Lilly was already composing the e-mail she was going to send to purchasing and carbon copy to legal. Someone was going to pay big for this fiasco today.

The most effective way to ensure organizational results is by partnering with all of our internal and external customers. Through partnering, relationships are built on trust and sustained by ongoing efforts of collaboration. We become aware of the interdependent nature of our work, and we seek ways to address the priorities, perspectives, needs, and concerns of everyone and not just ourselves.

The metaphor of an ecosystem provides us with some important insights. Almost any ecosystem is composed of a fragile set of relationships. When any one of an ecosystem's members is endangered all facets of the ecosystem are affected. An ecosystem thrives because of its dynamic balance of interconnected relationships. Ecosystems cannot easily be controlled, and the nested set of relationships between ecosystem members is a complex phenomenon whose interrelated pieces are very difficult to untangle, even for ecosystem experts. If we view our organizations as ecosystems, we may begin to develop the necessary respect and humility for the ongoing energy required to maintain the delicate homeostasis of our work environments.

Poor relationships contribute to poor performance and ineffective work environments.

Whether we realize it or not, we pay a tremendous price for poor relationships. All the contractual and legal agreements in the world are not going to help when it's critical for us to produce results.

Punitive measures provide some level of enforcement and motivation, but they are not sufficient. When our relationships are governed and managed exclusively by these explicit tools, we have to look at ourselves in the mirror and realize that we haven't done a good enough job of partnering with our customers. Their failure is our failure. Although the step of putting these contractual and legal agreements in place cannot be skipped, they are not a substitute for taking the time to develop strong partnerships.

Building relationships is the most important work we do. The most successful people cultivate strong relationships. They make relationships a priority. Focusing on relationships is a challenge. By nature we are out of sync with each other. It's hard to stay current. People's ideas, opinions, emotions, and priorities are constantly shifting. It's our job to keep up with them.

Whether they are internal employees, external vendors, or contractors, treat people as prized customers. This shifts our mind-set from one of entitlement to one of involvement. Instead of expecting people to understand us, we seek to understand them. Every customer becomes an opportunity rather than a headache. This approach also takes a burden off our shoulders. We do not need to have all the answers. T&D cannot possibly have all the resources, experiences, or knowledge to help every functional area or external vendor and contractor succeed. If we work in tandem with our customers by treating them as partners, we will discover ways to optimize our resources to solve the organization's challenges.

We have a horrible habit of drawing lines and boundaries to protect ourselves and simplify our work relationships. Although these boundaries have a place in clarifying roles and responsibilities, they can become limiting and may even function as justifications for our poor relationships. People are not machines, and we cannot relegate each other to boxes defined by utilitarian dictates.

Our success in T&D is inextricably tied up in the success of others. We are facilitators. Working hand in hand, side by side with our internal and external customers, vendors, and contractors is the only way we can ensure success. The very definition of success is a moving target. Partnerships provide not only a wealth of strategies to help us achieve shared objectives but they also produce the criteria by which we and our partners will jointly measure the success of our ventures. In this way we are in motion with our partners. Our tools, processes, approaches, strategies, and measures of success are not static. As the organization's goals and priorities shift we can leverage our partnerships to stay on track.

During the rest of this chapter I will

- Examine the top five critical success factors for successful partnerships.
- Explore ten strategies for building strong partnerships.

Top Five Critical Success Factors for Successful Partnerships

How can you tell when you have a successful partnership? You can evaluate these five key qualitative indicators:

1. Strength of the relationship
2. Flexibility
3. Facilitation skills

4. Results orientation

5. Business focus

Strength of the Relationship

Look around at the people you work with. How strong are your relationships with them? Weak or tense relationships are trouble spots. Although we may have an intuitive feel for the strength of our relationships, this is a difficult thing to measure. We can break the characteristics of strong relationships down into the following subjective components:

- Amount of trust

- Amount of dialogue

- Value we assign to the relationship

- Degree of reciprocity present in the relationship

- Level of respect

Amount of trust

Merriam-Webster's Collegiate Dictionary defines *trust* as "assured reliance on the character, ability, strength or truth of someone or something."

Take a moment to reflect on your closest relationships. What role does trust play in empowering those relationships? How would those relationships be different without trust?

Trust is the foundation of any relationship. Collegial rapport may create a friendly atmosphere, but at the end of the day it's not enough to get the job done. Unless others are willing to lower their defenses and let us know what's really on their minds, it's very difficult to build strong relationships. A certain degree of vulnerability is necessary. This of course means that we need to extend trust to others and model the same positive behaviors we seek in them. I'm not suggesting we divulge all of our deepest, darkest secrets and dreams, but no relationship will ever have the potential of becoming a partnership if we do not risk sharing a part of ourselves with others. Trust cannot be a one-way street. Trust is developed over time, and that time varies depending on the person. Some people are more ready to trust than others are. Some people give trust easily but quickly retract it at the first sign of doubt or unease. Some people need to share a common experience during which trust is established as result of that experience. And still others may never be willing to trust us, perhaps for some personal or political reasons. Whatever situation you find yourself in, do everything you can to win the trust of others.

Trust is synonymous with confidence. Partners have each other's best interests at heart. When you believe others want to work with you to ensure your success as well as their own, the dynamics of the relationship change. You and your partners will then go the extra mile to help each other. There may even be times when communication is hampered for one reason or another, and yet an individual acts as result of the presence of trust in the relationship. Even without the benefit of knowing your exact needs, a partner may act in a manner intended to benefit your interests. We are more creative and capable when we are in the mode of trusting each other. Think about driving your car down a street. How would your driving change if you did not trust people to stop at red lights? Partners know more is possible when a relationship is imbued with trust. This enables both parties to act with freedom and confidence.

Amount of dialogue

Relationships require lots of communication. As you scan your working relationships, look at how much dialogue exists between yourself and others. Dialogue implies two-way communications. I see a lot of asynchronous communication in the organizations I work with. These are one-way broadcasts, filled with lots of information and few opportunities for genuine exchange. Among other things, these broadcasts amount to requests, status updates, directives, and explanations. E-mails and voice mails are two of the most frequent forms of these communications. For example, we might assume that once we have a project plan in which all the project details have been clearly articulated and understood there is nothing to discuss. We lean on this project plan as a crutch, and we shy away from substantive conversations. Our worst nightmare might be that our customer's requirements will change and the whole T&D project will come undone at the seams. We are not interested in exchanging information. We either push or pull information depending on our perceived needs.

Dialogue, in contrast, is a two-way street that ensures agility. Nothing is taken for granted. As I have discussed, partnerships are based on relationships, and relationships are volatile by nature. However, our success in bringing value to an organization hinges on our ability to continuously and spontaneously generate new and alternative solutions with the aid of our partners. We and they are in it together. We either sink or swim based on what we and our partners do jointly. Partnerships succeed on the basis of dialogue. Partners who maintain good lines of communication have stronger relationships.

Value we assign to the relationship

Have we taken the time to understand the unique characteristics of our partner? Do we demonstrate our understanding of our partner's organizational and personal challenges through our actions? Partnerships succeed when the parties involved value each other. It helps if we like the people we are partnering with, but that is not necessary and probably not always possible. Appreciation is at the core of value. Through appreciation we take an interest in other people. We demonstrate that we are capable of wanting to see the world through their perspective. Even if we lack the proper experience or knowledge to construct an adequate representation of a partner's perspective, appreciation proves our sincerity. Oftentimes it's enough to show we have a desire to learn more about our partners. Our partners need to see our care. It sends a loud signal that we value our relationship with them.

Degree of reciprocity present in the relationship

The strength of our relationships with partners can be evaluated in terms of the amount of reciprocity present in those relationships. Are we willing to help our partners? Do we seek only to take from our partners or are we just as willing to give? Relationships where there is more taking than giving cannot be sustained. There are always inequalities in relationships so there will be times when we must be more in the mode of being a giver than a receiver. However, when we examine relationships that appear at the moment to be one-way streets, we discover that if they are strong and if we view them over a longer time period they are really two way. Establishing a relationship may demand that we be more generous with our time, energy, and expertise in the beginning. This helps us establish trust. Then, to be sustainable, the relationship requires a healthy amount of giving and taking. After time, if there is little or no reciprocity in the relationship, we need to step back and analyze what other factors may be compromising the strong relationship we are trying to garner. The good news is that most people who have been recipients of another's energy will look for opportunities where they can reciprocate.

Level of respect

Merriam-Webster's Collegiate Dictionary defines *respect* as "an act of giving particular attention" and as "high or special regard." Respect is the cornerstone of a relationship. Disagreements may be plentiful in any relationship, but without respect these disagreements will be destructive. Reflect for a moment on the significant people in your life. What role does respect play in maintaining those relationships? Respect gives others the benefit of the doubt. In doing so we also recognize that we will not always fully understand each other. It's impossible. When you add the dimension of often diametrically opposed organizational perspectives it becomes even easier to imagine the natural gaps that exist between us and others. For example, think about the inherent pitfalls of relationships with outside vendors. Profits, controlling costs, and proprietary attitudes lurk in the background of these relationships. Respect is our insurance policy for holding these natural but potentially dangerous attitudes at bay.

If we are going to have strong relationships that operate as partnerships, we must learn how to view others as at least equals. Hierarchy within the organization, or positional power relative to others, is not a sufficient condition for respect. People grant respect on the basis of their acceptance of others. Individuals like to be recognized by each other. When they feel scrutinized or challenged by others, relationships suffer. Respect protects the sanctity of every person. If we can keep our egos in check, respect is so easy to give to others and so critical for building strong relationships.

Flexibility

Becoming partners with our internal customers, vendors, and contractors requires flexibility. We can evaluate flexibility in four main areas:

- Flexibility in requirements
- Flexibility in design
- Flexibility in delivery
- Flexibility in measurement

Flexibility in requirements

Let's face it: requirements are a moving target. We've all been on both sides of the fence. We know how impossible it is to develop a T&D intervention when the requirements keep changing. Nothing sticks, and we go crazy trying to get our internal customers to focus on how we can help them. We have also probably experienced the flip side of the coin when we desperately need and want to change the scope or requirements of a project but our hands are tied. Additional information, a shift in priorities, or a new understanding of the problem domain after an initially poor understanding sheds a whole new light on a project's requirements. There has to be a middle ground. The size of the project does play a large role in how flexible we can afford to be, but we can be far more flexible than we tend to be.

Part of what makes a partnership work well is the degree to which our partners feel control and ownership of a project. Although we may not be able to throw out all of the requirements and start over every time a partner has a change of heart, we can sit down with partners on a regular basis and collaboratively prioritize what we do and how we are going to do it.

It is more important that everyone be on the same page than on the correct page. In other words, partnerships are focused on keeping people in sync with one another and not on whether T&D hits all its deliverables as defined in a statement of work (SOW) signed by both parties at the front end of a project. Partnerships thrive on people working together. Working with others always requires flexibility. We cannot ever predict what will come up and what will become important to us or others as we progress through the various stages of a project. Our flexibility with our customers' requirements mediates conflicts and potential disappointments. We should also not forget that there will be times when we have to go back to our partners and ask them to be flexible with some aspect of a project that we are having difficulty delivering on as it was initially defined. Flexible partners are successful in working through the inevitable chaos and uncertainty bound to be a part of any relationship.

Flexibility in design

As T&D practitioners we are involved in a variety of interventions, and it is the training ones that tend to be most rigid in their design. It's understandable but inexcusable. Instructional designers are challenged to take a series of high-level learning objectives and create a structured course with repeatable outcomes. Every training topic begs for unique treatment. Safety training, for instance, is very different from communication skills training. However, both courses can and need to be designed to allow for some flexibility.

I remember designing some technical instruction for a company preparing to replace all its green-screen, "dumb" terminals with computers. Everyone was required to go through training before receiving a new computer. On one end of the spectrum my colleagues and I had people who had never touched a computer mouse or used a graphical user interface before, and on the other end we had people with lots of experience. Because we didn't have the ability to group people into courses according to their experience level, we had to design a course that could be taught to everyone. So we were plagued by the following questions: Do we risk boring people who have the knowledge and make them sit through an unnecessary training? Or do we force people who may not be comfortable with the new technology to accelerate their learning? In the end we did neither. We ensured the design of the course had enough flexibility that it could accommodate different audiences and give an instructor an easy-to-follow roadmap. Diving into the instructional design practices that enabled us to do that is beyond the scope of the conversation here. The point for all T&D professionals is that our partners need us to make sure our interventions have enough elbow room in them. Flexible requirements and flexible design go hand in hand with one another. We can more easily accommodate shifting requirements when we design interventions that have the ability to conform naturally to the needs of our partners.

Flexibility in delivery

Our partners need us to be flexible in how we deliver learning solutions. Today we have a host of options (e-learning, blended learning, distance learning, Internet platforms, coaching, . . . and so forth). Even after we design an intervention, organizational conditions or priorities may change and force us to reconsider the design and delivery of our solutions. If we work together with our partner we can almost always jointly find alternative delivery strategies. Remain open to other possibilities. It's difficult because once we have expended the time and resources to architect a solution we are naturally going to be resistant to any changes or modifications. Sometimes the flexibility in delivery may be needed "just-in-time." For example, if we are facilitating a workshop and we have a group of participants with a particular set of needs, we may need to modify the content, length, or delivery of the program on the spot. Within T&D we have to help each other become dynamic facilitators who are simultaneously focused on the learners' needs and respectful of the learning objectives of the programs we are leading.

Consider the following scenario:

> Andy gave himself a pat on the back as he looked at his calendar. In two weeks he would be rolling out the largest end-user training program the company had ever seen. When he had started this job over a year ago, the training department did not have a good relationship with the information technology department (IT). The chief technology officer (CTO) had told

Andy's boss on numerous occasions that he did not need or want the help of the training department.

Having been a software engineer for five years and a data center operations manager for three years at another company, Andy spoke the language of IT. The project management office had been a key ally in helping Andy make a strong business case for training. Equipped with the best practices of other companies, Andy was able to successfully introduce training as a formal part of the software development project management process.

The CTO was sinking over $3 million into replacing a legacy application with a new Web-based one. Over 600 users would have the new application. With a complete overhaul of the network and upgraded PCs, end-users were going to access the new system from their Web browsers. Several legacy applications had been retired, and many business processes had been changed or completely eliminated. This was a high visibility project and all involved were holding their breath. It had become a sink-or-swim project for the CTO, but as far as Andy was concerned this was a golden opportunity to show how the training department could support the business's needs. Andy knew end-users would revolt without the proper support and training. Andy had had great access and rapport with all the subject matter experts, but he often felt out of the loop when it came to understanding the overall project's status. Andy glanced over to the corner of the office where the training materials for the one-day course, the job aids, and the technical support documentation sat in boxes, ready to fulfill their mission.

Andy jumped when his phone rang. He was surprised to hear the CTO on the other end.

"Listen, Andy, I have a crisis. This project is 15 percent over budget and at least four weeks behind schedule. I have the rest of the executive team breathing down my back to deliver. Everyone else has had to cut their budgets this quarter, and while this project is a top priority for the business, I need to offset my overexpenditures by cutting in other areas. We need to scrap the training for this application rollout. Our users won't have any trouble adjusting to the new software. It is better than the old system and easier to use. Besides if folks can't use a Web browser then they have no place in this company anymore. I'll have Jack, my Web master, give you a call. Let's just beef up the online help screens, and put the documentation on our intranet site. Sorry to do this to you. I really appreciate all the hard work you and your team put into this, but this is just how things are."

How would you handle this situation? How would delivery flexibility help you? (See Appendix 4 for the thoughts of some T&D professionals on this issue.)

Flexibility in measurement

When we partner with our customers we are constantly setting new priorities and strategies to achieve their organizational objectives. If the priorities and strategies change, it stands to reason that how we measure our success should also change. Although we need a starting point, these agreed-upon critical success factors are baseline measurements articulated on the basis of what we know at the time. As a project progresses and morphs so must our measurements. At the front end of any learning initiative, we need to set the expectation with our partners that we will later revisit how we will measure efforts. If we allow our partners to play a driving role in determining valuable measurements on an ongoing basis these measurements will always be meaningful and flexible.

Consider the following scenario:

Lewis thumbed through a pile of evaluations from a recent time management class for the company's knowledge enabling team (KET). Great scores, but what did they really mean? As a veteran instructional designer and trainer he knew that these participant evaluations were of limited value. However, for the moment the evaluations were the only metric he had.

Two years ago the KET team was chartered with capturing, documenting, and sharing successful business processes and best practices across the company. Due to KET's great results, the company's chief operating officer (COO) asked the team members to expand their services to external-facing customers and become a new source of revenue for the company. Jill, who had been heading KET, was thrilled by the COO's request but overwhelmed by the challenges facing her. According to a memo she had received from senior management, 65 percent of KET's work needed to be with external-facing customers by the end of the fiscal year.

Jill knew if her group was going to live up to the company's expectations she would need to provide the members with some professional development. She distributed a survey with a list of twelve soft-skill classes, which she had compiled by browsing through a training vendor's course catalogue. Jill analyzed the results of the survey and sent Lewis the training request displayed in Table 6.1.

Table 6.1. Jill's Training Request

Class	No. of People	No. of Events
Time management	75	3
Presentation skills	33	3
Communication skills	26	2
Negotiation skills	22	2

Through the grapevine Lewis had learned that the COO thought KET needed to develop better consulting competencies. Lewis had never met Jill, and because the director of training had been on vacation for the last three weeks, he wasn't sure if she was aware of KET's new charter.

Resources were tight in the training and development group, more than ever the group was being asked to demonstrate its impact on the company. Lewis and his colleagues knew that the company's internal training function was in danger of being outsourced if they could not begin to align their activities with business objectives and measure them. Jill's training request was an opportunity, if he could only figure out what to do.

If you were Lewis what additional pieces of information would you want? How would you use the information to develop a measurement and evaluation plan? (See Appendix Five for some ideas.)

Facilitation Skills

In his book *Masterful Facilitation,* A. Glenn Kiser (1998) describes the knowledge, skills, and personal qualities of a masterful facilitator. They are

- *Skills and abilities:* understanding of the drivers of individual behavior and knowledge of group process; observation skills, communication skills; teaching; directing.

- *Personal qualities:* self-awareness; credibility; congruence; empathy; acceptance; emoting; assertiveness.

T&D professionals specialize in the art of facilitation. It's an unusual blend of listening and communicating skills that works by leveraging the energy and ideas of a group. In my estimation, facilitation works when it connects people heart to heart with one another. A conversation becomes a dynamic flow where no one person dominates and no one idea monopolizes the intellectual real estate. Facilitation puts people in charge of their decisions. The process of facilitation creates a safe space where people can explore perspectives, brainstorm, solve problems, prioritize, and develop action plans. Facilitation brokers commitment in people because the ideas and solutions raised emerge out of the group's process.

The term *win-win* is another way to understand the importance of facilitation skills for partnerships. Real winning precludes the myopic attitude of trying to influence our partners to our way of seeing or doing things. Even when we are right we cannot force our ideas or solutions on others. Partners function as a synergized team where the sum of the parts is always greater than the whole. Facilitators look first to listen and understand their partners before sharing their own viewpoints. When we encourage sincere dialogue people find ingenious ways to dovetail each other's ideas and needs. Suddenly there is no longer one way of looking at things or getting things done. Due to the rich set of possibilities, the process becomes invigorating. Partners thrive on the energy generated by good facilitation.

A strong partnership requires good facilitators. Ideally, both sides of the partnership possess some facilitation competencies, but it is not necessary. In fact the responsibility falls on our shoulders to be good facilitators. In essence, to be good facilitators should be part of our charter as T&D professionals. Almost everyone in our industry has a passion for learning. We know we cannot be keepers of learning. Even when we are genuine subject matter experts we can act only as knowledgeable guides, helping others find a path of their own based on their own experiences, working constructs, and interests. The importance of facilitation skills to partnerships is similar. The nature of our work, how we do it, and how we help the organization succeed is ever changing. It's just not possible or even desirable for us to do our jobs with 100 percent unwavering certainty. We are challenged to adjust our course while we are in route to our goal. Our partners need our help to do the same. Our work can be accomplished only through the cooperative efforts of all parties involved. If we do not use our facilitation skills to encourage collaboration we will encounter resistance. We must use facilitation skills to nurture our working relationships.

Results Orientation

Partnerships focused on results are less prone than others to the perils of egos. Once strong relationships are established on the basis of trust, partners can help each other drive toward results. Short of causing anyone else purposeful pain, partners will do whatever it takes to succeed. With a strong interpersonal and emotional foundation, partnerships can be governed by objective evaluation of the topic in discussion. Partners can gently remind one another of the goals. If there is disagreement as to the best way to achieve those goals, partners will use their facilitation skills to negotiate their differences and decide on a jointly agreeable action plan.

Partners keep their sights on the target; everything else is superfluous. This is only possible because partnerships succeed on the basis of strong relationships not objectivity. We tend to put the cart before the horse. We assume that relationships are secondary to results, that if we could just get people to be objective then we could eliminate all the emotional, subjective nonsense and overhead associated with relationships. It's business after all; so what place do these things have in an organization? This thinking is dangerous and counterproductive. We can only be truly resulted oriented when we have dealt with all the subjective aspects of working with others.

Business Focus

Organizations need financial viability in order to exist. Having a business focus is a survival trait. Partners do not have the luxury of doing whatever they want and ignoring the overall health of the business. As T&D professionals we are exquisite learning architects. We are capable of building masterpieces if we are left alone to practice our trade, but our work has to be done within the business constraints of the organization. Imagine the organization as a living and breathing entity. Everything we do must somehow benefit the ongoing success of the organization. Success within our domain is not enough. Partners balance the drive to excel in their domain with the need to do what is in the best interest of the organization. This philosophy succeeds to lesser or greater extents based on the organization's structural and process-related factors, which are usually out of our control. For example, when there is built-in internal competition between divisions or within a functional area it may be very difficult to broaden a partner's focus, but we must do everything we can to do so. At the very least we can model the importance of aligning learning solutions and other activities with the organization's long-term interests.

Ten Strategies for Building Successful Internal Partnerships

The critical success factors I have just discussed show us what to look for in partnerships and what skills we need to develop. Now let's discuss specific things we can do to build successful partnerships. The focus of this section is on internal partners. (I discuss the additional points to consider when dealing with external partners and contractors later in the chapter.) There are ten key strategies for building successful internal partnerships:

1. Seek to be an integral part of every functional area.
2. Be proactive.
3. Reduce administration.
4. Streamline standard offerings.
5. Get to the executive table.
6. Support partner activities.
7. Establish liaison roles.
8. Align T&D with corporate communications.
9. Celebrate successes.
10. Reinvent the partnership.

Seek to Be an Integral Part of Every Functional Area

Every functional area T&D supports has its own set of business processes. We want our partners to view us as an essential resource so that we are invited to be a principal contributor during strategic and tactical discussions. In other words we want to be seen as an integral part of our partners' success. Two functional area business processes that stand out as prime candidates for our involvement are strategic planning and project development.

Strategic planning varies greatly from one organization to the next; however, every functional area needs to set goals, lay out projects, and determine priorities.

We can contribute to strategic planning discussions in two main ways. First, when we have strong relationships with our partners, we can act as a trusted, unbiased facilitator who leads the process and ensures that input from all the stakeholders is heard and taken into account. Second, we can articulate learning, performance, and communication activities to support the functional area's strategic plan. Why wait until a functional area comes to us for help? By that time it is frequently too late, and we may have lost the opportunity to understand the context of the challenges the area is facing. Our interventions will inevitable be more effective when we have more time, more information, and more influence.

Project planning is another opportunity for T&D. Every project in a functional area can be analyzed in terms of what role learning can play. If your organization has some sort of project management office and its project planning document template has a section dedicated to learning, don't make the mistake of assuming that section will act as a catalyst for functional areas and T&D to develop strong partnerships. It's a start and it certainly helps, but it's not enough. The goal is to have functional areas turn to T&D during the initial phases of their projects to ask for assistance with articulating a strategy for weaving learning into all areas of the project plan.

Our T&D mission of providing learning and performance solutions can be best accomplished when we are actively engaged by every functional area we support. We need their confidence. When we are perceived as an integral part of a functional area we cease to be a "nice to have resource" and become a "must have resource." When we are embraced as full-fledged partners our contributions are an indispensable part of how work is done. We must do everything we possibly can to get to this position.

Be Proactive

One of the fastest ways to eventually becoming an integral part of every functional area is to be proactive. Why wait for a request? Given your organization, how can you go out of your way to discover what people need? Simple gestures go a long way. For example, ask to be invited to some functional area meetings. Then go and listen. Absorb everything you can. This is usually not the time to offer ideas, but you will gain a wealth of insights. Use these insights to go back to key stakeholders in the functional area to ask further questions. The goal is to jump-start a dialogue and not to spout off ready-made solutions even if you have them. Another good way to tactically execute the "be proactive" strategy is to spend more time conversing with people from the functional area. This seems such common sense, but ask yourself, when was the last time you planned and budgeted time in your schedule just to mingle with your customers with no other goal in mind than to invest in relationships?

Being proactive takes imagination. Stop, think, and then act. Reflect on the current state of affairs of each customer. As you gather information stay abreast of developments in each functional area so that you can anticipate what will be needed. As T&D professionals we are like waiters in a first-class restaurant where every need is met before customers even realize they had it. As at a restaurant, when this is done well our customers will be unaware of our presence and the positive impact we are having on their work. Later on I'll discuss how to be sure our successes are recognized in order to win ongoing support for our work, but as we do our work it is best to be as unobtrusive as possible. There is no need to draw undue attention to ourselves. Our goal is to help our customers succeed and not seek accolades. Be sure your motivation is driven by an internal passion for excellence and supported by a strong, dedicated culture of service within the T&D department.

Reduce Administration

No one likes bureaucracy, but administration is necessary. There are certain things we need to do in order to manage and track our work; there really is no getting around it. However, how much do we really need? Can we streamline the ways our customers interface with us? And what can we do to reduce the amount of time and effort we spend on keeping our T&D shop running?

Learning management systems and other self-service systems have helped us automate some of the more routine but essential aspects of T&D. Although these are a step in the right direction, they are not enough. We need to do everything in our power to spend as little time on these things as we can. Administration shelters us from doing the real work of getting our hands messy in the unpredictable, unstable work of supporting our partners. When given the choice between uncertainty and predictability, there's no shame in admitting you favor work you've done before and know how to do. It's just not the principal way T&D adds value.

A certain percentage of our time is already occupied by organization-wide business processes that we cannot control. Therefore we should scrutinize every procedure, meeting, form, process, report, tool, and the like . . . that we institutionalize in T&D. Perform regular audits of these things, and ask each department member to offer feedback on which ones might be eliminated or simplified. Recognize that the need for these things changes over time. We all can do a much better job of purging the clutter of administrative tasks by getting rid of the ones that have outlasted their usefulness. Outsourcing certain administrative necessities might be another way of reducing administration tasks for T&D personnel. Ask yourself this guiding question about each task: Is there any competitive business advantage to this administrative business process? If it doesn't offer any such advantage, it may be a good candidate for outsourcing. In my opinion there are very few, if any, business processes in T&D that give the organization a competitive advantage. Competitive advantage for a for-profit organization means adding to the bottom line, and for a nonprofit organization it means furthering the organization's mission. T&D's ability to partner and to develop new learning and performance interventions is its competitive advantage.

Streamline Standard Offerings

In many organizations T&D provides a core of standard offerings. Although these courses may be necessary they are only a small part of the value we can bring to the organization. We need to evaluate what percentage of our time is spent in these routine activities. Because every organization is different I cannot pin down the ideal percentage of time we should be spending on designing, delivering, and managing these standard courses. Each T&D department will need to take into account the size of its organization, number of its employees, industry it is in, culture of its organization, and a host of other factors. Suffice it to say, whatever percentage of time we spend on these activities, it should not get in the way of our being proactive, integral partners offering just-in-time learning and performance solutions to our customers.

Start by working with your partners to assess how many of these standard offerings are really necessary. How much does each one cost? How do your partners prioritize these offerings? Are there any trends or seasonal demands for these courses? Are there any other ways of delivering the learning and information contained in them (and I'm not talking just about turning them into e-learning courses)? Can you use outside vendors? Answer these types of questions with input from your partners. Our time is best used creating learning, performance, and communication solutions tied to our partners' organizational objectives and real-time needs. Minimize broad-stroke, cookie-cutter course offerings wherever possible. Be aggressive about it. As a general rule our profession has been largely focused on these standard offerings. Times are different now. The future relevance of our profession is riding on our ability to transform ourselves into strategic partners.

Get to the Executive Table

Executive-level support of T&D facilitates our ability to effectively partner with our customers. I have highlighted the importance of building relationships at all levels, but the endorsement and commitment of executive-level management in particular makes our job easier. Although executive-level support is not enough in itself to build partnerships, it will open doors. New partners are far more likely to try working with us if we have strong, vocal allies in high places. Our challenge lies in getting on the bandwidth and winning the respect of executive-level folks. If we do not already have their support, we will need a combination of tenacity, patience, and entrepreneurial spirit to acquire it. Start by identifying highly visible, large-scale projects where training and development does not already have a role. Do your homework. Use whatever lines of communication are appropriate in your organization to offer concrete ideas about the ways T&D will help the project succeed. Work out your plan ahead of time, and get key people involved in the project to be your sponsors.

Another path to the executive table is through others. Lots of little successes with our strong partners will generate goodwill and positive word of mouth throughout the organization. When influencing executive-level people you do not need to be your own spokesperson. Oftentimes it's more effective to have others be your advocate. Remember, no matter how earnest and well intentioned your efforts may be and no matter how brilliant your plan, there are no guarantees that you will get executives' attention. Stay the course. Eventually, with some persistence and luck, you will earn your rightful place at the executive table.

Support Partner Activities

Our partners are involved in a multitude of organizational activities. We will not be directly involved in all these activities; however, many of them will provide us with opportunities to show our interest and support. It's a simple truth: people are more likely to support people who support them. Suuporting others is a good way to strengthen our relationships and encourage a spirit of community. We need to be aware of our partners' activities and, without diverting too much time and energy from our major initiatives, find ways to demonstrate loyalty. If it is not always clear how to support your partners' other activities, ask them. It's likely that they will have some good ideas. Maybe you can act as a sounding board, be a guinea pig, be an early adopter, or act as an advocate for what they are doing throughout the rest of the organization. Don't forget, however, that there may be political dimensions to supporting a partner's activities. So however we show support it needs to take such dynamics into account. We wouldn't want to alienate another partner or different part of the organization. There are times to take a strong stance, but we need to be shrewd about avoiding turf wars or getting unnecessarily involved in other people's political machinations. Besides, remember that our goal in supporting partner activities is to nurture our relationships. Here's a general rule of thumb: if our support creates more negative energy than positive energy, then we should find a different activity to support.

Establish Liaison Roles

Staying in sync with our partners requires a good communication strategy. Diplomacy offers us a good metaphor. Think of T&D as a diplomatic core and each functional area it supports as an embassy. We need to post an ambassador in each functional area. These ambassadors are people from our T&D team who act as trusted confidants and who are instrumental in building strong ties. They play a liaison role by shuttling information back and forth between T&D and its partners. These liaisons can also be influential in negotiating critical aspects of the partner relationship, such as priorities, strategic planning processes, project deliverables, and communication interfaces. It is their responsibility to know the pulse of T&D's partners. Treat this post as a rotating one. Select a term length that makes sense for your organization. In my experience a year is a good length. Move people in and out of the role. You want as many of your people as possible to build relationships with your customers. Although in the short run this may appear to weaken or compromise the potential strength of these relationships, in the long run you are cultivating a greater number of relationships. This will serve to diversify the support you receive from your partners, increase the depth and diversity of your knowledge of them, and create more shared history with them. You also gain more perspectives, and you do not have to be concerned that a partnership will diminish if a key ambassador leaves the company. You want to avoid having to start again from square one.

Align T&D with Corporate Communications

Corporate communications needs to be one of our closest allies. This functional area is an essential partner. From a philosophical point of view communication and learning are inextricably connected. Without communication there is no learning.

Many learning and performance interventions look very much like communication strategies. The tools and processes of corporate communications are vital assets to us in T&D. Why reinvent the wheel when we can leverage the assets of corporate communications, particularly its ready-to-go infrastructure, for reaching out to the organization? We have a wonderful opportunity to make sure communications are saturated with learning. In this way corporate communications benefits by having a partner who understands how to transform communication into learning.

If you do not have a strong relationship with corporate communications make it one of your first priorities. As with any partnership we need to learn the partner's cultural landscape. The individuals in corporate communications have a different way of viewing the world. We will benefit from a healthy dose of their perspective. They know how to grab people's attention and succinctly transmit information. People have even less time for digesting corporate communications than they do for traditional learning so we have a lot to learn from this area. Start your efforts to make corporate communications a partner by making it a central part of T&D. Invite individuals in this area to be contributors. Seek their advice and they will begin to do the same. Natural synergies will emerge. As each group becomes more aware of the other there will be more and more opportunities for collaboration.

Celebrate Successes

Our success is our partners' success. When we celebrate our successes we elevate our partners and generate a positive focal point for the entire organization. Because the work we do is achieved through collaboration, it is critical to exhibit public signs of appreciation and recognition of everyone's efforts. People are energized by celebrating achievements. Our partnerships will be strengthened by focusing on the positive. It also becomes easier to learn from experience and identify opportunities for improvement. Our partners are less likely to point fingers at us for aspects of a project that may not have gone as smoothly as everyone had hoped. Instead, we become better equipped to enter into a depersonalized dialogue where accountability is not an issue because it is shared jointly. These dialogues are a wonderful way for us to grow in knowledge, increase effectiveness, and create opportunities to share lessons learned.

Celebrating successes allows us to bring visibility to T&D and reinforce our importance to the organization. If actions speak louder than words, then results speak volumes. The best way to sell T&D and encourage others to seek us as a partner is to share stories that celebrate our successes. Let these stories be authentic ones. We are not in the business of advertising, and we do not need to hawk the features and functions of T&D, like the stereotype of the used-car salesman. If we get our partners to tell their stories of working with us, we will secure our role in the organization. Look for creative ways to build celebration into project methodologies. This is another good place for corporate communications to help us. Go beyond the obvious methods of sticking endorsements of courses on T&D's intranet site or in printed collaterals. As genuine as these endorsements may be they fall into category of advertising or "spinning." Everyone is saturated with such messages. By themselves they do not go far enough in promoting our value to the organization, and they do not enable our partners to celebrate success.

Reinvent the Partnership

The survival and continued relevancy of a partnership is contingent on our resolve to reinvent it. Partnerships are relationships. They are living, breathing entities that need to be continually nurtured and renewed. If we are not constantly investing time, energy, and creativity into our partnerships and thinking about ways to improve them they will become stale and irrelevant. By itself, no amount of processes, procedures, or even successes is going to permanently sustain a partnership. Staff changes, shifting priorities, and modifications of existing tools and processes or introductions of new ones are just a few of the sorts of things that can influence the characteristics and longevity of a partnership. Think of a partnership as possessing an almost infinite number of variations and configurations. Be guided by what is necessary and not by what is familiar. By treating partnerships as a two-way street rich in dialogue, we can discover new ways to optimize how we work with our partners. In this way the partnership will never exist as an end itself. It will always remain focused on bringing value to the organization.

A Note on Strategies for Building Successful External Partnerships

Overall the critical success factors and strategies for managing internal partnerships also apply to external ones. Vendors and contractors benefit from being treated as partners and not as objects. More and more the boundaries of our organizations are becoming porous. We cannot afford to be insular. We've already established the benefits and importance of breaking down the barriers of functional silos. So now we have to create a more dynamic flow between ourselves and all the outside people we work with on a regular basis. Let me try an analogy. Imagine the chef of a fine restaurant. Every meal fired by the chef has to be treated as though it were the only one. Why? You may never eat in that restaurant again. The chef wants every meal to be his finest. A performer feels the same way. Both the chef and the performer recognize the unique nature of each interaction and do everything they can to preserve the sanctity of each one. Would we want either a chef or a performer, once we have paid for the dinner or a ticket to the show, to treat us with circumspection? How would that compromise our experience? Sure it makes sense to keep our guard up higher while we are in the process of selecting and evaluating vendors and contractors, but once they are on board we need to treat them the same way we treat our internal partners. The two notable differences we can consider are that the duration of an external partnership may be shorter than the duration of our internal ones and that it is very unlikely that the external partnership will provide a competitive advantage to our organization. Follow the processes and use the tools of your organization, but remember, whether you are working in an internal or an external partnership, treat it as a prized relationship and you will never go wrong.

Key Points

- The most effective way for us to ensure organizational results is by partnering with all of our internal and external customers.

- If we view our organizations as ecosystems, we may begin to develop the respect and humility necessary to appreciate the ongoing energy required to maintain the delicate homeostasis of our work environments.

- Poor relationships contribute to poor performance and ineffective work environments.

- Treat people, whether they are internal employees or external vendors or contractors, as prized customers. This shifts our mind-set from one of entitlement to one of involvement.

- Our success in T&D is inextricably tied up in the success of others. We are facilitators. Working hand in hand, side by side with our internal and external customers, vendors, and contractors is the only way we can ensure success.

- The success of a partnership can be measured by five key qualitative indicators:

  1. Strength of the relationship
  2. Flexibility

　　　3. Facilitation skills

　　　4. Results orientation

　　　5. Business focus

- There are ten key strategies for building successful partnerships:

　　　1. Seek to be an integral part of every functional area.

　　　2. Be proactive.

　　　3. Reduce administration.

　　　4. Streamline standard offerings.

　　　5. Get to the executive table.

　　　6. Support partner activities.

　　　7. Establish liaison roles.

　　　8. Align T&D with corporate communications.

　　　9. Celebrate successes.

　　10. Reinvent the partnership.

Questions for Reflection

1. How would you rate the quality of your relationships within your organization?

2. What could you do differently to improve them?

3. Given the five key qualitative indicators for successful partnerships, how does your T&D team measure up?

4. Which of the ten key strategies for building successful partnerships can you start to use?

7

Partnering Inside T&D

CHAPTERS FIVE AND SIX discussed the importance of partnerships. The same philosophical underpinnings that make partnerships work can be applied within the functional area of training and development. Our staff will benefit from a relationship-based management style and our peer-to-peer relationships will be vastly improved. In this chapter I discuss two essential tools for instilling the practice of partnering inside the T&D team: leadership and performance management.

Leadership

T&D needs to foster a culture of leadership. The extensive body of literature on leadership agrees on at least one thing: we should encourage everyone to view himself or herself as a potential leader. As I see it, if we are going to achieve our organization's missions and objectives, we have no other choice. So how do we transform every person on our T&D team into a leader? From my experience of working with T&D professionals I have developed a list of eight key behaviors for emerging leaders. I believe the term *emerging leaders* is appropriate because it recognizes how little of our attention has gone to purposefully developing leaders at all levels of the organization. Unfortunately, T&D is no exception. These behaviors are interrelated with one another and support the critical success factors and strategies for building partnerships that I discussed in the last chapter. The eight key behaviors are

1. Cultivate trust.
2. Delegate.
3. Manage boundaries.
4. Share passion to instill passion.
5. Recognize talent.
6. Park the ego.
7. Stop and listen.
8. Know when and how to take risks.

I give a brief overview of each behavior and also offer some ideas on how to put each one into practice.

Cultivate Trust

An organization is bankrupt without trust. In order to leverage all forms of capital (monetary and social) leaders must cultivate trust. People need to believe in one another and be willing to engage in intricate and intimate exchanges of knowledge, idea generation, and team effort. Likewise, people need to believe in their leader. Maintaining a positive reputation and exhibiting integrity are core parts of any leader's work, as is accepting responsibility for people. All of this ensures the organization's success along with the ongoing personal growth of its members and their satisfaction, resulting in a perpetual loop of renewable, sustainable energy and innovation.

Model trust and it will be reciprocated. Our ability to be agile depends upon it. In an environment besieged with rapid changes, maintaining tight reins of managerial control, whether hierarchical or lateral, interferes with our ability to be responsive. People need to know we trust them to act, even if they make a mistake.

It's the only way to maximize the intelligence and experience of our team. In a supportive environment full of trust, any mistakes made by members of our team accelerate learning and seldom become stumbling blocks. When people know it's OK to fail, because they are trusted, they are likely to perform better.

The trust we show each other will also send a signal to our partners. How can we expect our partners to trust us if they see we do not trust members of our own team? People pick up on negative dynamics very quickly. We will not be able to hide any dysfunction in our T&D team from outside observers, therefore we cannot afford to undermine each other. Breaches of trust are inevitable, but they are not an excuse for us to withhold trust. Even when the culture of the organization at large is tainted by a degree of distrust, we can create a corner of the organization where trust reigns supreme. Our work succeeds or fails on the basis of relationships; and no relationship can thrive without trust.

Practice

- List the people you interact with in your organization. On a scale of 1 to 7, where 1 = little trust and 7 = lots of trust, rank the level of trust you perceive you have with each person.

- For any person with a rating of 4 or less, write down two to three things you believe you could do to begin to improve that level of trust.

- Identify any people on your list with whom it is unlikely you will cultivate greater trust (hint: look at anyone with a rating of 5 or higher). It's simply not possible to have the same degree of trust with everyone we work with. Some people may not be interested in or capable of high levels of trust, or we may have knowingly or unknowingly done something in the past to severely restrict a relationship.

- Before beginning a new relationship with anyone in your organization think about specific things you can do with this person to begin cultivating trust.

- The next time you have an opportunity to negotiate deliverables and a timeline for a project be realistic but modest in what you commit to doing—then surprise the recipient by giving more than he or she asked for and before the agreed-on deadline.

Delegate

Distribution of work is a passive form of delegation and only scratches the surface of this management tool. Delegation also means sharing the baton of leadership. When leadership is shared, talents are maximized in an organization. People become more aware and willing to assume optional responsibilities, tasks, or initiatives that lie outside their work-defined domains. Delegated leadership results in team members who seek to maximize the use of their unique gifts and talents by dovetailing them to the organization's current and future mission and objectives.

T&D professionals wear lots of hats, some of them better than others. We hope we have a good mix of talents and experiences on our team, but if we don't we need to develop a strategy for diversifying that team. When delegation operates well within our team, people are proactive. People naturally gravitate to the things they do well. We have a responsibility to bring out the best in each other. We do not need to compete with each other. Recognize and enable the gifts of others. If a member of our team shines we all benefit. The spotlight can move from one contributor to the next. None of us has the full set of talents that will ensure the team's success. Make a point of identifying the capabilities and strengths of everyone on the team. Enable people to take the initiative for deciding the best way to be an invaluable contributor to the team.

Practice

- During a staff meeting take a few minutes to ask everyone to write down strengths and skills that he or she has noticed and appreciated in other team members.

- Ask each person to make a note of how his or her strengths and skills complement those of others.

- Ask each person to write a list of things he or she currently does as part of the job that he or she could teach others to do.

Manage Boundaries

Boundaries are necessary and not necessary. As learning architects we are challenged today to develop a keen appreciation for the porous relation between an organization and its various ecosystems. Knowing how and when to construct and retain clear boundaries and also how and when to demolish unnecessary ones is an art without simple rules. Managing boundaries becomes even more complex when it comes to the realm of interpersonal relationships. Use this as a general rule: when a boundary is impeding the flow of communication, is eroding trust, has become an end in and of itself, or is in any way preventing us from achieving our objectives, then that boundary needs to be modified. Likewise, there may be times to erect boundaries in order to formalize relationships, protect our interests, or minimize confusion.

Practice

- Draw a map of all the natural boundaries that exist in your organization and that affect your role. Write a short description of each one. Determine which ones are out of your control.

- Identify any boundaries you have artificially created. How can you remove them?

- Are there any boundaries you feel are necessary but not currently in place? Think about how you will know if any of the boundaries that are either missing or in place will need to be changed.

Share Passion to Instill Passion

Tuning into the fires of the heart is a mission-critical ingredient for success. Without passion the organizational actors are just reading their lines from teleprompters on a bare stage. In whatever personal form it takes, leaders must find ever-new ways to share their passions. They must do this not simply for the purposes of rallying others to be illuminated by the leaders' brilliant blaze but to model and encourage others to stoke their own fires. Having lots of fires ensures that the organization is bright, alive, and warm and that it contains a plethora of inviting interpersonal places for people to gather around and share their stories of how things have been and dream about how things can be.

Practice

- Take a piece of paper and draw a large heart. In the center of the heart write down all the things you are most passionate about in your organization. Describe how the role you play in the organization relates and contributes to these areas of passion.

- During a team meeting ask people to share these pictures of their passions. Discuss how various team members' passions overlap. Discuss any gaps between people's passions and the organization's current goals and direction.

Recognize Talent

Talent is everywhere, and everyone has unique gifts and talents. Recognizing talent can be a challenge, however; requiring leaders to suspend their biases, values, judgments, worldviews, expectations, and perspectives. In order to recognize talent, a leader may have to work with what on the surface appear to be shortcomings or liabilities to the organization and transform them into positive skills.

Practice

- Make a list of people you find it challenging to work with. Next to each name write a short description of why you find it difficult to work with that person.

- Now imagine how some of these traits you see as negatives might be seen as assets. Can you develop a game plan for doing a better job of leveraging these traits?

Park the Ego

Conviction and self-confidence are key attributes of a leader, and as such they help her develop a healthy ego. However, when ego consumes a leader's perceptiveness and becomes a tool of power versus inspiration, it has ceased to serve the leader well and has become dangerous to all. Leaders must learn how to draw internal strength from their egos while simultaneously parking them out of the way. Leaders who put others first do so by attending to the egos of others and not to theirs.

Practice

- Reflect on things about yourself (skills, abilities, qualities, experience, knowledge, . . . and so forth) that you are very confident about. Then reflect on areas where you are less sure of yourself. Our egos tend to be more dominant in areas where we lack true self-confidence and self-esteem. Identify these areas in yourself and others, and be watchful. These are the areas where our egos can easily get out of control.

- Give other people the opportunity to take the lead in areas where you have more experience. Act as a coach rather than as a doer all the time.

Stop and Listen

The importance of this simple and powerful technique cannot be stressed enough. Leaders must learn how to listen on many different levels. Hearing others' words is only one facet of listening. Leaders must also discover techniques and practices for tuning into the actions of people around them and unscrambling their observations into insightful reflective patterns that guide their interactions with others. Self-reflection is another crucial form of listening that gets overlooked. Leaders with the capacity to retreat into the stillness of their heart, mind, and gut in the frenzy of change and chaos around them can act from a place of fuller knowledge than can leaders who work principally from their heads.

Practice

- Set aside ten minutes a day to rewind the day and review your interactions with others. Consider how any of your interactions with others might have altered your mental model of them.

- Look for any interactions that might have resulted in misperceptions. Determine the best way to follow up and alleviate the potentially negative impacts of these interactions.

Know When and How to Take Risks

Without risk and uncertainty very little can be achieved. Jumping into a situation with reckless abandon is seldom fruitful and may simply be a different face of the same malady afflicting those who are paralyzed with fear and unable to ever take a risk. So there is a delicate balance between risk and safety. A leader must learn how to decide when to take a risk and how to take it in such a way as to minimize its potential damage. Part of success in risk taking lies in allowing others to take risks and trusting their judgment, especially when the risky action being considered lies closer to their realm of experience and knowledge than to yours.

Practice

- Challenge yourself to learn or try something new. Look for opportunities to get out of your comfort zone.

- Seek people who can act as your coaches.

Review of Eight Behaviors of Emerging Leaders

Regardless of our formal positions in an organization all of us are leaders. These eight behaviors encapsulate all the little things we can do to develop our leadership capabilities. If you are interested in delving into other facets of leadership, I recommend the work of James Kouzes and Barry Posner and their classic book on leadership, *The Leadership Challenge* (2002), and also the Leadership Profile Inventory (LPI) developed by them. As with anything else, we have to exercise our leadership muscles if we are to strengthen them. I urge everyone in our industry to start thinking of himself or herself as a leader. We cannot afford to wait for others to step up to the plate. We know that continuous learning is at the heart of every organization's success. It is our responsibility to act as models. A major thrust of this book on business acumen is to pave the way for all of us to guide our organizations to new heights by transforming ourselves into leaders.

Performance Management

Imagine yourself as a major league baseball coach. It is the bottom of the ninth inning in the seventh game of the World Series. The bases are loaded, the game is tied, and you have two outs. You decide to put in your best hitter. He has an exceptional batting record, but he is facing the league pitcher with the leading strikeout percentage. It has come down to this one moment. The tension is thick on and off the field and everyone is watching you. Your star batter is hesitant and mentions that he is nervous just before you are about to send him in. How do you overcome this performance obstacle? What do you need to do to inspire your batter to rise above the challenge at hand and squeeze out his best performance?

In business the pressure may not always be this extreme, but you are always at the mercy of your employees' performance and needing to get their best performance. There are many potential pitfalls when tackling employee performance challenges. Managers are often caught up in the symptoms of the problem and fail to seek the actual root cause. Until the cause of the problem is understood, proposing a solution is premature and unlikely to bring long-term resolution. Before we look at solutions to these challenges, let's first define performance management and identify the parts of the process.

Setting Up Employee Performance Management Plans

The concept of evaluating employees based on performance is a departure from the traditional tell-them-what-to-do-and-get-it-done approach of the past. In this traditional approach, workers experienced *employee appraisals* or *employee reviews,* which were conducted after events took place, when it was too late to act upon them. These appraisals also focused on rewarding employees for activities performed rather than for doing the right things to reach specific objectives. *Performance management* is a more appropriate term for today's evaluation process, which assesses the ongoing effectiveness of employees' efforts in the context of expected results and accomplishments.

The performance management process is a collaborative and facilitated approach to getting tasks completed. Performance management ensures that the organization and the structures within it are working optimally together to achieve the results desired. The recognition of employees is an indispensable ingredient if they are to attain the organization's strategic direction and contribute to improved performance. Performance management produces a cascading effect in which employee objectives are derived from the division's needs and are also in line with the company vision.

The performance management process offers both employees and managers an opportunity to put forward their own performance objectives and development plans for reaching specific objectives while maintaining the performance expectations of the company. Each performance development plan must align with the strategic direction of the company while also incorporating the employee's professional and personal objectives and aspirations. There are eight steps in creating an effective *employee performance plan:*

1. Focus on the big picture.
2. Determine specific accomplishments to reach the performance goals.
3. Identify individual accomplishments.
4. Determine critical and noncritical performance measures.

5. Specify individual measures for performance.

6. Develop standards.

7. Monitor performance.

8. Build in a control process.

Step 1: Focus on the big picture

When planning to improve individual performance, rather than starting at the employee level, focus first on the ultimate objective—where is the company going? Answer these questions:

- What are the primary objectives in the strategic plan?

- What specific performance goals will help individuals and groups in this department to attain the strategic vision?

- What successful performance measures are already in place?

Step 2: Determine specific accomplishments to reach the performance goals

The second step is to determine what the job tasks are to accomplish. Identify the components of the work involved and how that work leads to tangible accomplishments. Understanding the workflow process allows you to maintain your focus on the big picture and leads to performance measures based on workflow objectives rather than on activities.

Step 3: Identify individual accomplishments

The performance elements measured in the employee performance plan should include both individual and group tasks and responsibilities. Your previous breakdown of the workflow process and associated accomplishments will help you to set goals for each employee. Other performance elements to measure in the workflow process include group dynamics and decision-making and problem-solving processes. The performance elements should be quantifiable or otherwise verifiable and clearly identified as accomplishments.

Step 4: Determine critical and noncritical performance measures

In a performance development plan each employee is measured in terms of elements in their workflow process and expected performance levels. Clearly distinguish the critical elements from the noncritical elements, and set specific and attainable performance measures within the workflow process.

Step 5: Specify individual measures for performance

For each critical issue identified, specify a measure that adequately demonstrates whether the employee is meeting the performance objectives. Measures can be quantitative (cost savings, reduction in complaints, increased sales, and so forth) or qualitative (production efficiencies, identification of product defects, improved workflow process, and so forth).

Step 6: Develop standards

Once critical issues are identified and measures are in place, set the standards the employee should strive to attain. Performance standards should be set at two levels. The first level is the minimum performance standard acceptable. If performance is any lower than this, corrective measures are warranted. The second level is the performance standard that the employee is rewarded for reaching or exceeding. This is the desired level of performance.

Step 7: Monitor performance

The performance measures should be fair, objective, and developed with the employee. Determining how to monitor performance, what is monitored, when to monitor, and who monitors is as important as the desired results. Identify the data to acquire for each performance element, the source of these data, and whether to use a data sample or to collect all the data. Create feedback mechanisms where appropriate or necessary to clearly communicate the results and to give employees feedback automatically.

Step 8: Build in a control process

The performance management plan is a tool to instill a sense of accomplishment and confidence in your employees and to ensure that the company arrives at its ultimate destination. It is important that you put control mechanisms into place for ensuring that the right performance issues are measured in a fair, quantifiable, and flexible manner. The performance elements you initially set must be attainable and in line with operational and strategic needs. Make sure that the performance plan developed for your employees adapts to the changing conditions of the company and meets employee needs. If you are off track in this, you will not only miss your performance objective but also confuse and frustrate your employees.

   The purpose of an effective performance management process and development plan is to make the company more flexible in attaining its objectives while allowing employees to strive to achieve higher expectations. It emphasizes decision making and accountability at the level where the work is done. Clearly defining the performance management process and outlining employee expectations will help you to avoid many potential challenges.

Resolving Performance Problems

Managing employee performance is the process of creating a work environment in which people are enabled to perform to the best of their abilities and provided with the support they require to do so. Managing an employee's performance begins once the individual in question assumes his or her role and does not end until he or she leaves the company. Performance management is about the importance of measuring and recognizing accomplishments rather than activities. To overcome performance obstacles, you need to develop elements and standards that center on what your employees achieve, not what they complete.

Employee performance is one issue that is a challenge for almost every manager. In particular, improving the performance of an employee who is exhibiting substandard performance can be a daunting task. A one-size-fits-all solution to resolving poor employee performance does not exist. The following discussion addresses some of the common issues that result in poor performance and describes a three-step process for overcoming them, but I recommend you consult local labor laws and legal counsel before taking any direct action.

Step 1: Identify poor performers

Just about every organization has its share of poor performers. But even though these employees may be partially responsible for their poor performance, there will be other contributing factors as well. The following are some of the issues that directly affect the performance of employees and eventually the organization.

Lack of knowledge Lack of knowledge is a common problem among employees for various reasons, but one common cause is that managers have failed to supply the needed knowledge, believing that employees can figure things out for themselves. Every employee deserves to receive the proper knowledge and training to effectively function in his or her role. Without functional and cultural knowledge of the company, employees cannot be expected to attain any type of performance objective.

Poorly defined performance objectives Employees may understand what is required for them to do their jobs but may not have been given any performance expectations. Individuals tend to equate *performance* with doing as much as possible rather than with accomplishing tasks in relation to specific performance and organizational objectives. It is your responsibility to define the critical elements to be accomplished and to set the specific performance standards to be achieved.

Lack of support Employees state that having support from their company and superiors is essential for them to have confidence in their jobs. When asked if they receive the desired support, many answer that they do not. When employees receive support it helps to build their confidence, gets them more involved, and allows them to strive to do better in their jobs. Your role is to create a supportive environment for your staff. Discuss with them what they require from you to become better performers.

Inconsistency from superiors Another annoyance for employees is management inconsistency. Mixed messages, unclear directives, and a lack of defined performance measures are just some of the issues that are at the root of poor performance. The demands on a company and its employees require clarity and consistency from managers. By supplying both you will remove one of the main obstacles to achieving your performance management objectives.

Inadequate tools Think back to a recent time when you had to work on something and did not have the right tool at your disposal. What did you feel? Frustration? Anger that you could not finish what you had started? Essentially, you were unable to accomplish your task and you did not meet your performance objective. Now think of your staff when they are asked to do something or have to meet specific performance objectives set forth by you or the company. They will also experience frustration if they do not have the right tools at their disposal. This frustration will prevent them from attaining the expected performance levels. Ask them what they need to do a better job. Provide the right tools, infrastructure, and environment so that they can reach their goals.

Not having a clear direction If the company or department does not have a clear direction, how can you expect your employees to achieve any type of performance objectives? Effective performance management begins with the organization setting a clear strategic direction. We derive from this the critical elements and specific performance measures and then we set attainable standards for employees to meet.

What these points have in common are their links directly back to the organization and to management. This is not an exhaustive list of issues that can affect employee performance, but it shows the value of asking if you are providing the appropriate resources and measures to give your team the support it requires to reach performance goals.

Step 2: Ask the difficult questions

Motivating employees to achieve performance objectives requires that the company have a focus and direction and that its leaders are accountable to performance measures. Your performance is dependent on your own actions and behavior as well as on your ability to address the right issues. The primary issues a performance-based organization addresses are these:

- What do we want to achieve one year from today?
- What are the company's long-term objectives (three to five years from now)?
- Can we see clearly the direction to take?
- What do we need to accomplish to realize the company objective?
- When can we expect to arrive at our goal?
- Can we create an environment to leverage employee performance?

This company destination, the overall vision, is a starting point for developing performance objectives leading to a proper performance management process. With the vision defined, you can easily determine what is required to communicate the end results to your employees.

A gap between your team's current performance and potential performance may still arise if you are unable to create an environment conducive to performance-based behavior. It is important to think strategically about how to provide your team members with the resources to overcome any type of performance challenge. They need to know how to build and implement processes that will facilitate and execute realistic performance results. The only guide employees have is you—their manager. If they do not receive direction, communication, or feedback about their performance objectives then expect them to become increasingly dissatisfied, frustrated, and disillusioned. There are simple ways to overcome some of the challenges in creating a performance-based environment, such as the following:

Communicate your vision For employees to see how performance measures relate to their jobs they need to understand where the company is going. Communicating the company and the department visions is a challenging task for a leader. Too often, leaders do have visions and do know where they are headed, but they do not communicate what they know to others. Reflect for a moment on how often you communicate explicitly to your staff. When was the last time you spoke to them about your performance objectives? Have you ever told them that the company depends on the success of their efforts? Have you explained some of your actions and how they relate to the bigger picture?

Focus on employee behavior It is human nature to stick with the status quo. People would rather not change things for fear of the unknown. We all tend to follow the mantra "If it works why fix it?" Also, employees tend to get mired in the daily routine of the company. They begin feeling that they are a commodity rather than a valued asset. Complacency is a disease that affects many companies in America, and if allowed to spread it creates an indifferent workforce and an exponential rise in poor performance. In order to avoid complacency and performance monotony, push your employees out of their comfort zone. Lead by example and encourage them to do new and different things that will lead to improved performance.

Encourage accountability An integral part of performance improvement is ownership and accountability. When one of your employees comes to you with a problem, he or she is not seeking just a solution but also guidance. Good employees want to take ownership of the problem. If you solve their problem then you are negatively affecting their confidence and performance. They become overly dependent on you to solve issues. This does not contribute to building a performance-based environment. Allow them to arrive at their own conclusions. Stimulate this process by asking the questions that will lead them in the direction of achieving their performance objectives. The performance of your team is a reflection of your management style and behavior. It is your responsibility to shape and influence their performance behaviors.

Step 3: Handle the employees who lack motivation

You've communicated the strategic direction of the company, broken down the tasks your team is required to accomplish, set out the critical elements for each person, and set the standards each one needs to attain to meet his or her performance plan. You have even put into place a rewards and recognition incentive to motivate employees. But for unexplained reasons you still have some team members unmotivated to perform. What do you do now to overcome the biggest obstacle—unmotivated employees? Here are some tips that can help employers work through performance management issues:

Attend to the situation immediately Don't wait too long to address the poor performance of the individual. You may lose an excellent opportunity to resolve the situation and help the employee to become a better performer. Set sufficient time aside to show the employee that you recognize there is an issue and that you will address it in short order.

Recognize the issue Be certain that you understand the issue affecting performance. Prepare yourself with examples of an individual's poor performance behaviors prior to meeting with him or her. Be able to describe how this behavior affects other areas of the department and its impact on the company. Document all of your thoughts and arguments so the employee will know you are serious about resolving the issue.

Set up a meeting with the individual Provide a safe, secure, and neutral environment where the employee will feel comfortable speaking with you. Use the notes you prepared in the previous step to address the situation, and provide ample opportunity for the individual to state his or her concerns and perceptions.

Get the employee to buy in People want to control their environment. This applies to employees in their role in improving performance. Because employees know their jobs best, let the individual share his or her ideas and provide suggestions on how to improve the situation.

Reinforce positive performances outcomes If possible, reinforce what the employee has done well and the ways in which he or she has met some of the performance expectations of the job. Then outline the results that are required from the employee to meet the standards initially set forth in the performance plan. Be clear about your expectations and ensure that they are specific, attainable, and realistic. Complete your discussion by reviewing what is expected and agreed upon between the two of you, and show the employee how meeting these expectations will make his or her tasks more focused and efficient.

Set goals and timelines Together, break the performance expectations for the employee's tasks into manageable chunks. Obtain a commitment from the employee about the time within which he or she will accomplish the objectives. Make sure that you arrange time to assess the employee on his or her progress.

Provide a written summary After the meeting summarize the issues and objectives discussed and accepted. Provide a copy to the employee, asking him or her to review it and to confirm that these were the points agreed upon. Give the employee a copy of the summary, and keep a copy for yourself for future reference.

Assess employee progress Many of your employees have good intentions and may require only the one meeting and a follow-up to ensure they are on track. But in some cases you may have to conduct a regular review and performance evaluation.

Dismiss or reassign the employee If your efforts at working with the employee fail, then you may want to consider assigning the person to a different responsibility if you believe he or she has potential, or you may decide simply to let the person go from the company. Don't be too quick to judge, and be sure to consult with the appropriate human resource staff regarding the dismissal process.

Business needs and goals change quickly, and the demands you and your staff face are constant. Often these demands bring with them obstacles that stand in the way of improving employee performance. Your responsibility is not only to help employees grow or to facilitate their tasks—it is to help them attain higher levels of performance and to manage that performance to the expectations of the company. Find out precisely what the company's objectives are and what it is most important to accomplish to meet these objectives. Realize that true performance is about what you and your team accomplish and not about the activities completed. And remember that performance obstacles may simply be an employee's call for help—so make sure you answer it.

▶ OVERVIEW OF THE PERFORMANCE MANAGEMENT PROCESS AT TDS TELECOM

Figure 7.1. TDS Telecom Performance Management

Performance Management is . . . a year-round process of two-way communication between you and your supervisor to work together toward improved performance and career development.

Source: TDS Telecom.

The TDS Telecom performance management process (Figure 7.1) uses the documents listed in Table 7.1. This list is part of the materials given to employees. The roles and responsibilities of the supervisor and the direct report (DR) are outlined in Table 7.2. This list is also given to employees. And the cycle of events that make up performance management at TDS Telecom is illustrated in Figure 7.2.

Table 7.1. Documents for Performance Management

Action plan	Provides a place to document performance goals, quarterly progress reviews, performance ratings, and comments regarding daily activities and behaviors.
Development plan	Identifies activities that will help you achieve your performance and career goals.
Peer/customer feedback	Used to obtain feedback from those with whom you interact daily or on specific projects.
Direct report feedback	Used to provide feedback regarding your supervisor's performance.

Source: TDS Telecom.

Table 7.2. Performance Management Responsibilities of Supervisor and Direct Report

Supervisor Role	Direct Report Role
Set the stage for two-way interaction.	Communicate openly regarding performance and development needs.
Work with direct reports to create performance goals and development plans.	Work with supervisor to create your performance goals and development plans.

Table 7.2. Performance Management Responsibilities of Supervisor and Direct Report, Cont'd

Supervisor Role	Direct Report Role
Provide continuous feedback and coaching.	Be open to feedback and willing to give it.
Document discussions and progress.	Document discussions and progress.
Conduct, review, and supplement documentation for annual and quarterly performance discussions.	Prepare documentation for and participate in annual and quarterly performance discussions.
Maintain performance documentation file for each direct report.	Maintain personal documentation file to provide examples of performance.

Source: TDS Telecom.

Figure 7.2. Cycle of Performance Management Events

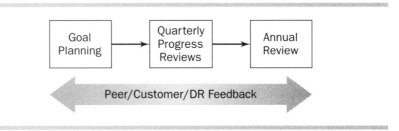

Source: TDS Telecom.

Renee Stoll, manager of Training, Education, and Employee Development at TDS Telecom, whom we met in Chapter Five, offers the following account of her personal experiences with performance management at TDS Telecom.

Before I became a manager, I saw performance management solely in terms of the end-of-the-year review. After all, that was my experience with the process. I worked hard all year and hoped and prayed that my boss noticed and gave me a good review.

When I became a manager, I decided I didn't want my folks to be afraid of annual reviews. After all, if we are communicating consistently through-out the year, the annual review should be a simple, no surprises wrap-up of the conversations we've had along the way. At around the same time, TDS Telecom was revising our performance management process to the one out-lined earlier in the case study, which provided the tools and processes nec-essary to make this an ongoing development conversation.

A typical year goes something like this:

January
Set goals for the upcoming year with the employee. We use SMART crite-ria (specific, *m*easurable, *a*ttainable, *r*ealistic, *t*ime-framed). We also take time at this stage to align these goals with department goals all the way to the top company goals. This shows the employee how his or her individ-ual contributions impact the success of the company.

April
Quarter 1 progress review. We use this time to discuss results of the goals we have set, review and revise goals based on organization or team changes, and review feedback received from customers, peers, or direct reports. The purpose of these reviews is to understand where the employee is doing well and where he or she needs to continue to grow.

July
Quarter 2 progress review. We use the same process as in Quarter 1, including again reviewing goals. I've found that one of the stressful pieces of performance management is the fear that a goal set in January can't change. We spend time in these quarterly discussions talking about what, why, and how a goal needs to change to keep the action realistic and attain-able. This does not let employees off the hook on deadlines but rather empowers them to set realistic deadlines that actually get accomplished from quarter to quarter.

October
Quarter 3 progress review. Same process as Quarters 1 and 2.

January

Quarter 4 progress review and annual wrap-up. This meeting has two purposes: (1) as a Quarter 4 review, which is run much like the reviews of Quarters 1 to 3, and (2) an annual wrap-up and performance rating. This is really simply a paperwork piece, to make sure we've met our obligations with HR. At this time, the employee is given a rating for each goal on the action plan and an overall rating for the year. Because we've had conversations about performance and results throughout the year, the rating is rarely a surprise or disputed.

Throughout this process, I am adamant about "no surprises." Nothing goes in writing on the action plan until we've talked about it. This way, the employee never has to dread or fear the progress reviews.

The Benefits

- I and the employee always know what the expectations are by the goals written out on the action plan.
- Reviewing progress quarterly ensures things don't get too far off track. A goal can be reestablished and new milestones created to reflect our changing environment.
- No surprises means the employee doesn't waste time fearing performance reviews. This leads to more open and honest discussions about performance and allows us to focus on development not fear.
- Because results are tracked quarterly, they are more accurate and more detailed. With our previous process, you sat down in December and tried to think of all the results you accomplished over the past year. The process was time consuming, inaccurate, and very frustrating. ◀

Key Points

- T&D needs to foster a culture of leadership.
- The eight key behaviors of emerging leaders are
  1. Cultivate trust.
  2. Delegate.
  3. Manage boundaries.

    4. Share passion to instill passion.

    5. Recognize talent.

    6. Park the ego.

    7. Stop and listen.

    8. Know when and how to take risks.

- People need to believe in one another and be willing to engage in intricate and intimate exchanges of knowledge, idea generation, and team effort.

- In a supportive environment full of trust any mistakes made by members of our team accelerate learning and seldom become stumbling blocks. When people know it's OK to fail, because they are trusted, they are likely to perform better.

- Delegated leadership results in team members who seek to maximize the use of their unique gifts and talents by dovetailing them to the organization's current and future mission and objectives

- In order to recognize talent, a leader may have to work with what on the surface appear to be shortcomings or liabilities to the organization and transform them into positive skills.

- Leaders must learn how to draw internal strength from their egos while simultaneously parking them out of the way.

- Leaders with the capacity to retreat into the stillness of their heart, mind, and gut in the frenzy of change and chaos around them can act from a place of fuller knowledge than can leaders who work principally from their heads.

- The performance management process is a collaborative and facilitated approach to getting tasks completed. Performance management ensures that the organization and the structures within it are working optimally together to achieve the results desired.

- There are eight steps in creating an effective employee performance plan:

    1. Focus on the big picture.

    2. Determine specific accomplishments to reach the performance goals.

    3. Identify individual accomplishments.

    4. Determine critical and noncritical performance measures.

5. Specify individual measures for performance.

6. Develop standards.

7. Monitor performance.

8. Build in a control process.

- Managing employee performance is the process of creating a work environment in which people are enabled to perform to the best of their abilities and provided with the support they require to do so. Managing an employee's performance begins once the individual in question assumes his or her role and does not end until he or she leaves the company.

Questions for Reflection

1. What actions do you plan to take to develop your leadership qualities?

2. If you begin viewing yourself as a leader in your organization, how will that change the way you do your job?

3. Working within the parameters of your organization's performance management process, how can you make that process more collaborative?

4. Are there some new ways you can leverage your performance plan to facilitate better communication with others? What are some ways you can use it more effectively to drive results?

8

Human Performance Technology and Business Acumen

I **NEED TRAINING,** and I need it now!"

As the T&D manager (actually, the whole department) at the A-Z Catalog Company, Karen was used to this type of call. This time, the call was coming from Ed, the vice president of sales.

"How can I help you, Ed?" asked Karen.

"Our customer satisfaction scores are very low. They've dropped by 25 percent over the last two months! I think our customer service agents need some more training. Can you arrange for that?"

"I'd be happy to, Ed, but they just had training six months ago. Are you sure you want the expense of putting them through training again so soon?" asked Karen, concerned about the effectiveness of another training session. She suspected something else might be going on.

"I don't care what it costs. We need to get them trained now. That's the only way to get our customer satisfaction scores back up," barked Ed.

"OK, Ed. I'll start arranging for the training today," said Karen, reluctantly. She didn't feel that training would work, but after all, her job was to develop and deliver training. So when someone asked for training, she had only one option.

Karen conducted the customer service training for the customer service agents the next week. The following month Ed called again.

"What kind of training did you give our agents?" asked Ed, obviously irate. "Our scores haven't improved a bit! In fact, they've dropped by another 2 percent! When I ask for training, I expect results!"

One of most common solutions to organizational problems is training. When that solution doesn't fix the problem, the failure is blamed on the T&D professional. Instead of focusing on training, we need to focus on meeting expectations and delivering results. First and foremost we need to understand what the expected result is. After all, if we don't understand the result, how can we deliver it?

In order to deliver results, we must offer comprehensive solutions, of which training is just one option. The *human performance technology* (HPT) process will help us achieve this objective.

What Is HPT?

Human performance technology (HPT) is a systematic and systemic process that addresses performance issues in an organization by focusing on results. The goal of HPT is to improve performance by aligning it with the business goals of the organization.

Why Is HPT Important?

It is an organization's responsibility to ensure that barriers to performance are removed so employees can perform to their true potential. HPT provides that opportunity by ensuring that the right problem is addressed and that the solution or intervention works. HPT helps the organization by

- Aligning business and individual performances with business goals
- Looking at the whole system instead of just one piece
- Focusing on results to ensure that performances add value to the organization

Principles of HPT

HPT begins by understanding the problem. For example, thinking back to the case study at the beginning of the chapter, if Karen were an HPT specialist she would have asked if there were any customer comments about the service. Karen and Ed would have discussed the gist of these comments and discussed what caused the undesirable customer service situation. Karen would have known that training is appropriate only for skills and knowledge deficiencies, and she would have been listening for Ed's explanation of what the customer service agents didn't know or weren't able to do. Karen and Ed might also have discussed other issues, such as a sales planning process, support for sales, policies, delivery, product quality, or management coaching. Karen would have known that lack of feedback can be one of the most important workplace deficiencies, and she could have discussed how the customer service agents are provided with coaching and positive feedback when things are going well. Karen would have offered to include realistic scenarios and job aids in the training sessions. She could have suggested on-the-job support from Ed as the customer service agents practice and institute the new ideas from training. Karen would also want to support Ed with ways to institute ideas so that the training "works." In this way, training and sales management would become partners in improving customer satisfaction scores.

There are four main principles of HPT that can guide us as we create workplace improvement:

- Focus on results
- Take a systems view
- Add value
- Collaborate

This chapter contains a summary of each step that we use to determine the problem and its cause, create ideas for improvement, implement the improvement, and then evaluate the improvement and the HPT process.

Focus on Results

Stated more fully, this principle is *focus on results and help clients focus on results.* This principle means we always have to align performance with business goals. When looking at performance issues, always keep the end result in mind in order to achieve the desired performance.

In order to focus on results, we must clearly understand the business goals. Business goals are often communicated in business terms and use business definitions. Without a proper understanding of these terms, we cannot communicate effectively with key stakeholders or understand annual reports or other company documents and therefore we cannot understand the business goals. Without a clear understanding of the business goals, it is impossible to focus on results.

Take a Systems View

Look at situations systemically, taking into consideration the larger context, including competing pressures, resource constraints, and anticipated change. This principle means that we always have to look at the big picture when looking at performance. People and departments do not operate in a vacuum; they are linked to one another. When one part of an organization changes, a ripple effect often appears in other parts of the organization. By being systemic we will be able to address these effects.

In order to take a systems view we must be able to understand different departments and functions, competitive pressures, organizational culture, and all the ins and outs of the business. Without business acumen, we could never understand the complexities of an entire organization and be able to take all parts of that organization into consideration when effecting change.

Add Value

Add value in how we do the work and through the work itself. This principle means that we should always be positively contributing to the organization through the HPT process. This standard is linked to the first standard in that we can add value only by aligning the work with business goals. If the work does not contribute to the organization in ways that bring about positive change, then it does not add value.

We must be able to effectively communicate to key stakeholders that value is being added to the organization, especially financially. Adding value means not just affecting the organization and people positively but also increasing profits.

Collaborate

Use partnerships or collaborate with clients and other experts as required. This principle means that working with others is often the key to successful performance. We need to work with the client to get the job done. We also need to recognize when to call in an expert for assistance.

We must be able to communicate with clients using their terminology in order to collaborate with them. Possessing business acumen is also essential when collaborating with experts. If we cannot communicate effectively, then collaboration cannot occur.

Phases of HPT

Basing our efforts on these four HPT principles, we use the five phases in the HPT process to guide our understanding of the problems and causes, design improvements, change the workplace to benefit from the improvements, and then evaluate to see if we actually made a positive difference. The five phases are

- Performance analysis (also known as needs or opportunity analysis or new performance planning)
- Cause analysis
- Intervention (improvement) selection, design, and development
- Implementation
- Evaluation

These phases are not always in step-by-step order, and we will often go over steps if we think we need to adjust what we did in any phase. In fact, as we go through the process, we may become aware of something that was not apparent at first. With that new knowledge we may need to make adjustments through the HPT process. The relationship between these stages is illustrated by the HPT model shown in Figure 8.1.

Performance Analysis

Two separate analyses are part of the performance analysis: the *business (or organizational) analysis* and the *needs (or environmental) analysis*.

Business analysis

The business analysis, or organizational analysis, is a search to determine the vision, mission, and goals of the organization. This analysis is the beginning of the HPT

Figure 8.1. Human Performance Technology (HPT) Model

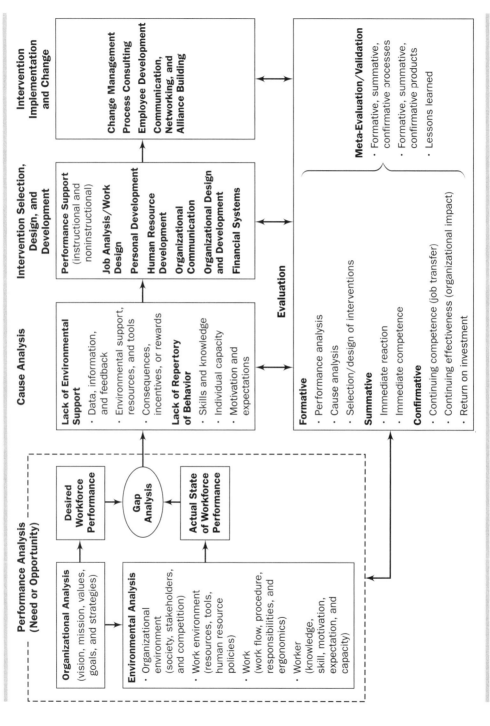

process and is extremely important because all future steps of the HPT process will be conducted with the business goals in mind. Annual reports, company Web sites, and interviews with key company personnel are good sources of information when conducting the business analysis. Without a business analysis, our efforts are unfocused, and the results will not meet the expectations of senior management.

Needs analysis

Once the business goals have been established, it is time to determine if there is a need for HPT. The purpose of the needs analysis, or environmental analysis, is to identify whether any performance deficiencies or new performance opportunities exist in the organization and, if so, the extent to which they exist. By following a defined analysis process, we will ensure that we analyze the entire business and collect all the data necessary for a thorough needs analysis. Based on the results of this needs analysis, a recommendation to proceed or not to proceed with improvements (interventions) will be made. (If there is a new performance opportunity, this step is often called an opportunity analysis or new performance planning.)

The goals of the needs analysis are to determine

- If a performance deficiency (gap) exists
- If the performance gap is related to the business goals
- If further action toward improvement is recommended

To determine whether a performance gap exists, compare the current performance to the desired performance. If they are not in line, then a gap exists.

Next, determine if the gap (deficiency) is affecting the business goals. If reducing this gap would bring the organization closer to achieving its business goals, then the issue affects those goals.

Last, determine if further action is recommended. In other words, if a gap exists and it affects business goals, then proceed with the HPT process.

Cause Analysis

Once it is determined that a need exists to improve performance, the root cause of the performance issues must be identified. Cause analysis considers workplace (environmental) factors such as information and feedback, resources and tools, and consequences, incentives, or rewards. Worker (behavioral) factors are also considered, such as individual skills and knowledge, intellectual capacity, motivation, and expectations. Identifying the correct root cause of each performance issue will help determine which ideas or interventions will resolve those deficiencies.

By following a defined analysis process, we will ensure that we analyze the entire business and collect all the data necessary for a complete cause analysis. The cause of the issue may be linked to other areas of the business, so a thorough understanding of the complete picture is required. Being systematic ensures we will thoroughly analyze all possible causes of a performance issue.

Analysis is one the most sensitive aspects of HPT. Organizations don't want to pay for analysis; they believe that they know the problem and want simply to resolve the situation. We need to be sensible. We definitely need the analysis information, yet organizations often believe that they only get from analysis what they already know. It is often important for us to do this work unobserved. If it is available, begin with the annual report; it is a gold mine of information, such as the mission, vision, business goals, financial targets, and so forth. Using our business acumen, we can translate the lofty organization-wide goals into the activities of any department and understand how those activities affect the overall goals. To illustrate the point about beginning analysis unnoticed, I can report that a senior manager once told a software implementation manager, "I don't care if you do an analysis, as long as no one knows that is what you are doing." People don't like to be examined, but you need certain information to make your case. Sivasailam Thiagarajan (Thiagi) points out that it is often best to begin quickly with a little data and then continue to ask questions. As you question you will gradually conduct your analysis and develop targeted ideas that really help the organization improve. You want to minimize attention to what you are doing, not because you are trying to discover clandestine information or covertly influence the organization but because you are working to understand a problematic situation well enough to respond to it and you want to do the preliminary investigative work without raising worries for your internal or external client.

Intervention Selection

Interventions, or improvement actions, are selected based on the needs and cause analyses. When selecting interventions, take into account the following criteria:

- Issue(s) the interventions will address
- Cost to implement each intervention (low, moderate, high)

- Impact or effectiveness of each intervention (low, moderate, high)
- Opportunity cost or economic consequence if interventions are not implemented (low, moderate, high)
- Time frame in which the interventions could be implemented

Note that in many (or even most) situations, more than one intervention is needed to resolve the problems. For example, consider the case study at the beginning of this chapter. Karen may need to help Ed and the customer service agents with a sales planning process and create a job aid to help the customer service agents and a coaching process to help Ed as the entire department practices the new process. In fact it is very likely that the customer service agents and Ed may see that the sales and customer support process could be "tweaked." Karen can make modifications to the process and the job aid to make the process even better.

Intervention Design and Development

Once interventions are selected, they may need to be designed and developed if samples (prototypes) are not readily available. This design and development must be properly done if the intervention is to be effective. Design takes into account such issues as the audience, resources, time frames, cost, and usability, to name a few. By following a defined design process, we can ensure that we take into consideration all such issues in order to create an effective intervention design. The design should be complete enough that another person could develop the intervention solely from the design specifications.

The development of an intervention is just as critical as its design. A poorly developed intervention will not be effective. By following a defined development process, we will ensure that the intervention is developed effectively.

Interventions often include training or references, job analysis or work design, personal development, human resource management, organizational communication, organizational design and development, or financial systems. The wise T&D professional *does not design an intervention if he or she does not possess the expertise to do so!*

Intervention Implementation and Change

Effective implementation is critical to the success of an intervention. Without proper implementation even the most carefully planned intervention may fail. Implementation often involves several people and departments as it affects everyone.

Implementing any intervention permanently alters the way an organization does business, so it is critical that it is done with the whole organization in mind. Therefore an implementation and change management plan is necessary for each intervention that will be carried out. By following a defined implementation process, we will ensure that we design the implementation plan thoroughly and that the implementation is effective and efficient.

An implementation plan has three main components:

- Introducing the intervention
- Supporting the implementation and testing it
- Minimizing resistance to the intervention

Introducing the intervention

The first step in successfully implementing an intervention is properly introducing it. Introducing the intervention does not mean simply communicating the change to employees; it also involves ensuring that everything is ready for the implementation to begin. A communication plan, required materials, schedules, and defined roles are necessary for introducing the intervention effectively to employees.

Supporting the implementation and testing it

The second step in successfully implementing an intervention is the most critical one. During this step the implementation team ensures the implementation process is going smoothly and removes any barriers from successful implementation. The intervention is also thoroughly tested during this phase, to ensure that it will work for the organization. Testing, marketing, delivery, and maintenance are part of this step.

Minimizing resistance to the intervention

The last step in implementing an intervention is minimizing the resistance from employees. All change is met with some level of resistance. The key is managing the resistance to keep it at acceptable levels so it does not interfere with the implementation.

Intervention Evaluation

The evaluation of any intervention is an important last step to determine whether the intervention has had any impact on the organization and, if so, what type of impact. Evaluation is critical because it helps prove that an intervention has added value, is resolving the identified performance issues, and is not causing other issues. Because one intervention can affect all parts of an organization, it is essential to learn what these effects are. By following a defined evaluation process, we ensure that we thoroughly evaluate every part of an organization that could have been affected by the intervention.

There are three phases of evaluation:

- Formative
- Summative
- Confirmative

Formative evaluation considers the success of analysis, design, and development. *Summative* evaluation considers the immediate impact and success of the intervention. *Confirmative* evaluation considers the long-term impact and success of the intervention.

Each intervention should be individually evaluated to determine if it has changed employee behavior and organizational results. If the interventions have affected the employees and organization positively, they will be considered successful. If they have had no effect or a negative effect, they will be discontinued or modified.

In addition, organizations often don't want training or other interventions to be evaluated beyond the initial participant reactions to training. As trainers we can observe positive changes in skill level during the training sessions and jot down the improvements. We can talk with managers and workers before training about the situation prior to the training or other intervention. We can also talk with managers and workers after the training or other intervention. We can write down improvements and also problems (such as Ed's report that customer service scores had not improved). We can ask if managers (such as Ed) have any idea what problems remain.

As we learn more about HPT, we can make more suggestions about next steps. We will remember that most adverse situations will benefit from more than one intervention. We can keep our evaluation notes in a single computer file so that we gradually create a detailed report of the impact of training and other interventions in the organization, especially as it relates to the business goals.

How HPT Relates to Business Acumen

HPT and business acumen are intertwined (as displayed in Table 8.1, which also presents the related American Society for Training and Development [ASTD] competency areas). Those who are well versed in business acumen understand the language of business. Throughout the HPT process, business acumen is essential for communicating with key stakeholders and employees. In order to present the performance issues, implement interventions, and evaluate interventions, we must understand the organization's business model and financial goals and be able to use appropriate business terminology in order to be understood.

Table 8.1. Performance Technology Standards, Business Acumen, and ASTD Competencies

PT Standard	Business Acumen	ASTD Competencies
Focus on results	Financial skills Communication skills	Interpersonal Business/Management
Take a systems view	Partnering skills Communication skills	Interpersonal Business/Management Personal
Add value	Financial skills Communication skills	Interpersonal Business/Management
Collaborate	Partnering skills Communication skills	Interpersonal Personal
Needs analysis	Financial skills Partnering skills Communication skills Leadership and personnel management skills	Interpersonal Business/Management
Cause analysis	Financial skills Partnering skills Communication skills	Interpersonal Business/Management

**Table 8.1. Performance Technology Standards,
Business Acumen, and ASTD Competencies, Cont'd**

PT Standard	Business Acumen	ASTD Competencies
Design	Partnering skills Communication skills Leadership and personnel management skills	Interpersonal Business/Management
Development	Partnering skills Communication skills Leadership and personnel management skills	Interpersonal Business/Management
Implementation	Partnering skills Communication skills Leadership and personnel management skills	Interpersonal Business/Management
Evaluation	Financial skills Partnering skills Communication skills	Interpersonal Personal

Financial skills are vital to managing the HPT process. We must be able to focus on results, add value, and evaluate interventions, often in the light of financial data. The easiest, and often most effective, way to prove added value is to show increased profits. We must also be able to work within a budget and understand the expenses and costs associated with a project as well as make decisions regarding vendors.

Partnering skills make up another vital component of the HPT process and are involved in almost all the ten PT standards. We must be able to work effectively with others in order to achieve the best results. Working with clients, customers, key stakeholders, and experts is necessary to effectively address performance issues.

Communication skills are absolutely essential to the HPT process. If we cannot communicate effectively with others, the HPT process will fail. Effective communication is the cornerstone of the HPT process.

Revisiting the Case Study with an HPT Viewpoint

Now let's revisit the case study situation this chapter began with, but this time let's approach it from an HPT viewpoint.

► MAKING SURE TRAINING SOLVES THE RIGHT PROBLEM

"I need training, and I need it now!," barked Ed, the vice president of sales.

"How can I help you, Ed?" asked Karen, the T&D manager.

"Our customer satisfaction scores are very low. They've dropped by 25 percent over the last two months! I think our customer service agents need some more training. Can you arrange for that?"

"Well, I could arrange for training, but our customer service agents just went through training six months ago. Before I send them through another training, I'd like to see if there's something else going on," said Karen thoughtfully, trying to remember HPT and taking into account the big picture.

"I don't have the time for you to go poking around to see if there's another problem," said Ed. "I already know the problem; our customer service agents don't know how to handle customers properly. Obviously they need a refresher course. And I need results now!"

"Well, Ed, I could go forward with the training, but if there are other issues going on, it won't increase our customer satisfaction scores," said Karen convincingly. "Besides, we have twenty agents and the customer service training is three days. If the average wage of our agents is $15 an hour, that's $7,200 in lost wages plus the cost of the training itself to try to address an issue that may not even be the root problem," continued Karen, trying to appeal to Ed's fiscal sense. "Why don't you give me a week to assess the situation? If I feel the agents need training after that, I will gladly train them. What do you say?"

"At this point I don't care how you fix the problem," said Ed, "just fix it!"

Karen was excited as she hung up the phone. This was her first chance at trying HPT. She hoped it would produce the results Ed was looking for.

Needs Analysis

First, Karen had to conduct a needs analysis. This time the analysis would be very quick. She had gotten some information from Ed, and she knew the company's business goals. She began by asking herself the following questions to make sure HPT would be needed.

- Does a performance gap exist? The answer was yes. Ed had said that the customer satisfaction scores had dropped by 25 percent; this was the performance gap.

- Is the performance gap related to business goals? The answer was yes. Karen knew that one of the company's business goals was to provide outstanding customer service to all customers. Because customer satisfaction had dropped, the company was not meeting this goal.

- Is further action recommended? The answer was yes. There was a performance gap that related directly to business goals, so further action would be warranted.

Karen knew that every needs analysis would not be this easy, but she was glad she could quickly start looking for the cause in this case. She would try to see the customer satisfaction data and comments because this would help her to create activities (such as role plays, games, or simulations). In a friendly, informal manner she would try to catch a few customer service agents at lunch to find out what they thought of the previous training and what training would be helpful for the future. This way Karen would get sufficient information to begin the cause analysis.

Cause Analysis

Karen needed to continue her needs analysis and also to develop a plan to do a thorough cause analysis. The cause analysis was important because it would help her get to the root cause of the problem. Karen knew she needed to start in the customer service department, but she also knew she had to be flexible in case her analysis sent her elsewhere. Karen decided the best approach would be to begin with some interviews and observations.

Karen began by meeting with the customer service manager, Joan. She wanted to explain to Joan what she was doing, why she was doing it, and what she hoped to accomplish at the end. She also wanted to establish a good relationship with Joan so she could have easy access to the information she needed to complete her analysis.

Karen wanted to be prepared for this meeting, so she made a list of the information she thought she would need to obtain:

- Customer satisfaction scores for the last fourteen months
- An understanding of the customer service process
- An understanding of the customer complaint handling process
- The turnover rate in the department
- An understanding of any changes that have occurred in the last six months
- A copy of the customer complaint log over the past two months
- The name of a "star performer" she could interview

Karen had a brief meeting with Joan where she was able to obtain the information she was wanted. Joan expressed appreciation that Karen had "kept her in the loop." She also told Karen to come back if she needed anything else.

At this point Karen wanted to look over the information she had obtained, before she moved on to the next part of the process.

- Karen reviewed the customer satisfaction scores and confirmed a 25 percent drop over the last two months. The scores had pretty much been steady over the last year at around 90 percent—the company objective. The scores had dropped sharply two months ago, by 15 percent, then they had dropped another 10 percent last month.

- Joan had explained the customer service process. When a customer called in, the agent entered the customer's catalogue order into the computer system. The order was then automatically printed out in the shipping department, where the items were packaged and shipped to the customer. Karen made a mental note that she might have to involve the shipping department to complete her analysis.

- Joan had explained the customer complaint handling process. When a complaint came in, the agent looked up the customer's original order and did whatever it took to resolve the issue. If the agent could not handle the issue, he or she would refer the customer to Joan.

All complaints were recorded in an electronic log, which was reviewed at the bimonthly staff meeting so agents could learn from customer complaints.

- Joan said that the turnover rate in the department was pretty low. The last new agent was hired six months ago when another agent retired.

- Joan said there hadn't been any major changes in the last six months. The only change was that the computer system had been upgraded two and a half months ago. However, this was simply an upgrade and the system functioned the same way as before, so no new training was needed. In fact, Joan said, the agents seemed to like the new interface on this upgrade better because it made the system more user-friendly.

- Karen reviewed the customer complaint log. After weeding out some standard complaints, she realized that about 85 percent of the complaints were from customers who had items on back order. Karen made a note to ask Joan about the back-order policy.

- Joan had given Karen the name of a star performer, Tom. Tom had been with the department for five years, and Joan said that all the other agents deferred to Tom when there was a problem.

After reviewing all this information she had obtained, Karen went back to Joan. First, she asked about the company's back-order policy. Joan explained that if an item was on back order for longer than a week, the rest of the order would ship immediately to the customer. Karen asked how someone would know that. Joan said it was all handled by the computer; everything was automated. Next, Karen asked Joan to introduce her to Tom. She also asked Karen if it would be all right to interview one other agent at random; Joan agreed.

When Karen met with Tom, she asked for his explanation of the customer service process, the complaint handling policy, the back-order policy, and information on any changes. Tom's answers were the same as Joan's. Karen asked if there were any problems with the new computer upgrade. Tom replied that he loved the new system; he thought it was better than the last version. Karen asked Tom if he had handled more complaints lately regarding back-ordered items. Tom replied that there were a few more complaints, but the customers were just upset that their orders didn't arrive sooner.

After talking with Tom briefly, Karen observed him doing his job, to make sure he was following the company's policies. Tom followed the policies perfectly. Karen thanked Tom for his time and moved on to another agent. Karen wanted to make sure that a random average performer performed and understood the job as well as Tom.

Karen randomly selected another agent, Mary, and introduced herself. She explained what she was doing and asked if Mary would answer a few questions. Mary agreed. First, Karen asked Mary about her background with the company. Mary explained that she had been there for a year and this was her first job out of school. Karen was pleased because Mary would be a great example of an average performer—no prior work experience and relatively new to the job. Karen asked Mary the same questions she had asked Tom. Mary gave her basically the same answers. Karen observed Mary for a while; Mary also performed the job to the company's expectations.

After interviewing and observing employees in the customer service department, Karen thought the problem might be elsewhere. After all, the policies were pretty clear and the agents were following the policies. Karen decided to look in the shipping department next.

Karen went to the shipping department where she met with Roger, the shipping manager. She explained to Roger what she was doing and asked if she could ask him a few questions. Roger wasn't as pleasant as Joan; he said he was very busy and only had a few minutes. Karen asked how they received customer orders. Roger took her over to a large printer where orders were printing out. Roger explained that the shippers would grab an order, pack it, label it, and send it to an inspector before final shipping. Then the inspector would stamp the order as complete and place the paper in the bin; this paper would later be filed in the shipping department. Karen thanked Roger and asked if she could stick around and observe for a few minutes. Roger said it was fine, as long as she didn't get in the way. Karen observed the work process long enough to see that the shippers were following the policy.

Karen went back to her office; she felt confused. The problem didn't appear to be in customer service or shipping, so where could it be? Karen decided to call a few of the customers to ask them more questions about their complaints.

Karen contacted five of the customers who had complaints about back orders and said she was following up on complaints they had filed. She asked them to explain their problem in more detail. Each of the customers said he or she had been told that even though one item was on back order, the rest of the order would ship out immediately. Instead, all of them had had to wait for their back-ordered item to be filled before the rest of their order was shipped. A few of the customers had called twice, and both times the customer service agent said the computer showed that the rest of the order had already been shipped and that they should receive it shortly.

Karen finally felt as though she were getting somewhere! For some reason the orders with back-ordered items were not being shipped immediately, as the company policy stated. Now she needed to figure out where in the process the problem was occurring.

Karen went back to Joan and explained what she had found out so far. She asked Joan to pull any orders from today that contained a back-ordered item that would take longer than a week to be ready. Karen selected ten of the orders that contained both a back-ordered item and other items. The orders indicated that the other items had been shipped. Karen thanked Joan and went back down to shipping.

In shipping, Karen told Roger she needed to locate these orders. Roger told Karen she would need to look for them because he didn't have the time. Karen started with the orders on the printer; the ones she was looking for weren't in there. Next she looked at the orders in progress; they weren't there either. Lastly, she looked at the orders marked as complete; she still couldn't find them. So even though orders like these were being processed correctly, they were not printing out in shipping. Karen decided she needed to talk to one more person who might be able to help her.

Karen went to see John, the IT manager. She explained the problem to him: the orders were being processed correctly but were not printing. She also reminded John that the computer system had recently been upgraded, and asked if that could be the problem. John looked at the coding in the computer system and discovered an error. The system was not sending the order to the shipping department printer if any back-ordered item was listed. John said the settings must have been reset to default when the system was upgraded. Karen was just glad that she had finally uncovered the problem! Before going further she met with Ed to keep him informed of her progress and her ideas for improvements (interventions). She was careful to get Ed's buy-in and commitment to support her efforts to resolve the deficiency issues.

Design and Development

Karen asked John what it would take to fix the problem. John replied that it was a simple fix in the coding once he got the right specifications to put in. Karen asked about the orders that were currently stuck in the system. John said he would have to write a new program to correct that problem and that would take a couple of hours, but he didn't have the time until tomorrow morning.

Karen gave John the specifications to do the simple fix now; she told him that an order with both a back-ordered item and other items should print if the out-of-stock item would be on back order for longer than a week. John corrected the settings so that the orders would now print correctly. She also asked John to develop the other fix in the morning and call her when it was completed; John agreed. Karen thanked John for his assistance.

Karen went back to Joan and apprised her of the situation. Joan was ecstatic that the problem was fixed but concerned that this could have happened. Karen told Joan that this was something they needed to remember the next time a computer upgrade happened; they needed to have testing procedures in place to make sure the new system was working properly. Joan agreed and said this would go on the agenda at the next department head meeting.

Implementation

Karen told Joan they needed to verify that the fix was now working. She asked Joan to print any more orders that came through today with back-ordered items. She also asked Joan to print any outstanding orders with back-ordered items. She told Joan she would check tomorrow to make sure the system was working properly, after John had developed the new program.

John called Karen late the next morning to say that he had put the fix in place. Karen again thanked him for his assistance.

Karen went back to Joan to get the printed orders. Joan told Karen she wanted to go with her to shipping to make sure the system was now working. Karen checked that all the orders that had come through after the fix were processed properly; they were. Joan checked to make sure that all the outstanding orders had printed; they had. Joan thanked Karen for all her help in resolving this problem. Karen said she would be back to make sure this action helped bring the customer satisfaction scores back up.

When Karen got back to her office, she phoned Ed. She recounted what she had discovered, the steps that had been taken, and that they had to wait to evaluate the situation until the next set of customer satisfaction scores came out.

Evaluation

Because Karen had already checked to make sure the computer system was now working properly in the implementation phase, she did not have to do this during the evaluation phase. She just had to wait for the customer satisfaction scores.

The next month the scores had gone up by 10 percent. Ed called to say he was pleased, but he wanted the scores to be back at the original level. Karen told him to wait another month, that there were probably still some residual effects of the computer problem in those scores. Ed reluctantly agreed.

The following month the scores had returned to their original levels. Ed called again.

"Well, I don't know how you did it, but you certainly fixed the problem! I guess we should try more of this nontraining stuff again. So does this mean you don't do training anymore?"

"I still do training," said Karen. "But instead of just training, I now do total performance solutions." ◄

Key Points

- Human performance technology is a comprehensive solution to performance issues in today's organizations.

- As T&D professionals we need to go beyond training and offer total performance solutions. HPT will help us achieve this objective.

- The better we understand the process, the more effective we can be at using HPT to resolve performance issues in the workplace.

- The four main principles of HPT are

  1. Focus on results.

  2. Take a systems view.

  3. Add value.

  4. Collaborate.

- HPT removes barriers to performance by ensuring that the right problem is addressed, that the solution or intervention works, and that the solution helps the organization.

- HPT aligns business and individual performance with business goals, looks at the whole system instead of just one part of it, and focuses on results to ensure that it adds value to the organization.

- The five phases of an HPT intervention are

  1. Performance analysis

  2. Cause analysis

  3. Intervention (improvement) selection, design, and development

  4. Implementation

  5. Evaluation

Questions for Reflection

1. Reflect on some of the recent training initiatives you have been a part of. How many of them might have been different if you had applied the principles of HPT?

2. How will you approach future training assignments?

Section 3
Communication Skills

9

Writing Business Messages

THE FIRST TWO SECTIONS of this book introduced the critical components of working with the tools of finance and the soft skills of cultivating strong relationships and partnerships. The third area of skills often overlooked, or assumed to be already strong, involves written communications. In this chapter we will explore the best practices for writing effective business communications.

All of us in training and development are writers, but we are not all good writers. We need to be, though, because the business world is increasingly dependent on written communication. And with the popularity of e-mail, writing has now become a huge part of almost everybody's job.

Most T&D professionals read and write business messages—e-mails, memos, and letters—every day. Although these messages are not, perhaps, the most significant documents we write, they are certainly the documents we produce most often.

Given the frequency with which we compose business messages, there are plenty of reasons to become better at writing them. An ability to produce well-written messages will increase your efficiency in the following ways:

- You will get the results you want more often.

- You will reduce the number of mistakes resulting from miscommunication.

- You will need to send only one message instead of three.

If increased efficiency isn't reason enough, here is an appeal to your ego: good writing will improve your image. When you communicate you are sending a representation of yourself out into the world. You want to make sure that representation is one you can be proud of.

Like other skills that you can acquire on the job, effective writing can be learned. The first step toward improvement is to develop an understanding of what constitutes superior writing. To that end, some of the ideas in this chapter might challenge your beliefs about what makes writing "good" or "bad."

The first part of the chapter explains the fundamentals of good writing. The second part is a workshop designed to hone particular skills. It will focus on a few specific strategies for writing effective business messages.

Good Message Writing in Five Simple Steps

To get started, here are five steps that I recommend you cycle through every time you write a business message (any e-mail, memo, or letter).

1. Make sure you need to write a message. Maybe you should make a phone call or arrange a meeting instead.

2. Focus on your reader's point of view. All writers must focus on their audience in order to be successful.

3. Use simple, direct language. No one wants to have to read a stuffy e-mail twice to decipher what you're saying.

4. Structure your message strategically. Following a few simple structural guidelines will make your message clear.

5. Remember that grammar always matters. Even though your memo will not be returned with red marks, you will still be judged by how your writing reads.

You might want to post these guidelines by your computer and consciously walk yourself through them several times as you compose your next few business messages. Soon enough, you will have internalized the steps and become known as the Hemingway of your office.

Now let's examine these guidelines in more detail.

Make Sure You Need to Write a Message

E-mail plays a huge role in our professional lives for obvious reasons: it is convenient, efficient, and quick. Yet for all its virtues, e-mail (and its older cousins, the memo and the letter) is not always the best way to communicate. That is why you should always begin the message-writing process by considering whether a written message is in fact the appropriate medium for whatever it is you have to say.

Let's look at an example that illustrates this principle:

> Jody e-mailed all her department staff about an upcoming national conference in Hawaii. She asked for volunteers to attend the all-expenses-paid event. There was one catch: there were only three openings. The first three to respond were the people who would go.
>
> Upon reading Jody's e-mail, Ted became very excited. He loved Hawaii and he was interested in the conference anyway. He quickly hit Reply, confident that one of the three spots was his.
>
> But Jody, who was catching up on paperwork, didn't check her e-mail for several hours. Meanwhile, several other employees who were eager to go telephoned her and filled the slots. When she finally read Ted's e-mail, she let him know the openings had been filled.

Written messages are not a particularly reliable form of communication. You cannot, for instance, predict any of the following variables:

- When your reader will actually read your message
- How carefully he or she will read it
- When he or she will reply
- Whether he or she will respond in the way you had hoped

For these reasons (and others), you will need to assess whether a written message is the best form of communication that is available to you before you write anything.

Written messages are not a good medium for matters that require a timely response. If a matter is extremely urgent and you require a response right away, a phone call is almost always your best bet.

Similarly, complex matters are best handled using alternative forms of communication. For instance, if you have an open-ended question that requires a thoughtful response, you're more likely to get helpful information during a meeting or an informal brainstorming session than in response to a written message.

A written message is an effective communication tool when its subject matter is relatively straightforward and can be easily digested. Also, an effective message should focus on a single topic. If you try to cover too much ground, your reader is less likely to absorb whatever it is that you are saying.

When you decide to write a message, limit the number of questions you ask. For example, if you are sending an e-mail to a colleague with questions about an upcoming recruiting event, try to ask one or two solid questions (for example, "What is the schedule?" or, "Will we have time to speak to candidates individually?"). However curious you may be about the topic at hand, show some restraint. You can always ask follow-up questions later.

Good topics for messages are limited and straightforward, like these:

- The itinerary for an upcoming trip
- Praise for a recent project
- A request for the minutes of a meeting

Bad topics for messages are complex or require immediate responses, like these:

- Brainstorming for a new project
- An annual performance review
- A request for a phone number that you urgently need

The guideline categories in Table 9.1 will help you decide whether you should or should not write a message.

Table 9.1. Should I Write a Message?

Yes	No
Nonurgent matters	Urgent matters
Straightforward topics	Complex topics
Limited questions	Open-ended questions

Focus on Your Reader's Point of View

Writing is a solitary affair. There is of course the stereotype of the reclusive novelist typing in a dim room. But even when you are writing a short message surrounded by the commotion of a busy office, writing is a solitary act: it is just you, your thoughts, and your computer.

Because we write in relative isolation, it is no surprise that we tend to focus on ourselves while we're doing it. We may be preoccupied by thoughts like these: What do I know about the topic? What do I need from the reader? This focus on "I" makes it easy for writing to become a self-centered activity.

To become a better writer, you must learn to focus on your reader. If you approach your message from a purely self-centered perspective, your writing (and by extension your professional life) will suffer. Before you begin writing, think about your readers. Ask questions like these:

- Who are my readers?
- What do they need to know?
- What do they want?
- Under what circumstances will they be reading what I write?
- What will make them more likely to give me what I need?

The answers to these questions will vary each time you compose a message because your audience will probably change from one message to another. One morning you might write a memo that will circulate to everyone in your department. That afternoon you might e-mail a single colleague in another department. Before you leave for the day you might send another e-mail to a client. In each instance you are writing for a different audience.

Although your various readers will differ in important ways, there is one assumption you can make when you are writing a business message: you are writing to a busy person who has many things to do. Your message will probably not receive the full attention of the reader; he or she will likely be distracted by something while reading your message.

As a result you have a difficult task whenever you write a business message: to break through your reader's busy day, to bang the reader over the head with whatever it is you have to say. The rest of this section of the chapter is designed to help you do just that.

Use Simple, Direct Language

In most areas of our lives we are comfortable with messages that use simple, direct language. Consider the content of messages that you write outside of work. You might send a quick e-mail to a friend asking, "Would you like to have dinner at 8:00?" You might leave your daughter a note that says, "Walk the dog. I'll be home at 6:00." Although these are just short, informal notes written in a hurry, they reveal an important principle that we intuitively know: plain language is the best way to get our point across.

Sometimes this common sense abandons us when we sit down to write a business message. Suddenly, we feel compelled to use formal and cumbersome phrases such as "per your instructions" and "at this point in time." For some reason, we have come to associate wordiness with intelligence. We may even believe that being long-winded somehow creates a more professional tone. In fact this type of writing is inefficient, and simply put, it is bad business writing.

Simple, direct language is extremely important because it will hold your reader's attention. Consider this sentence:

> At the present time, it is my belief that the addition of an associate to the team would be beneficial to our future endeavors.

The writer intends to recommend hiring a new employee, but the sentence is so weak that the recommendation is all but lost. Its meaning is buried beneath a host of unnecessary phrases. Its wordiness fails to engage the reader, and because the reader's phone is ringing and a colleague has stepped in for a chat, the point is probably forever lost.

Now consider a simplified version of the same sentence:

> We should add a member to our team as soon as possible.

This plain language drives home the writer's point because the recommendation is not buried by lengthy, formal phrases. The reader does not have to read the sentence twice. Even if her phone is ringing and the colleague is knocking, the message has gotten through.

Simple, direct language is one of the most important keys to writing well in the business world. Remember to be as plain as possible in your messages. If you find yourself writing sentences that sound as though they belong in someone's last will and testament, stop yourself and begin again. Even though this may seem awkward at first, it will quickly become second nature.

These two paragraphs contain the same information. Which one do you think is easier to read?

> In view of the fact that there have been company-wide changes in expense processing, the department has accordingly adjusted the submission procedure. Attached please find the new guidelines in their entirety. Your understanding and patience as the new procedure is implemented is greatly appreciated. In the event that you have any questions, please refer them to me via phone or e-mail.

> Our expense-processing guidelines have changed. The new procedure is outlined in the document attached to this e-mail. Please be patient as we all grow accustomed to the new guidelines. Let me know if you have any questions.

The first paragraph uses a lot more words to say what the second paragraph says more economically and more clearly.

Structure Your Message Strategically

To structure your messages to communicate efficiently and effectively, use these four techniques:

Keep your message brief

Because your message will focus on a single topic, it should be relatively short. If it creeps over the one-page mark, you should probably consider using a different form of communication.

Place vital information at the beginning

For most of your messages, include all vital information in the first few sentences. Think of it this way: if your reader were to read only the first paragraph, would he or she have the most important information?

Because people receive so many messages, they often skim and skip sections. The first paragraph is the part most likely to receive your reader's full attention. Therefore the main thrust of your message should be fleshed out in those first few sentences. Use the remainder of your message to fill in the details.

Place your questions near the end

Position any questions for your reader in the final paragraph of your message. If you include questions at the beginning, your reader might forget about them by the end of the message. Similarly, questions embedded in the body of the message might get overlooked.

Place actions the reader must take in the last paragraph

Use the last paragraph to point out any action that your reader must take. Highlight what comes next. Do you want your reader to write a report? Are you hoping your reader will follow-up with a prospective client? Even if you made these requests earlier in the message, make sure they are repeated before you sign off.

Good business writers also pay particular attention to structuring effective paragraphs. I discuss this issue at the beginning of the second major section of this chapter, "Further Refining the Content of Your Messages."

Pay attention to all the ways in which this sample message is strategically structured.

Ben:

I'm writing about the interviews we have scheduled for next week. My hope is that a little planning will make the process run smoothly for everyone who is involved. Since these interviews will be your first with the company, I would like you to send me a list of the questions you'll be asking in advance.

As you know, we'll be talking to six candidates for Bob's old position. We have scheduled 2 hours with each person, so try to keep your interviews under 30 minutes.

We will meet next Friday at 2:00 to discuss the candidates. Please come ready to discuss the two who most impressed you. Can you send me your list of questions by 5:00 Wednesday?

Best,

Sharon

Remember That Grammar Always Matters

No matter how laid back your office is, even if it is the most casual of casual Fridays, my guess is that you do not wear sweats to work. No matter how late you were up last night, you probably managed to comb your hair before your breakfast meeting.

You dress a certain way for work even though you know it has no direct bearing on your performance. Why? Because you know that people judge you by your appearance, just as you judge people by theirs.

Despite these superficial tendencies, how many times have you received an e-mail like this one?

> Yes . . . the meting might be good for a different time Ask sandy if she can schedule something, by the way good job with the new client yesterday.

If this e-mail were a person, he would be wearing sweats, have tangled hair, and maybe even have toilet paper stuck to the bottom of his shoe. Grammatically speaking, he is a mess.

Let's face it: many of us have sent such e-mails. We have let correct spelling and proper punctuation slide. We have forsaken complete sentences and capital letters. The rise in the popularity of e-mail has led to the death of grammar, or at least to some very bad grammatical habits. With e-mails flying fast and furiously, who has time to make sure everything looks the way it should?

Before you answer that question, consider this example:

> At the request of her manager, Sam had been working on some ideas for improving internal training procedures. Although she had been developing the ideas for a long time, she wrote them up in a hurry. She was about to go on vacation, so she wanted to get the e-mail off before she left.
>
> When she was finished, Sam skimmed the e-mail and noticed a number of mistakes. She pressed Send without correcting them, knowing that her manager would forgive any mistakes. They exchanged e-mails about 100 times a day anyway.
>
> Upon her return a week later Sam was surprised to learn that her manager had forwarded the e-mail to an operations VP who had asked for input about training improvement. Sam, recalling the many mistakes she had made in her rush, was mortified.

In the worst cases bad grammar can obscure your meaning or (if it's truly terrible) make it impossible for your reader to understand you. But even when your reader can make out the gist of your message, bad grammar leaves a bad impression. Fairly or unfairly, your colleagues and clients might assume that sloppy writing reflects low intelligence or competence.

If you send shoddy e-mails, now is the time to reform. Take a few extra seconds to quickly read over all your messages, including short e-mails. Doing so will guarantee that you are projecting an image of professionalism and competence through your writing.

Further Refining the Content of Your Messages

The first section in this chapter focused on five principles that will help you write better business messages. The following section will show you specific strategies that will sharpen the content of your messages. Watch for the CD-ROM Resource note. It will guide you to exercises designed to help you further hone your writing skills.

Crafting Effective Paragraphs

There are three keys to crafting effective paragraphs: use topic sentences, supply supporting details, and choose an appropriate length.

Use topic sentences

Every fourth grader knows that a paragraph should begin with a topic sentence. A topic sentence orients your reader; you make a point and then back it up with supporting details. In theory topic sentences are simple and sensible: they summarize the main idea of the paragraph. In practice, though, many people do not use topic sentences. Why?

Maybe it's because topic sentences run contrary to the way our adult minds work. As Mike Markel explains in *Technical Communication* (2006), the way we process information when we think differs significantly from the way we process information when we read. When we think, we gather evidence *before* we draw a conclusion. If our thinking process were written out formally, it might, for example, look like this: "The sky seems cloudy. The forecast predicted storms. I therefore conclude that a storm is brewing." When we read we prefer to take in the writer's conclusion first and then evaluate that conclusion based on the evidence presented later. Our response to reading the sentence, "We must cut expenses," for example, is likely to be, "What are the reasons behind this?" We like to have the writer's conclusion in mind so we can better test its validity.

As a result topic sentences are counterintuitive; we need to make a special effort to ensure that they are inserted at the *beginning* of the paragraph rather than the end. Consider the difference that the position of the topic sentence makes in the following examples:

We expect the new training program to increase productivity up to 25 percent during its first year. There have been three major changes. The first months of our employee referral program have brought in exceptional new talent to the training department. Two trainers have been added to the employee orientation program, which will create new opportunities for one-on-one training sessions. Also, the new cross-training matrix and continuing education program will help existing employees fill in for absent colleagues.

The first months of our employee referral program have brought in exceptional new talent to the training department. Two trainers have been added to the employee orientation program, which will create new opportunities for one-on-one training sessions. Also, the new cross-training matrix and continuing education program will help existing employees fill in for absent colleagues. For all of these reasons, we expect the new training program to increase productivity up to 25 percent during its first year.

The first paragraph is more effective because the topic sentence comes first and is followed by supporting details. The second paragraph is more difficult to read because the details are stated before the topic sentence, which is positioned at the end of the paragraph.

CD-ROM RESOURCE

Open the "Writing Exercises" file on your CD, and take the opportunity to practice this skill by completing "Exercise 1: Writing Topic Sentences." (The "Writing Exercise Answers" file presents sample answers.)

Supply supporting details

A topic sentence is the cornerstone of an effective paragraph; however, the rest of the paragraph is also important. Support your topic sentence with details; these details should either support or expand on your initial claim. It is crucial that every supporting sentence relates back to the topic sentence. This will prevent you from accidentally wandering off the topic.

Choose an appropriate length

Finally, length is an important consideration as you craft effective paragraphs. In a business message, paragraphs should contain no more than five sentences. Shorter paragraphs are also OK. In fact, even one-sentence paragraphs are useful when you have a point that you really want to hammer home, as in this example:

> If you can't make Tuesday's training session, please attend the makeup session on Thursday at 3:30.

As you can see, the brevity adds emphasis to the content.

Writing a Descriptive Subject Line

No one understands the importance of the subject line quite as well as spammers, the people who send random, annoying e-mails that try to sell you things. Consider how many times you have received spam with a subject line like one of these:

> Subject: Diet pills for less
> Subject: You've been chosen!
> Subject: Girls gone wild

You probably delete these e-mails without opening them because the subject line tells you the e-mails are useless.

But some of the more clever spammers have found a way to fool the discerning e-mail reader. Consider how many times you have received spam that was disguised with a subject line like one of these:

> Subject: RE: Your recent purchase
> Subject: I'm sorry we lost touch
> Subject: Urgent request

Spammers know that these misleading subject lines are more likely to trick you into opening their messages.

These examples from spamming dramatize the importance of the subject line. Its function is to inform readers whether or not they *really* need to read your message. Make sure that your subject line is as descriptive as possible about the content of your message. That way your reader can make an informed decision.

Let's look at an example that demonstrates the importance of the subject line.

> Adam, a trainer, was notorious for circulating e-mails containing bad jokes and for sending boring forwards around his office. His colleagues had learned to ignore these messages. Out of habit they instantly deleted anything with a subject line like, "You know you need a trainer when . . ."

> When Adam was experiencing class disruptions from a problem employee, he knew he needed to register a complaint with the employee's manager. He typed out an e-mail and, for laughs, gave it the subject line, "5 signs someone needs the boot."
>
> Upon receiving the e-mail the manager assumed it was another of Adam's unbearable joke e-mails. She immediately put it in the trash unread. When Adam reported a similar disruptive incident at a meeting the following week, she had no idea what he was talking about.

As this example suggests, the subject line should accurately and concisely describe the main thrust of your message. Specificity is key. If, for instance, you are writing an informative memo about the quarterly budget, try to zoom in closely on the exact content:

Subject: Quarterly budget information [Vague]
Subject: Quarterly budget projections [Specific]
Subject: Quarterly budget meeting agenda [Specific]

An e-mail subject line can be a good opportunity to remind your reader of something you want him or her to do. If, for example, your e-mail includes questions that need answers, you might use the subject "Questions about the quarterly budget." Similarly, you might use the subject "Today's 3:00 meeting" to remind your reader of something he or she needs to bear in mind.

Finally, you should use the subject line to help yourself stay focused as you write the rest of your message. Make sure that everything you write relates back to the subject line. (Think of the subject line as the topic sentence of the entire e-mail.) This will keep you from losing focus. Table 9.2 offers more examples that show the difference between vague and specific subject lines.

Table 9.2. Vague and Specific Subject Lines

Vague	Specific
Workshop	Adobe workshop 3:00 today
Questions	Questions about July 7 fundraiser
Request	Feasibility report request

Delivering Good, and Bad, News

Ideally, if you must deliver important or sensitive good news (like a job promotion) or bad news (like downsizing), you will do so in person. With less personal or dramatic news, a written message can get the job done. Just be sure to pay careful attention to the structure that you use.

You can use the order of the details to enhance good news and soften the blow of bad news.

People like good news and dislike bad news, and there is nothing you can do to change that. Still, the way you position the news in your message can help your reader digest whatever it is you are telling him or her.

The technique is simple: position good news at the beginning of a message and bad news toward the end. That's all you need to remember.

Why put the good news first? Because people like good news, they will be glad to receive it. Delivered at the beginning of your message, it will have a more immediate impact. The reader can revel in the good news as he or she reads the remainder of your message.

By the same token, if you put the bad news first your reader will focus on it for the remainder of your message. He or she will have a hard time processing anything that comes after the bad news. For this reason it is best to state any additional information you really want your reader to notice before you deliver the bad news.

The following case example illustrates this principle:

> Karl sent an e-mail to his department personnel that began, "Unfortunately, we were denied our conference attendance request. I am not sure why." He thought it best to get the bad news out of the way before he shared the good news, which was that he had made alternate arrangements.
>
> Mel had spent a lot of time putting together the conference attendance request. When she read the bad news, she stormed into the HR department to demand answers.

Of course, had Mel continued reading, she would have learned that Karl had arranged for everyone to attend key conference workshops via WebEx. Participants would enjoy catered lunches for both days of the event. Also, he had arranged for two professors of new media from a local university to attend and assist with debriefings after each workshop.

Finally, remember that it is always best to end a message on a good note. Include a positive sentence or two directly after the bad news whenever possible. Consider this message:

For all of these reasons, we did not approve your request for an increase in the training budget. *Know that your hard work has not gone unnoticed, and we hope to increase the budget next year.*

By delivering modest praise directly after the bad news, the writer manages to end on a positive note, without sounding condescending. Table 9.3 suggests how to categorize some specific kinds of news.

Table 9.3. Delivering Good News and Bad News

Good News: Put News Like This at the Beginning of Your Message	Bad News: Put News Like This Toward the End of your Message
Approved requests	Denied requests
Budget increases	Budget cuts
Praise	Criticism

CD-ROM RESOURCE

Open the "Writing Exercises" file on your CD, and take the time to practice this skill by completing "Exercise 3: Writing Good-News and Bad-News Messages." (The "Writing Exercise Answers" file presents sample answers.)

What Comes Next?

You have learned five steps that can improve your writing. You have also learned how to shape the content of your message to make your writing both clear and effective.

Now it is time to put these principles into practice. Reading this chapter is only the first step toward becoming a better writer. Like all skills, writing requires practice for it to improve.

You have many interesting ways to go about this. First, take a look at the writing exercises on the CD that accompanies this book. After that, try critiquing old messages that you have written or received to see where improvements could be made. (Where is the topic sentence? Is the language clear and direct? Is the message written in complete sentences?) Take an active role by making notes in the margins as you review these messages.

Finally, apply the principles you have learned to every message you write, short or long. Remember that even brief messages deserve your full attention. The few extra minutes you spend writing messages that are clear and effective will ultimately improve both your efficiency and your image.

Business Message Examples

The following sample business messages and commentary are shared with us by Renee Stoll, manager of Training, Education, and Employee Development at TDS Telecom (staff names in these e-mails are pseudonyms).

▶ E-MAILS SENT BY A MANAGER AT TDS TELECOM

This first example is an e-mail we sent to our Training Team to keep them up to date on how we were handling being short of our coordinator (a critical position on the team).

Subject: Help is on the way!

Hi All—Just a quick update on how we'll care for some of Cindy's critical work processes in the interim as we look for a new Coordinator.

With some creative help from our friends, we'll be getting some assistance from Nancy until we can find a permanent replacement. Nancy and Julie will work with Cindy to learn the Registrar import process and/or technical external request process so we can keep the team afloat. As you can imagine, there will most likely be a few snags along the way, so your patience and understanding is appreciated.

Just wanted to let you know of our plans and to send a HUGE THANK YOU to Nancy, Beth and Julie for helping us in our time of need.:-)

This second message is one that we sent to the team to communicate our overbudget status and at the same time keep things in perspective. As you can see, I use a lot of humor to defuse bad news. I also tend to keep things simple, straightforward, and clear—in my experience, the more I try to explain, the worse the situation seems to be.

Subject: 3% over budget

Yep, you read that right. For the first time in at least 5 years, the training budget is over! No need to panic, just keep a few things in mind as you close out the year.

- If an expense is for next year, please try to wait to submit the expenses until January. I realize this isn't always possible, but if it is, please do so.
- Do not order extra course materials for 2005 with 2004 budget dollars.
- Continue to be careful with expenses. I prefer the term frugal to cheap.:-)

Thanks—Let me know if you have any questions or concerns.

This third example is an announcement we sent when one of our associate managers was taking a new job.

Subject: Alice announcement

Hi All—Many of you have probably already heard, but in case you haven't, Alice has accepted a position with the Recruiting Team. While this is really bad news for training, it is a good fit with Alice's past experiences and career goals, and a wonderful opportunity for the Recruiting Team.

Alice has been a part of the Training Team for over 5 years and in that time has contributed in many ways to the TDS Invest in People shared values. To name only a few of her many accomplishments:

- Transitioning separate DESI and SABRE classes into a comprehensive process-based CSSR Basic Training Program

- Leading a team of 6 limited-term employees to develop position-specific training to 10 Metrocom Call Center Teams
- Taking on a new role and a new team as Associate Manager of Functional & Technical Training
- Teaching Situational Leadership and MDP while juggling all of her other projects
- Managing oodles and oodles (yes, that's a technical project management term!) of projects for key business units

Alice has left her mark and very large shoes to fill. Luckily, her talents will continue to support TDS, and I imagine she'll stop by to say hello from time to time! Please join me in wishing her the very best in her new challenge.

I will be working with the Training Team to determine the best way to back-fill this critical position and will keep you all posted on progress. Until then, please ignore the loud weeping from my office!:-) ◄

Key Points

- The five steps for writing a business message are
  1. Make sure that you need to write a message.
  2. Focus on your reader's point of view.
  3. Use simple, direct language.
  4. Structure your message strategically.
  5. Remember that grammar always matters.
- To become a better writer, you must learn to focus on your reader. Ask: Who are my readers? What do they need to know? What do they want? Under what circumstances will they be reading what I write? What will make them more likely to give me what I need?
- A message is an effective communication tool when its subject matter is easily digestible and relatively straightforward.
- Simple, direct language will hold your reader's attention.
- There are four ways in which you can structure your messages to communicate efficiently and effectively:

1. Keep your message brief.

2. Include all vital information in the first few sentences.

3. Position any questions for your reader in the final paragraph of your message.

4. Use the last paragraph to point out any action that your reader must take.

10

Developing a Business Case

BUSINESS CASES are one of your most important tools for communicating with business management. Although business cases come in all shapes and sizes, they have five common goals they must achieve:

1. Articulate the objectives of the project in clear concise language.
2. Identify the drivers, needs, and impact of the project.
3. Demonstrate the value of the project to the business.
4. Analyze the potential risks of the project.
5. List outstanding questions.

The formal business case is only a small part of the equation. The real success of a business case comes from our ability to speak the language of the business. Our powers of communication; the quality of our partnerships throughout the organization, especially in the upper echelons; and our political acumen factor into our success. If we can demonstrate value to the business and link our projects to major organizational initiatives we will get the support we need. Writing business cases and thinking in terms of the questions to be addressed is something everyone in T&D needs to be doing; not just managers and leaders. I am appalled by the number of T&D professionals I run into who have never had to write a business case and have no desire to do so. Gone are the days when we could hang out in the sanctuary of the classroom. Of course that is still a large part of what we do, but until we also step out and become an integrated part of the organization's value chain, we will always be seen as second-rate citizens. Business cases represent tangible, low-hanging fruit we can pursue to demonstrate our relevancy. Exhibit 10.1 defines some of the key elements in a business case.

Exhibit 10.1. Definitions of Key Elements in a Business Case

Business Case Element	Description
Executive summary	Offers a short sound bite summarizing the context of the proposed recommendation, cost and resources requested, and benefits to the organization.
	Everything in the proposal in four sentences or less.
Background	Describes and details key circumstances, events, and pieces of contextual information relevant to the business case. You can also think of this as the problem domain being addressed.
	What conditions have brought about the need for this proposed solution?
Business drivers	Highlights how the organization will be fundamentally improved by the proposed business. Business drivers and background information are often combined. The background or business driver section is a good place to use an organizational story (think of it as a mini compelling-use case that succinctly illustrates the need and opportunities addressed by the business).
	What new opportunities, competitive advantages, or cost savings are offered?

Exhibit 10.1. Definitions of Key Elements in a Business Case, Cont'd

Business Case Element	Description
Proposed solutions	Presents the core part of the proposal, laying out solutions. Be sure to present more than one solution. Identify the option you favor and why. This is a good place to present pros and cons of the options presented. Budgets, a bill of materials or resources that are being requested, high-level timelines, and work breakdown structures can be included here. *What are your recommendations?*
Measurement	Provides a collection of critical success factors and criteria for evaluating the impact of the proposed solution. These should relate back to the business drivers. Depending on the nature of the proposal you may have a strong quantitative component in this section of the proposal, including return on investment (ROI) information. This section also needs to include qualitative measures. For a complex project, measures need to be tied to the various project phases and should demonstrate that stakeholders directly affected by the project have had a voice in articulating the measures. *How will you measure the success and impact of the project?*
Risk analysis	Details the factors both foreseen and unforeseen that might affect the success of the project. Provides details on how you plan to mitigate these risks. *What are the risks?*
Outstanding questions	Lists questions that need to be answered and the ways in which potential answers may affect the project plan. *What questions still need to be answered?*
Next steps	Details the steps that need to occur next. *What needs to happen next to move the proposal forward?*

Anatomy of a Model Business Case: TDS Telecom and Learning Management System Replacement

The remainder of this chapter presents a business case example based on a case used at TDS Telecom. First, Renee Stoll, manager of Training, Education, and Employee Development at TDS Telecom, offers some background information about the effort of the training function at TDS Telecom to build this business case for a learning management system replacement.

▶ RENEE'S LESSONS LEARNED ABOUT BUILDING A BUSINESS CASE

The introduction of our learning management system (LMS) was one of the first true HR synergies across our enterprise. Three parts of our enterprise were involved: TDS Corporate, TDS Telecom/Metrocom, and U.S. Cellular. All three groups do separate training. We began holding meetings about two and a half years beforehand to see if we could all work off the same LMS.

We had to make the business case to three separate organizational entities and then also present it to a committee responsible for the approval of all new capital expenses. Since the largest percentage of capital funds is given to revenue-generating initiatives, we had to be clear about the fact that there were no hard benefits and at the same time we had to make the soft benefits tangible to financial decision makers. I discovered you need to think differently when you are speaking with the VP of operations.

Be sure to find a cheerleader within your organization; he or she had better be at least your own boss. Our VP of sales and marketing was part of the committee. I went to her and presold the business case to her. She gave me her fantastic advice. She told me to do presale meetings with a couple more folks. By shopping the business case around to key stakeholders I was able to gather critical intelligence about them.

For example, I learned that for one operations group reporting capability was a hot button—what they were having do to get data to generate reports for auditing purposes was a nightmare. The new LMS would put almost real-time data in the hands of those managers. That's a huge business benefit that I would have never learned about if I hadn't met with the operations group.

Meeting with our information technology group I learned that they were supporting the hosting of U.S. Cellular's LMS. Because our new LMS was going to be hosted by a third party, it was going to free up the information technology group to do more revenue-generating activities.

I was fortunate that our management team is pretty accessible. I can schedule a meeting with a VP by sending a meeting invite and highlighting the points I want to make. In the process I learned so much about how the officers interacted with one another.

When I finally made a formal presentation of the business case in front of the committee and to all of the officers about how the LMS fits with the TDS vision, they understood it and were 100 percent behind the project.

My last words of advice are these: see T&D through the eyes of the business. I am a career trainer so I had to work really hard to understand the business impact. It's more subtle than you might think. I spent a lot of time trying to understand how other people work. See the organization through the eyes of other people. Put yourself out there. Be open-minded. Try not to judge things as you see them happen. ◄

► BUSINESS CASE FOR A NEW LMS

Situation

TDS Telecom currently has a learning management system (LMS) of sorts. This LMS has limited functionality and isn't currently meeting our needs. We wanted to replace it with something more robust that has the capability to help us reach our strategic goals.

Business Drivers for the Learning Management System Overall

1. Provide a flexible learning management framework that can incorporate all types of training: e-learning, classroom, Web-based, CBT, and so forth.

2. Provide a secure, centralized online repository for training and development resources and opportunities.

3. Streamline training coordination by implementing more efficient training administration processes.

4. Provide management with tools to effectively coach their employees for skill and career development.

5. Empower employees with a self-service ability so they can manage their unique training and career development plans.

6. Track the impacts of training activities and report them to senior management: that is, class interest, time spent in class, accomplishments, evaluations, and so forth.

7. Clearly link competencies to training and development activities and resources, and then report on them.

8. Reduce duplication of training efforts across the TDS Enterprise so purchasing, development, delivery, and measurement can be shared.

Drivers for an Enterprise LMS (Telecom/Metrocom/USLink Perspective)

1. Give employees the ability to attend courses offered by TDS Corporate and U.S. Cellular. TDS Corporate has numerous courses that benefit the Telecom organization. At present, employees have to log into two different systems to find them. As a result, employees do not always know these classes exist, which means they either (a) pay higher costs to take the course outside TDS, or (b) don't take the course at all and miss out on an opportunity to enhance their skills.

2. Gain the ability to share our courses with TDS Corporate and U.S. Cellular. We may have internally developed courses and technical externally delivered courses that would benefit TDS Corporate or U.S. Cellular. The current system does not allow employees outside Telecom to view or register for our courses. As a result, we may be spending more on courses than we need to or not getting all the development training that we could as an enterprise.

3. Reduce duplication of costs and resources across the enterprise. Each organization currently spends money buying or developing and delivering content also offered by the other organizations in such areas as change management, leadership skills, communication skills, and so forth. With an enterprise system we can work together to select, negotiate, develop, or deliver a particular course or content area that could be shared across all companies. This will save costs, development time, and so forth.

4. Gain the ability to track all training on employees' transcripts. Currently, when Telecom employees take a corporate course it isn't tracked on their training transcript unless they complete a Web form and the training team enters it into Registrar manually. As a result, training and development cannot currently be completely or accurately tracked for all employees.

Business Needs

One of the main drivers and known factors for employee retention is whether employees feel they have development opportunities. Therefore, as enterprise training and development continues to grow, it becomes increasingly important to streamline delivery, development, contract negotiations, and reporting. An enterprise LMS will enable TDS Corporate, TDS Telecom, and U.S. Cellular to share training programs across the enterprise, report on progress at an enterprise level, consolidate course offerings to gain more cost-effective contracts, and provide employees with a streamlined central portal for all training-related information, course registration, and resources. More specifically, it will provide

- Streamlined training coordination; we will be able to implement more efficient training administration processes across the TDS enterprise and within each business unit

- Tools that allow leaders, managers, and supervisors to coach their employees effectively for skill and career development and to interface with performance and goal-setting tools

- A self-service learning system that allows associates and leaders to manage their unique training and career development plans

- Reports that track the impact of training activities: that is, class interest, time spent in class, accomplishments, evaluations, and so forth

- Alignment of training and development to organizational competencies and goals

- Reduction in duplication of training efforts across the TDS enterprise, so purchasing, development, delivery, and measurement can be shared and streamlined

- A flexible learning management framework that can incorporate all types of training, that is, instructor-led, face-to-face, Web-based, computer-based, and so on

- A secure, centralized online repository for training and development resources and opportunities

- The capacity to handle increased requests for department-specific learning plans and to track progress toward these plans

- The capacity to handle increased requests to identify the skill set base needed for future projects and organizational goals and to complete skill gap analyses.

Current Issues and Impacts

The following tables summarize the drawbacks of our current systems and the benefits of a new LMS.

Table 10.1. Limited Tracking and Reporting Capability with Current System

Issue	Impact
Minimal reporting capability exists today for all types of training. We can report on course completions, cancellations, and no shows without enhancing the system. We can't quickly report on who still needs to complete a given course, what progress an individual has made toward a learning plan, or assessment results from a given course.	• Increased time and costs are required for Training Administration to manually determine who hasn't taken a specific course. • Increased time and costs are required for learners and/or managers to manually track progress toward a learning plan. OR a missed opportunity for coaching and higher employee performance because this progress isn't tracked. • Opportunities are missed to enhance skills and/or improve course materials because we're unable to report on skill development as a result of training. • This may lead to inefficient or unnecessary follow-up training time and costs.

Table 10.1. Limited Tracking and Reporting Capability with Current System, Cont'd

Issue	Impact
Reports are difficult to read and time consuming to reformat.	• Increased time and costs are required for Training Administration to manually reformat the information to present data in a way that is easy for frontline managers to understand and analyze. • An increase in data errors is possible when information must be manually rekeyed into a usable report format. • Inefficient or unnecessary follow-up is possible if results are misunderstood due to poor formatting.
E-learning programs do not integrate with our current LMS.	• For more robust reporting on our e-learning programs, Training Administration has had to build interfaces to capture data from Web-based training and deliver them in a format that the current LMS can understand. • IS [information system] time and costs are required to build data translation programs that continue to require manual effort on the part of Training Administration. • Additional time and effort is required for Training Administration to pull data from multiple sources because they are not integrated in the current LMS.
No tools exist in the current LMS for the creation of learning plans or skill gap analysis, for reviewing employee transcripts and skill assessment results, or for monitoring learning plan progress.	• Managers and employees do not have the resources and tools to coach and develop in the most efficient ways. • Additional time and costs are required to manually build training plans formatted for the intranet, and because these intranet resources are separate from the Training Registration system, learners don't always know they exist and the registration and tracking must be done manually.

Continued

**Table 10.1. Limited Tracking and Reporting
Capability with Current System, Cont'd**

Issue	Impact
	• Training Administration does not have the ability to batch register students in multiple modules within a training program. They must be manually entered for each module, which significantly increases administration time. (For example, the new employee orientation program at TDS Corporate has over 20 modules.) • Managers have to request reports from Training Administration, which creates a time delay and potentially missed coaching opportunities.
The current system is unable to create employee learning plans; to identify skills, knowledge and abilities, and progress toward completing those plans; or to identify skills vital to current initiatives.	• Data to support LCP (Leadership Continuity Planning) is compiled through anecdotal evidence or guesswork rather than solid data from training records. • The Finance Leadership Team–People Training Team (an enterprise-wide team) is struggling to identify, provide, and track courseware that is consistent and available for all finance employees in each business unit. A system is needed to facilitate this. • Information is needed to support talent management program. • Customer Support Center's Training Model requires the ability to track module completion and to measure progress on skill development.
We are unable to report on certifications and recertifications that are critical to the business. We do not currently have a system	• The Corporate CSC Training Model and the future vision of a CSC global help desk require the creation and tracking of certifications and recertifications for specific customer needs (that is, DSL, printers, and so forth) so that calls can be routed more efficiently.

Table 10.1. Limited Tracking and Reporting Capability with Current System, Cont'd

Issue	Impact
that tracks professional certifications (that is, CPA, CIA, and so forth)	• Company X recently instituted certification and training reporting requirements to maintain provider discounts at TDS Telecom. Our current LMS is unable to meet these requirements, so the process of data gathering has been entirely manual. • Some reports must track data manually as part of development analysis.
We are unable to produce training-related reports on the total TDS enterprise.	• The TDS family is unable to identify areas of opportunity and possible reduction of costs or resource use across the enterprise. • Training opportunities are inconsistent and often duplicated unnecessarily across the TDS enterprise. • TDS Telecom transcripts are not automatically updated when employees attend training at the business units.
TDS Corporate is unable to track e-learning course history in the current system.	• This is critical, as e-learning is becoming an important learning medium due to its cost effectiveness and flexibility. • A separate reporting system is required to track e-learning usage, and it is not integrated into student transcripts.
Data for registrations, completions, and evaluations are currently stored in several unrelated files.	• IS must maintain multiple homegrown databases. • Pulling data into one source is very time consuming and labor intensive. • It is difficult to make real-time decisions based on the data. • Confidence in data integrity is reduced.

**Table 10.2. Inefficient Organization of
Training Resources with Current System**

Issue	Impact
Employees from all TDS Telecom business units attend training provided by TDS Telecom and also courses provided by TDS Corporate. These courses are currently housed in separate registration systems.	• Employees spend additional time learning and accessing more than one registration system. • Not all Telecom employees realize they have access to the TDS Corporate courses, because they are used to going to Registrar. • This, in turn, may be generating additional costs to the organization as TDS Telecom employees look outside the company for development opportunities. The reverse is true for TDS Corporate employees, who may be missing out on TDS Telecom internal classes and classes held at U.S. Cellular in the Madison/Milwaukee area. They too are missing out on local, inexpensive internal options at TDS Corporate.
Training and development resources are not centralized.	• Employees spend unnecessary time searching for information and may never find it due to multiple systems. • At TDS Telecom, resources are currently housed in one of three ways: (1) through Registrar (instructor-led courses); (2) through StarNet (Web-based training courses); and (3) through Start/Programs network connection (computer-based training courses). Additional information may be found on product Web sites, paper-based manuals, or external Web sites. • At TDS Corporate, resources are currently housed in multiple locations, including Education Toolbox, varying locations on the intranet, and within specific departments.
Employees and managers do not have a way to manage	• At TDS Corporate, employees searching for a new course cannot see which classes they took in the

Table 10.2. Inefficient Organization of Training Resources with Current System, Cont'd

Issue	Impact
training and development plans effectively.	past, and managers do not have a system to effectively plan for their employees' future development. • Employees may inadvertently take duplicate classes because they do not have access to a current transcript with their entire history. • As an enterprise, we are moving toward a self-service philosophy with our information and systems, and our LMS does not support this vision.

Table 10.3. Missed Opportunities to Share Resources with Current System

Issue	Impact
There are missed opportunities and inefficient processes to leverage development, resources, delivery, and vendor contracts across TDS Telecom business units.	• The TDS enterprise has three versions of similar content areas, such as time management, change management, and basic leadership skills. • Time and costs are wasted duplicating efforts across the enterprise business units. • Separate vendor negotiations are conducted by the units for the same content or course.
There is no uniform access to courses across the enterprise.	• Time and costs are increased owing to duplicated efforts. • Opportunities to combine and align resources are missed. • TDS Telecom employees fail to take full advantage of courses offered at TDS Corporate. Similarly, they may fail to benefit from courses delivered at U.S. Cellular. In U.S. Cellular's case, TDS Telecom does not have access to its registration system and therefore doesn't even know what opportunities may exist.

Continued

Table 10.3. Missed Opportunities to
Share Resources with Current System, Cont'd

Issue	Impact
	• We are missing the opportunity to have employees from across the enterprise attend the same courses and learn the same messages and language so that all employees can work more effectively with each other.

Table 10.4. Hard-Dollar Benefits of New LMS

Who Benefits	Description of Benefit	Financial Benefit ($) or Nonfinancial Benefit	How Benefits Will Be Tracked and Measured
TDS Corporate and TDS Telecom	Purchasing LMS Vision LMS license under the current USC enterprise contract will save $32 per license. (Price per license stand alone, $60; price per license for USC contract,$28.)	$123,200 one-time savings. (3,850 licenses × $32 per license saved.)	N/A
TDS Corporate and TDS Telecom	Annual maintenance costs (22% of purchase cost) will be reduced under USC enterprise contract due to reduced purchase cost. ($231,000 stand-alone purchase cost = $50,820 maintenance versus $107,800 USC contract purchase cost = $23,716 maintenance.)	$27,104 annual savings. ($50,820 − $23,716.)	N/A

Note: This table has been modified for this case study; it does not contain the vendor's real name or pricing information.

Table 10.5. Soft-Dollar Benefits of New LMS

Benefit	Description of Benefit
Improved performance	Managers' ability to assess and develop employees' knowledge, skills, and abilities will increase, allowing managers to strengthen employees in their current roles and to assist them with future development. Better knowledge will help managers and the HR/Learning organization to better plan, develop, and implement training and performance solutions to close identified gaps. Managers can "push" necessary and or required learning activities to all employees throughout the reporting structure. Real-time tracking of all learning activity throughout a manager's organization will increase accountability for associate development at all levels.
Enhanced reporting capability	We will be able to track informal and formal learning activities in one centralized location, which will help us as an organization make better purchasing, development, and implementation decisions and identify more cost-effective modalities. We could have consistent evaluations using one evaluation tool. Having a consistent scale could help us to better evaluate our course effectiveness across the enterprise. Reports will be available to the manager (rather than having to be requested from HR/Learning), which will provide more timely and efficient data.
Updated system and support	We will have one of the best systems on the market, with the latest training support tools available. In addition, our system will be consistently upgraded and supported for the entire enterprise. The current systems at TDS Corporate and TDS Telecom (Mainframe and Registrar) are reaching the end of their support terms and will need to be significantly upgraded within the next two years regardless of the outcome of this business case.
Improved self-service	Employees and managers throughout the enterprise with be empowered to manage their own unique training and development

Continued

Table 10.5. Soft-Dollar Benefits of New LMS, Cont'd

Benefit	Description of Benefit
	plans while receiving proactive, secure goal-attainment feedback on a need-to-know basis. This will, in turn, reduce each business unit's administrative burden of manual data retrieval and information sharing. Information will be in the hands of the people who need the data in real time; they will not have to request reports from Training Administration.
Time savings for employees	Instead of having to hunt across two or three registration systems, multiple intranet Web sites, and various network-based locations for a course or training resource, employees will be able to locate all training- and development-related information from a single source. This not only will save employee time but will ensure that employees have access to all the training and development available at the TDS enterprise. We will also realize travel time and cost savings if employees are able to find local or internal courses that meet their needs and do not have to look outside the organization for their training needs.
Increased confidence in data integrity	The accuracy of user registration can be ensured through the provision of a central course catalogue that can be viewed by individual users, their supervisors, and department managers. There will be more confidence in the data if we have the registration and evaluation data all located in the same system, and this will produce more accurate reporting.
TDS enterprise vendor leverage	The three training organizations use multiple outside vendors to provide training courses. With an enterprise LMS, we can negotiate content with one vendor and take advantage of volume discounts. For example, currently TDS Corporate and TDS Telecom contract with Vendor X for CBT courses; USC has a similar contract with Vendor Y. There will be potential cost savings when we have one contract with one vendor for all three companies.

Table 10.5. Soft-Dollar Benefits of New LMS, Cont'd

Benefit	Description of Benefit
Time savings for Training Administration	An improved LMS will reduce each business unit's administrative burden of manual data retrieval and information sharing by providing a secure, centralized online repository of organizational training and development data. Information will be in the hands of people who need the data in real time; they will not have to request reports from Training Administration.
Possible lower cost per training class seat and higher employee development	With classes available to the enterprise and not just individual organizations, there is a better chance of filling each class. For example, TDS Corporate recently sponsored a vendor class with a total on-site cost of $7,000. The class had only 8 participants, at a cost of $950 per person. If we could have filled the class, with 15 participants, the per person price would have been $500. That is, we could have trained an additional 7 participants for the same total cost.

Note: This table has been modified for this case study; it does not contain vendors' real names or pricing information.

Linking the LMS Business Case to the Strategic Goals of Training, Education, and Employee Development

- Alignment to the needs of the business.
- Business results drive all training efforts.
- Learning systems not learning events.
- Manager involvement is critical to success.
- Enterprise-wide synergies.

Alignment to the Needs of the Business

Learning Plans. The beauty of the LMS is that this functionality will allow efficient creation of an enterprise plan and also put this tool in the hands of managers and employees. For example:

- As part of the Finance Leadership Team, we will be developing an enterprise-wide training plan for new staff accounts.

- In addition, our VP Finance will be able to create learning plan components specific to the staff accounts at Telecom.

- Further, a Finance Manager will be able to create learning plan components specific to his or her team.

- And finally, an individual Staff Accountant will be able to create learning plan components specific to his or her needs.

Competency Alignment. This additional future functionality (included in the initial cost of the LMS but not planned for the initial rollout) will allow us to align training programs more concretely to our TDS company competencies. In addition, this assessment capability may allow us to begin to assess our level of competency across teams, departments, and even the company as a whole.

Business Results Drive All Training Efforts

Reporting Capability. Reporting in the old days was butts in seats. Now we've set a higher standard for ourselves—programs have to have an impact on performance and business results. Our current tools make this type of reporting difficult. We've invested hours and hours to cull through the data we can gather, and still have fallen short. The LMS will kick reporting up a notch and allow us to more efficiently pull out and format the data we need to analyze to judge the effectiveness of our investments.

Higher Levels of Evaluation. Coupled with this will be the ability to create evaluation and assessment tools within one system. Today this is done manually in a number of different systems. It's costly, inefficient, and inconsistent. The LMS will allow us to streamline a number of evaluation processes we use currently and provide tools for getting to evaluation levels 3 and 4.

Learning Systems Not Learning Events

One Portal for All Learning and Development. Our Management Development Program is the perfect example here. Today you go to the current

LMS to sign up for the instructor-led workshop piece of the course; Outlook to accept meeting invites to the follow-up conference calls; and the intranet page to take the Web-based training that is part of the program. We give participants a map to their training resources just to help them stay organized. Having all this in one place will save time and ensure that everyone has access and knowledge of all the resources needed to build a particular skill. It will also enable blended learning throughout the organization of the tools and resources for a particular program.

Manager Involvement Is Critical to Success

Access to Data. The LMS will give managers access to more data; they will, at a glance, be able to see learning progress for all employees reporting to them. Today they have to type in each employee's ID and look at each one individually.

Improved Reporting. Reporting will also be improved and in managers' hands. They'll be able to track progress at a team level and run some general reports in real time. Today a request has to be made to the training department for such information.

Learning Plans. Can be created by the manager for his or her team.

Enterprise-Wide Synergies

Sharing Courses. We'll be able to build a TDS Family of Companies domain within the LMS that will allow us to share resources across the enterprise (due to firewall issues, this is not possible today). This will save each company time, effort, and money and eliminate some duplication of courses.

LMS Business Case E-Mails to Stakeholders

To round out this business case example, here are two of samples of a key e-mail message that Renee Stoll sent to major stakeholders during the process of preselling the business case (see her introduction to the case at the beginning of this chapter). These e-mails cover nearly the same points, but note how each one is customized to its reader (staff names have been changed to pseudonyms).

E-mail to Neil, VP Metrocom Operations

Hi Neil—I'm hoping I can snag a few minutes of your time to discuss the LMS Business Case Ben and I will be presenting to the STC on February 10th. I see some specific benefits to your group and am not sure these come out clearly enough in the generic business case form. If this time works for you, I would really appreciate it. If there is a better time, or you feel this meeting is unnecessary, just let me know.

Benefits to Metrocom Business Operations:

- **Location for Training Resources:** The enhanced capability of this LMS provides a Learning Portal that can also house training materials and resources. Your teams will be able to house all their On the Job training materials and resources in the LMS, which will provide employees a "one-stop shop" for all learning. This will improve efficiencies and ensure that none of the necessary training falls through the cracks.

- **Learning Plan Ability for Contact Center Employees:** While we already have learning plans for many of the contact center positions, they are cumbersome and manual. We also currently have no way to track an individual's progress toward his or her plan. LMS Vision will house these plans within the learning portal and will facilitate better tracking, better budget planning, and a better sense of who has taken what in your organization.

- **Assessment Results Tracking:** The LMS will allow us to automate assessment tools that measure an employee's learning of the material presented in a course. These assessment results can be accessed by the employee and the employee's supervisor at any time. Eventually, this could provide some measurement and tracking of competency levels of certain employee groups.

I look forward to hearing your thoughts and questions on this business case. Thanks in advance for your consideration!

Renee

E-mail to Dan, VP Information Systems

Hi Dan—I'm hoping I can snag a few minutes of your time to discuss the LMS Business Case Ben and I will be presenting to the STC on February 10th. I see some specific benefits to your group and am not sure these come out clearly enough in the generic business case form. If this time works for you, I would really appreciate it. If there is a better time, or you feel this meeting is unnecessary, just let me know.

Benefits to IS:

- **Potential Reduction in Support Hours for HRA:** The enterprise LMS will be hosted by USC—after the initial rollout, this should reduce Telecom IS support hours for HRA—Training; implementation support may also be minimized as USC and Corporate will take on the majority of this work.

- **Learning Plan Ability for IS Employees:** The LMS provides the ability to create learning plans by workgroup, manager, salary grade—whatever fits. We will be able to show employees which classes they need to take and when, and track their progress. This will make Sue's job much easier—better tracking, better budget planning, better sense of who has taken what in your organization.

- **Increased Efficiency:** the Enterprise LMS is a learning portal where employees can come to find ALL of their training resources. In this system, they will be able to register for ALL classes (classroom, e-learning, courses offered through Corporate or USC), review transcripts, find other training resources (prework, job aids, FAQs), review learning plans for their job or department, and participate in evaluations on training they've completed. No more searching around StarNet or calling the help desk to figure out where a program or resource resides.

- **Enterprise Synergy:** The enterprise system will give us the ability to share courses across the TDS companies, which will give our managers access to more leadership courses and our employees access to more interpersonal skills courses. We may also be able to leverage some technical external training across the enterprise: for example, training on IS programming languages and telephony topics that are consistent across all companies.

I look forward to hearing your thoughts and questions on this business case. Thanks in advance for your consideration!

Renee ◄

Key Points

- All business cases have four common goals they must achieve:
    1. Articulate the objectives of the project in clear concise language.
    2. Identify drivers, needs, and impact of the project.
    3. Demonstrate the value of the project to the business.
    4. Analyze the potential risks of the project.
    5. List outstanding questions.

- The formal business case is only a small part of the equation. The real success of a business case comes from our ability to speak the language of the business.

- If we can demonstrate value to the business and link our projects to major organizational initiatives we will get the support we need.

⑪

Writing Reports

❶N THIS THIRD SECTION I have explored the principles of good written business communications and dissected the intricacies of writing business cases. I conclude this overview of employing business acumen through the written word by examining good report writing techniques.

Business reports come in many shapes and sizes. You'll probably work on many different types as your training career progresses. Look at the list that follows, and think about the reports you have created in the past. How were they similar to each other? How did they differ? Business reports go by many names and differ in subtle ways. Here are a few types:

- Progress report
- Feasibility report
- Recommendation report
- Proposal
- Annual report

- Quarterly report

- Periodic evaluation

- Informal report

- Field report

To a certain extent the specific situation surrounding any given report will dictate its form and content. For that reason I'll take a general approach, zooming in on the stages you progress through as your report comes together. I'll concentrate on strategies you can use to figure out exactly what kind of structure and substance you need to develop.

Accordingly, this chapter is divided into two sections that correspond to the two phases of creating a report.

The first, and most often neglected, is the planning phase. This includes the time you set aside for strategizing and for mapping out your report. Good planning can save you considerable time and trouble when it becomes time to write.

The second phase involves the actual assembly of your document. I'll present a breakdown of the various sections that make up a formal report. Then I'll share some advice for effective drafting and revising that will help you streamline your writing process

Let's get started.

Planning the Report

When Sarah was assigned to prepare a feasibility study about a new training program, she tried to plan it as best she could in the little time she had. An important part of her research was a survey she distributed to five colleagues. Sarah put off e-mailing the survey until the last minute, fully expecting to receive everyone's reply the next day.

When she discovered that two of her five participants were on vacation that week, she became worried. She requested an extension, but management wasn't willing to wait. They advised her, "Give us what you have and extrapolate from there." It seemed like a reasonable request, given the circumstances.

Sarah conscientiously described her results as incomplete. Still, basing her decision on its success in other firms, she recommended that the company go forward with the plan.

> Decisions were made and the plan went forward. Several hundred thousand dollars later, Sarah's organization had a brand-new training program with no buy-in from the expected participants. No one attended, and the project was deemed a failure.

The planning phase of report writing is often neglected or ignored. This is regrettable, because the benefits of good planning are many. Devoting time at the beginning of the process to thinking about the purpose and reach of your report will help you better meet your readers' expectations. It will also help you research and write more efficiently.

For these reasons the first part of this chapter is devoted to teaching you the art of planning. This important stage consists of two main tasks:

- Identify and confirm expectations.
- Gather information.

After examining these tasks in more detail, I will discuss strategies you can use as you actually write the report.

Identify and Confirm Expectations

Writing a good report necessitates having a clear understanding of what your readers expect and require. Your report will be of little use if it does not meet their needs. It is vital that you identify and confirm their expectations in the early stages of your planning.

Identifying your readers' expectations involves three main steps:

1. Identify the purpose of your report.

    Why will people read your report?

    How will they use the information in their jobs?

2. Identify your audience.

    What is your readers' knowledge level?

    What is their attitude toward your subject?

3. Identify the formal requirements.

    What do your readers expect your report to look like?

There are essentially two ways to go about identifying expectations:

- On your own
- With the help of the person who assigned the report

Let's consider two examples that illustrate these methods.

> David, on the one hand, has been with his department for many years. He is responsible for putting together the annual student statistics report every December. From years of experience David is very familiar with his readers' expectations; in fact he could probably write the report in his sleep. He should have no trouble identifying his readers' expectations on his own.
>
> James, on the other hand, is a new employee who has been with the e-learning department for only a few months. His senior tech manager has asked him to write a report about the feasibility of adding a new course to the training site. She mentioned that members of upper management will read the report. It may even reach the desks of the board.
>
> Because James is not yet familiar with what his manager (or anyone else in his company for that matter) would consider a good report, it is important that he *identifies* and *confirms* her expectations and needs (see Exhibit 11.1).

Exhibit 11.1. Where to Begin

If you are assigned a report and you have no idea where to begin, don't panic. Start by asking simple questions that will help you pinpoint your boss's expectations:

- Who will read it?
- Why will they read it?
- Are there any examples of similar reports that I can look at?
- Approximately how long should the report be?
- What should it look like? Is a special format required?
- Are there any recommended sources?

James can go about this in several ways. Ideally, he would request a sit-down meeting where he and his manager work through the initial stages of the planning process. Together, they could identify the report's purpose, audience, and formal requirements.

Of course in the real world such a meeting is not always possible. The manager might be busy or might favor a hands-off approach. James might have to answer the questions about purpose, audience, and formal requirements on his own. If that is the case, after James has identified his readers' expectations, he should send the manager a quick e-mail to confirm that they are correct.

Now, let's look at the three steps in greater detail.

Identify your purpose

The first step in determining your readers' expectations is to pin down the purpose of your report. Before you begin writing anything you should always ask yourself *why* you are writing. This is the planning step that will most shape the rest of your project.

When you ask yourself why you are writing the report, go beyond the obvious; "because I am required to do so" is not a very useful response. As you learned in Chapter Nine, focusing on your reader makes you a more effective writer. So ask reader-oriented questions like these:

- What information do my readers need?
- In what way(s) will my readers use that information?
- Must I convince my readers of something? If so, what?

Broadly speaking, all reports share one purpose: to inform. Some reports will require only that you inform your reader about your topic. This type of report is akin to an encyclopedia article in that it is entirely factual; you gather information, and then you present it in a straightforward manner.

Other reports will require that you go beyond encyclopedia mode. You may have to evaluate or analyze information. You may even be asked to give an opinion or a recommendation. Although this type of report requires critical thinking, it must be grounded in factual information.

After you have identified the purpose of your report, articulate it in a single sentence or a short statement (Exhibit 11.2). Use this sentence at some point within the actual report. You can even post your statement near your computer to help you stay focused as you write.

Exhibit 11.2. Defining Your Purpose

Begin by defining your purpose broadly, like this:

- The purpose of my report is to inform my reader.
- The purpose of my report is to evaluate something.
- The purpose of my report is to recommend something.

Next, define your purpose more specifically, like this:

- The purpose of my rcport is to inform my reader.

    The purpose of my report is to describe a recent project.

    The purpose of my report is to inform my reader about an ongoing project.

- The purpose of my report is to evaluate something.

    The purpose of my report is to evaluate a procedure.

    The purpose of my report is to evaluate options for a new program.

- The purpose of my report is to recommend something.

    The purpose of my report is to recommend a new procedure.

    The purpose of my report is to propose a future project.

Identify your audience

When you think about who will read your report, it is useful to think of yourself as an advertiser trying to reach a specific market. The way you pitch your product depends on who your potential "buyers" are.

As you write a business report you must appeal to your target demographic— your readers (also known as your audience). Otherwise you aren't going to have any buyers.

There are two main reader traits you need to bear in mind as you identify your audience:

- Knowledge level (what they know and what they don't know)
- Attitude toward your topic

Knowledge level The knowledge level of your readers is a very important consideration during planning. It will direct the amount and type of information you provide.

Your readers' prior knowledge will also help you decide what kind of language to use and what kind of background information to include. Your job will be easiest when your readers have a knowledge base that is similar to your own. It will be more difficult when your readers have a different background.

Let's look at an example that illustrates this point.

> Susan is an instructional design PhD who is writing a report. Her readers are also ID people. As a result, Susan can use the jargon of her field with confidence; she knows her readers will understand. She does not need to provide a lot of background information because her readers are already familiar with the topic.
>
> However, if Susan's audience were made up of people who are *not* in the ID field, her job would be different. Because her readers would not be trained in her field, Susan would need to present technical terms in a way that makes sense to outsiders. She would also need to include ample background information to bring her readers up to speed on the topic at hand.

Whenever your readers' knowledge level differs significantly from your own, your challenge will be to put yourself in their shoes. Try to examine the topic from their perspective. Make sure that you define terms that your readers may not know. Assume the role of an educator instead of a technical colleague (see Table 11.1).

Table 11.1. Adjusting Content to the Audience

Type of Content	For Expert Readers	For Lay Readers
Background	Unnecessary	Extensive
Language	Highly technical	Not technical
Graphics	Complex	Simple

CD-ROM RESOURCE

Open the "Report Writing Exercises" file on your CD, and practice this skill by completing "Exercise 1: Adjusting Content to Suit Readers' Knowledge." (The "Report Writing Exercise Answers" file lists the answers.)

Attitude In a perfect world, we would know each of our reader's exact preferences and opinions. Ideally, we would tailor a copy of the report for each individual reader based on this knowledge.

Of course it is not a perfect world and the circumstances under which we write reports are rarely ideal. Sometimes you will know your readers personally, and other times you won't.

In any case you should be able to broadly classify your readers' attitude toward your topic. There are four basic attitudes that affect the way you craft your report (also see Table 11.2):

- *Hostile.* The reader is opposed to your view.
- *Skeptical.* The reader doubts your view.
- *Neutral.* The reader doesn't have a strong opinion about your view.
- *Enthusiastic.* The reader supports your view.

Table 11.2. Typical Attitudes Toward Key Topics

Attitude	Example Topic
Hostile	Budget increase; negative evaluation
Skeptical	Restructuring proposal
Neutral	Conference planning
Enthusiastic	Budget decrease; positive evaluation

Let's examine these types of readers in more detail.

Hostile readers Hostile readers include those who are opposed to your view or otherwise antagonistic to your topic. You will have to work extra hard to convince these readers of what you are trying to say. Above all, strive to give your topic a balanced and thorough treatment. Anticipate the objections and questions of your hostile readers. Respond to their concerns in a way that is respectful and diplomatic. Also, keep in mind that you might have to devote more space to justifying your point of view to these readers. Additional background information might be necessary to develop your argument. As you explain your perspective, maintain a professional tone to avoid sounding condescending.

Skeptical readers These readers doubt your view or have serious reservations about your topic. It is your job to rid them of doubts and concerns. For your purposes, skeptical and hostile readers are very similar. Both require you to predict their objections and respond to these objections in the body of the report. Both require a full justification of your point of view. Tread carefully around controversial points.

Neutral readers Neutral readers are those who have no firm opinion about what you have to say. Your primary task is to maintain their interest throughout your report. For these readers a lengthy introduction and extensive background information are unnecessary. Jump into your discussion after a snappy opening. Woo them with interesting graphics and convincing statistics. A great way to engage neutral readers is to focus on how your topic affects them. Throughout your report, highlight the reasons why they should care about the issue. Show them ways in which the subject affects their work.

Enthusiastic readers Enthusiastic readers are every writer's dream. The problem is that people are rarely excited to read a business report. Even readers whose views align with your own would probably prefer not to have to read your report. For this reason it is useful to approach your enthusiastic readers as neutral. Reach out to them in the same ways. Keep them engaged, and demonstrate the topic's relevance to their own jobs whenever you can.

Let's take a look at an example that illustrates the connection between your content and your readers' attitude.

> Lee is writing a report recommending a budget decrease to management. In the introduction he explains that in the past it has taken a three-person team to keep the employee manual current. Lee recommends moving the manual to a Web server and updating it only in that online form.
>
> To build enthusiasm for his idea, Lee focuses on the benefits of his recommendation. His emphasis is therefore on the conclusion section of his report. He stresses that there will be no further need for expensive printing and production costs. The savings will extend for many years to come.

CD-ROM RESOURCE

Open the "Report Writing Exercises" file on your CD, and practice this skill by completing "Exercise 2: Identifying Your Audience." (The "Report Writing Exercise Answers" file presents sample answers.)

Identify the formal requirements

Formal requirements—governing the components of your report and the way it should look—will vary across projects and organizations. Your report may have no formal requirements. In that case its structure, design, and length are entirely up to you.

Many organizations, however, have established report formats for employees to use. For example, a large company might have created a template for its annual sales report. In that case you should model your report on that template. Try also to get a copy of last year's report, if possible.

Even if your office does not have a strict format for you to follow, your boss might want your report to contain certain features. She may, for instance, require that you use bar graphs to illustrate data. She may think that certain information should be included in the appendix. Make sure that you ask about such particulars while you are still in the planning stage.

Above all other design considerations, try to pin down how long your report should be. The length of your report will always shape your treatment of a topic. In a five-page project report you do not have space to describe your topic in much depth. A twenty-page project report, however, gives you enough space to go into much greater detail.

After you have completed these three steps, you should have a firm grasp on your readers' expectations.

Gather Information

Now you are ready to begin gathering the information you need to write the report. This is actually a three-step process, during which you

1. Identify information gaps.
2. Identify information sources.
3. Gather information.

Many people are so eager to get their project underway that they launch into their research without giving a thought to what types of information they need or what sources they should consult. Although it is natural to panic when a deadline is looming, you will find that your research will be far more productive if you can stand back for a moment, stay cool, and do a little planning.

Identify information gaps

The best way to get started is by identifying information gaps; these are the portions of your report that require research (see Exhibit 11.3). To fill these gaps you will need information that you have to request, look up, or otherwise reference.

Exhibit 11.3. Sample Information Gaps

- Employees' opinion of company restructuring
- Minutes of a recent meeting
- The potential cost of adding a new training course
- Sales statistics of competitors

If you are working on a large project, you should begin by making a *prioritized* list of your information gaps. This technique will help you allocate your research time wisely. Also, it will ensure that you don't forget any of the gaps when you begin gathering information.

CD-ROM RESOURCE

Open the "Report Writing Exercises" file on your CD, and practice this skill by completing "Exercise 3: Identifying Information Gaps." (The "Report Writing Exercise Answers" file presents sample answers.)

Identify your sources

Identifying your sources might be as simple as saying, "I already have all the information I need." Writing a report about a small-scale project that you directed, for instance, will not necessarily require any outside sources of information. You will be your own best resource.

But most of the time you will have to look to outside sources for information. Whenever research is required you should make a list of all the sources that you might need to consult to fill in your information gaps. Beside each entry on your information gap list, write the place (or places) where you can look for the information you need.

Potential sources for your report might include the following:

- Interviews or informal chats with

    Colleagues

    Customers

- Surveys distributed to

    Colleagues

    Clients or customers

- Past reports (written by you or someone else)

- Internal data, such as your company's sales figures or meeting minutes

- External data, such as a competitor's sales figures

- The Internet

- Print sources (books, trade journals, magazines, or newspapers)

Keep in mind that there might be more than one potential source for each piece of information you seek (also see Table 11.3).

Table 11.3. Example of Prioritized List of Potential Sources

Information Gap	Potential Source(s)
Sales projections for next year	Interviews with colleagues; sales figures from past years
Cost of creating a continuing education program for existing employees	Internet; trade magazines
Results data: have we fulfilled the goals we set three years ago?	Past reports; survey of colleagues

Gather information

Now that you are equipped with a list of the information you need and the places where you should look for it, you are ready to gather that information. Again, make sure that you prioritize your list. If, for instance, you need to distribute an internal survey, keep in mind that it will take time to create, distribute, and analyze.

Remember that you need not scrutinize every source you consult. In some cases, especially when you are dealing with print media (like books or magazines), you should skim the material initially to determine whether it will be useful. An effective skim includes reading the title, the subheadings, the first few paragraphs, and the last few paragraphs. From that, you should be able to determine whether a close read is required.

It is a good idea to take notes as you research. Your memory is probably not as good as you imagine. Notes will come in handy when it becomes time to assemble your report.

The way, or ways, that you choose to take notes depends largely on personal preference. Some people prefer to take highly detailed notes, and others want to remember only the main thrust of a source. If you haven't yet developed a system that works for you, Table 11.4 offers some ideas.

If you are collecting a lot of information, you may find it helpful to make a note of how you intend to use each source. This note should indicate which section of the report the information will appear in. You might label an article "background information for introduction" or highlight a statistic as "support for recommendation," for example.

Table 11.4. Note-Taking Methods

Source	High-Detail Note Taking	Low-Detail Note Taking
Web site	Print out relevant portions of the Web site; highlight and make marginal notes on the printouts as needed.	Record the Web site address; write a sentence that summarizes the type of information the site contains.
Trade magazine article	Make a photocopy of the article; highlight relevant sections make any necessary notes in the margin.	Write a few sentences that summarize the main thrust of the article.

To ensure that you complete all the steps in the planning stage, you might want to use the checklist in Exhibit 11.4.

Exhibit 11.4. Report Planning Checklist

☐ Have I identified the purpose of my report?

☐ Do I know who will be reading it?

☐ Do I know how long the report should be?

☐ Am I familiar with the required format?

☐ Do I know what information gaps need to be filled?

☐ Have I identified the best sources to fill these gaps?

☐ Did I record the information that I will need to write the report?

Assembling the Report

After you finish planning you will be ready to progress to the assembly stage, which is when you actually write the report's content.

First, I'll examine a method you can use to organize your document. It's a modular system, so please tailor it to suit your needs. Then, I'll present some practical tips you can use as you draft and revise your report.

Organizing Your Report

I'll start by discussing the sections you might find in a typical report. The core sections—the introduction, discussion, and conclusion—are features of most reports, informal or formal.

The other sections are "bells and whistles" that you can include or omit according to your own needs and judgment. You might not, for instance, need to include a table of contents with a three-page report. An executive summary might not be necessary if no executives will read your report.

Here are the basic components of a formal report:

- Title page
- Abstract
- Table of contents (for longer reports only)

- Executive summary
- Introduction (which may include background information)
- Discussion
- Conclusion
- Graphics
- Extras: glossary, index, appendix, references

Now let's examine each section in more detail.

CD-ROM RESOURCE

Open the "Report Template" file on your CD for a section-by-section guide that might prove helpful as you write your next report. Also see the "Quarterly Report Example," supplied by Renee Stoll, manager of Training, Education, and Employee Development at TDS Telecom.

Title page

The title page, as you know, includes basic information about your report. You have two tasks to accomplish on the title page (also see Exhibit 11.5):

- Write an effective title.
- Make sure the page looks both attractive and functional.

Exhibit 11.5. Title Page Checklist

☐ The report title

☐ Your company's name

☐ Your company's logo (optional)

☐ The date of submission

☐ Your name

An effective title will succinctly and precisely describe the contents of your report. If you have trouble composing titles, try using the two-part technique of writing the subject and then the purpose. For example:

Subject   Purpose

Improving student enrollment   Three recommendations

In other words, simply describe your subject, insert a colon, and describe your purpose. (Table 11.5 illustrates the difference between vague titles and titles that precisely describe a report's content.)

Table 11.5. Choosing a Descriptive Title

Vague Title	Improved Title
Project Proposal	Updating Departmental Learning Plans: A Project Proposal
Employee Survey Results	Why Are Classroom Evaluations Low? An Analysis of the Annual Survey of Learners
Program Evaluation	Repeat Customer Incentives: A Program Evaluation

Finally, make the title page pleasing to the eye. First impressions are important, and this page will be the first thing your reader sees. Make sure it is balanced and uncluttered.

Abstract

The abstract is a brief summary of the information contained in your report. It should be about one paragraph long (that is, no more than four or five sentences). Though you won't have space, at this length, to go into a high level of detail, be as specific as possible.

Your abstract should always include your statement of purpose and a brief summary of your conclusions. You may find it useful to summarize each of the core sections—the introduction, discussion, and conclusion.

Ultimately, the abstract will help your readers decide whether they really need to read your report. Make sure that yours gives your readers the right information so they can make an informed decision.

Table of contents

The table of contents (TOC) is a guide that helps your readers make their way through your document. Typically, TOCs are necessary only in longer documents. If you decide to use one, choose an appropriate level of detail. Subheadings can help readers easily find the information they need in a long report, but such headings might seem superfluous in one that is short.

Executive summary

The executive summary is essentially a fuller version of the abstract. It is designed for upper management or other readers who might not have time to read the report in its entirety.

The length of the executive summary will depend in part on the length of the report. One page is a good standard length. This can be adjusted for particularly short or long reports.

An easy way to go about creating an executive summary is to write a summary paragraph for each major section of your report. In other words, one paragraph will correspond to the introduction, another to the discussion, and another to the conclusion. If these sections are particularly long they might require more than one paragraph.

Introduction

The introduction is the first of the three sections that form the core of a business report. It should give an overview of the contents and ease your readers into the topic. It will also summarize your major findings or conclusions.

Your main goal in the introduction is to identify the report's subject and purpose. You should also include any background information that your reader might need. If extensive background information seems necessary, you might want to create a separate "background" section and place it immediately after the introduction.

Discussion

The discussion section is the heart of your report. It is useful to think of the discussion as divided into two sections: one that describes your methods and another that describes your results.

Methods Scientists include a methods section in their reports so that other scientists can duplicate their experiments. This principle should also guide the composition of your methods section. Essentially, the methods section should describe the trajectory of your research. Include any sources that you consulted and explain where they can be found so readers can duplicate your research if they wish. Tell your readers how you decided that certain sources or methods were valid (see Table 11.6).

Table 11.6. Information to Include in the Methods Description

Research Method	Corroborating Information to Include in the Methods Section
Survey or interview	How you decided which questions to include; how many copies were distributed and how many were returned; when they were distributed.
Print sources or Web sites	How you chose each source; where it can be found.
Evaluation	What variables were factored into your analysis; how those variables were quantified.

Results The results section should provide an objective report of the information you gathered. It describes the data that you examined to arrive at the conclusions that you will explain in the final section of the report (see the next paragraph). For instance, if you distributed a survey, you would write a succinct description of the responses you received.

Conclusion

The conclusion should bring your report to a graceful and logical close.

This section is the most subjective portion of your report because it contains your recommendations or opinions. It is also a place where you can tie up any loose ends.

The conclusion is also the logical place to talk about next steps. Is further research needed? What course of action should the company take? How should the reader go forward? Make sure that you leave your reader with a sense of what comes next.

Graphics

Whenever possible, use graphics to punch up your text. A great graphic can simplify a difficult concept, clear up a confusing point, or emphasize vital data. It can also break up long blocks of text and summarize expansive points.

You'll find that graphics will make your writing more interesting to almost all readers. Graphics attract the eye and keep people focused. They add impact to any topic, however mundane.

Graphics are especially useful when you are working with a lot of numbers. An illustrated statistical analysis is far easier to understand than one that is pure text. A table, for instance, can effectively consolidate data, as the example shown in Table 11.7 does. Although this table provides an effective visual summary, consider how the bar chart in Figure 11.1 emphasizes the trends of the same data.

Table 11.7. Example of a Numerical Table in a Report

Student Enrollments	
Month	**Sign-Ups**
January	46
February	92
March	116
April	145
May	110
June	75

Figure 11.1. Example of a Graphic Chart in a Report

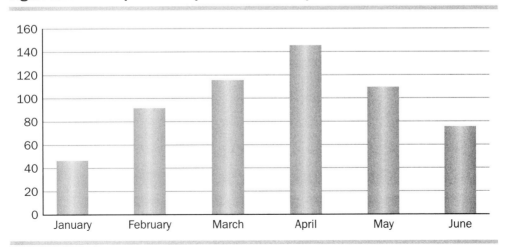

Keep in mind that graphics must be referred to and discussed in the text of your report. You have to introduce graphics and give them a context so they will make sense to the reader. Try to place each graphic close to the point in the text where you discuss it so readers can easily look back and forth between the text and the graphic and understand the connections.

Of course graphics do not always involve numbers. Microsoft Word and most other word-processing programs provide drawing tools that allow you to create with features like the ones displayed in Figure 11.2.

Figure 11.2. Some Graphics Created with Software Drawing Tools

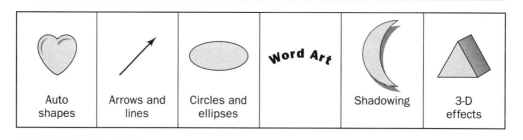

| Auto shapes | Arrows and lines | Circles and ellipses | | Shadowing | 3-D effects |

If you don't have much experience with graphic design, delegate illustrations to others whenever possible. Many organizations have graphic designers who can work from your sketches, scrawls, and descriptions.

Extras

The extras are optional sections that might appear at the end of your report; they include the glossary, index, appendix, and references. These sections can be added to your report as needed.

- A glossary is an excellent feature to include if your report contains unfamiliar or technical terms.
- An index helps readers find information they need in a long report.
- A list of your sources, or references, helps readers who want further information.
- An appendix is a great way to include material that does not fit in the body of your report. Readers can look at it only if they choose to.

CD-ROM RESOURCE

Open the "Report Writing Exercises" file on your CD, and check what you know about report organization by completing "Exercise 4: Organization Quiz." (The "Report Writing Exercise Answers" file lists some of the answers.)

Developing the Report Content

Now that you are familiar with the standard layout of a business report, I'll offer some tips that will help you as you develop the content of your report. Whenever time allows, you should use a two-step writing process: drafting and revising.

Drafting tips

Although everyone drafts differently, I recommend that you *write the first draft as quickly as possible.* That way, you get your ideas on paper without worrying about how they sound. The revision stage will provide an opportunity to fine-tune and to make sure that everything sounds all right.

Because your goal is to work quickly, *do not worry about writing the sections linearly.* In other words, write the report sections in whatever order you like. You do not have to write the introduction first. In fact many writers prefer to write it *last.*

Remember that momentum is everything when you write a draft. For that reason, you should always *begin with the section that seems easiest to write.* If you find that a certain section or idea is giving you trouble, *skip it.* You'll find it will be easier if you come back to it later.

Finally, do yourself a favor and *allow time for your draft to sit before you revise it.* A little distance will go a long way. You'll be able to spot mistakes much more easily if you can pull yourself away from the report for a short time (also see Exhibit 11.6).

Exhibit 11.6. Drafting Tips

· Write as quickly as possible.

· Don't worry about writing the sections in order.

· Begin by writing the section that seems easiest.

· Skip any section that is giving you trouble; come back to it later.

· Wait a day or so before you begin making revisions.

Revision tips

It is vital that you leave yourself enough time to check over and refine your draft. If you wrote the draft quickly, you will probably want to rewrite large portions of your text. The ideas will probably remain the same; you will simply make them clearer and stronger.

Even if you took your time with the draft, the very least you need to do is to read through your report for spelling and grammatical errors. Even though word-processing software will help with this, it can't catch all your errors. If you have a colleague who is willing to help, having another person proofread your report is even better.

If you are lucky enough to have another pair of eyes, ask your proofreader to give you general feedback on the content. You might, for instance, request that he or she mark passages that seem unclear.

If you are not pressed for time, you might have time to make a more substantial revision. Such a revision might include reorganization or the fleshing out of underdeveloped points. You can also check that your paragraphs are structured appropriately (refer to Chapter Nine for more information on this topic).

Another great way to evaluate your content is to do a paragraph check. A paragraph check involves writing a word or phrase beside each paragraph. This word or phrase should describe the contents of the paragraph. If you cannot effectively summarize a paragraph in this way, you should revise it.

What Comes Next

You now have all the tools you need to put together an excellent report. If you want to make sure that you have fully absorbed the tips and strategies discussed in this chapter, try the exercises on the CD that accompanies this book. Also remember that you can use the report template that is featured on the CD. Keep in mind that it is just a model. Feel free to modify it to suit your needs.

Finally, keep in mind that starting the report is always the hardest part. Keep a cool head and don't skimp on the planning, and you'll be well on your way.

Key Points

- There are two phases to creating a business report: planning and assembly.
- Devoting time to planning at the beginning will help you better meet your readers' expectations. It will also help you research and write more efficiently.

- The planning phase consists of two main tasks; identify and confirm expectations and gather information.

- Writing a good report necessitates having a clear understanding of what your readers expect and require. It is vital that you identify and confirm their expectations in the early stages of your planning. Identifying your readers' expectations involves three main steps:

  1. Identify the purpose.

  2. Identify the audience.

  3. Identify the formal requirements.

- The knowledge level of your readers is a very important consideration during planning. It will direct the amount and type of information you provide.

- There are four basic attitudes that affect the way you craft your report:

  1. *Hostile.* The reader is opposed to your view.

  2. *Skeptical.* The reader doubts your view.

  3. *Neutral.* The reader doesn't have a strong opinion about your view.

  4. *Enthusiastic.* The reader supports your view.

- Information gathering for a business report is a three-step process:

  1. Identify information gaps.

  2. Identify information sources.

  3. Gather information.

- If you are working on a large project you should begin by making a prioritized list of your information gaps. This technique will help you allocate your research time wisely.

- The basic components of a formal report are the following:

  Title page

  Abstract

  Table of contents (for longer reports only)

  Executive summary

  Introduction

Background (which may include background information)

Discussion

Conclusion

Graphics

Extras: glossary, index, appendix, references

12

Making Effective Presentations

YOU'VE SPENT the first eleven chapters of this book learning the nuts and bolts of training—and developing the business skills it takes to excel in this profession. You could read no further and you would be well armed for your task. But you know very well that there are others, competitors and colleagues, who are using powerful electronic tools to enhance the training experience. They have progressed from 35 mm slides and flipcharts to electronic whiteboards, and at the heart of the electronic presentation arena is one program—Microsoft PowerPoint.

There are an unbelievable number of PowerPoint presentations given every day (or minute?), and many of them are horrible. But you've probably seen some effective presentations, using video and images and professionally staged to greatly accentuate a presenter's message. By the way, many of the examples given in this chapter apply not only to PowerPoint but also to some of the competitive products, like Apple Keynote.

But using technology is a double-edged sword. It can certainly help you convey complex information, but it can also serve as an alternative to preparation (when used incorrectly) or even blow up in your face if you're not careful. It's impossible to teach everything there is to know about electronic presentations in one chapter, so I have chosen to highlight the key components of communicating effectively with a presentation program on a laptop computer (with PowerPoint as the model).

If we think back to the case study on the Pogo Insurance Company and its beleaguered training director, Stanley (presented in the Introduction to this book), we can conceptualize some ways that PowerPoint presentations might help Stanley and his colleagues.

- *Details.* PowerPoint graphs are a great way to show the costs involved in losing training personnel, allowing direct comparisons of critical numbers before and after employees are reassigned. Financial information clearly shown is a key component of solving Pogo's problems.

- *The big picture.* A flowchart or diagram sequentially animated in PowerPoint slides might be a powerful way to show the interrelationships of the various corporate departments and drive home the message that better communication is necessary for an impact on the bottom line.

- *Motivation.* Video interviews with some of the claims adjusters, describing their in-the-trenches issues, would dramatize the human issues involved in turning Pogo's new offices around. These interviews could be the basis for facilitation or brainstorming sessions run by Norma.

- *Action items and solutions.* Whatever business strategy Tim and Stanley finally determine, they will need to communicate it throughout the company. In some cases this might be done in face-to-face sessions with the aid of a laptop computer and a projector, as in the scenario described later; but Power-Point presentations can also be distributed online or on video—so the visual tools and thematic concepts covered in this chapter might well be an excellent way for Pogo to effectively distribute training and motivational packages throughout the organization.

Just as Pogo might use PowerPoint effectively, the preceding ideas and the following tips and techniques will, I hope, trigger your own imagination and point the way to the aspects of presentation software you will want to explore further, whatever level of expertise (or lack of it) you may currently have.

Getting Started

First, let's address some of the issues that influence the most aggrieved party in the PowerPoint process—the audience.

Oh, yeah, the audience. Remember them?

Because PowerPoint is used mainly for speaker support, thousands of people every day are subjected to PowerPoint presentations, and many of these people are not happy.

What are the issues that you (or your boss) may face in satisfying your audience and thereby making the final product of PowerPoint—the presentation itself—a rousing success? By dealing with these issues up front, you should be able to increase your self-confidence and minimize the risk of turning off your audience or disappointing your colleagues. Let's keep the ultimate objective at the forefront of our attention—to communicate as effectively as possible.

Work Backward from the Objectives

Few things annoy an audience more than self-centered presenters. Take into account what the audience members hope for or expect to gain from giving you their valuable time. Then think about how their goals may coincide with yours.

For example, they may need to solve a problem for which using widgets effectively is the perfect solution. Telling them your life story or the history of widgets is probably not as good an idea as dramatizing their dire need to solve their problem and then demonstrating how your widgets can do the job.

Always think about what audience members' main needs are first, and then how what you have to offer can help people achieve what they need to do. Then you can go back and create your presentation to dramatize those needs and solve their problems, not yours.

Be Aware of the Top Six Audience Annoyances

Dave Paradi is known as the Office Technology Lifeguard because he rescues people from "Death by PowerPoint" and other electronic sins. Respondents to his Web-based survey listed the following as the most annoying features of bad PowerPoint presentations (the numbers show the percentages of respondents who cited each item as one of their top three annoyances):

The speaker read the slides to us	62.0%
Text so small I couldn't read it	46.9%
Slides hard to see because of color choice	42.6%
Full sentences instead of bullet points	39.1%
Moving/flying text or graphics	24.8%
Overly complex diagrams or charts	22.2%

Source: Courtesy of Dave Paradi, 2006.

Remember the Stakes

My colleague Jim Endicott of Distinction Services (http://www.distinction-services.com) is a highly respected speaker coach and trainer. He teaches his clients that the reason for every presentation, what makes it necessary, is something that is more than an annoyance; it is something with the potential for real pain. In a sales situation the source of the pain is obvious—not getting the sale. In other situations it may be more subtle, but it's something that requires learning a skill or measuring up. In any event it's always about your audience and what they want and need.

The presentation's message needs to be framed in terms of why what the presentation has to offer is vitally important, and once you find that hot button, plan your presentation around it.

Use the AutoContent Wizard

PowerPoint can be a big help in overcoming writer's block. Start a New Presentation or open the New Presentation Task Panel, and locate the link to create a presentation using the AutoContent Wizard.

Under Presentation Type (the second step in the wizard) you will find all kinds of fully scripted slide shows on a wide range of common topics. When the wizard is completed these slides provide prompts for filling in your own information, just by editing what is already on the slides to suit your own needs. Each content presentation template has its own integrated design, and some come with diagrams and other creative elements to help you deliver your own message.

With the AutoContent wizard you come away with a multislide presentation that will give you plenty of ideas, let you get comfortable editing materials in PowerPoint, and even practice presenting a series of slides (Figure 12.1 displays an AutoContent Wizard screen).

Figure 12.1. AutoContent Wizard Can Help You Brainstorm a Presentation from Scratch

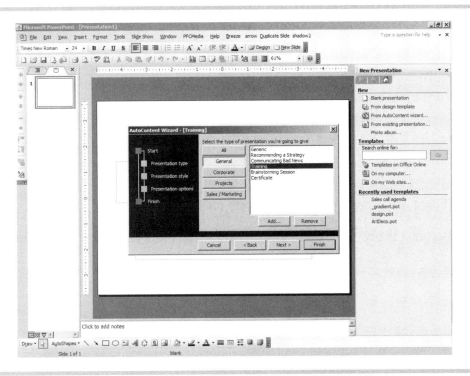

Research Your Audience

There is no excuse for not knowing something about the audience you're going to address. Demonstrate to your audience members that you've put some thought into considering and understanding their specific needs. This will help you build your case for whatever solution or message you want to deliver.

Send your Handouts to Word for Revision and Printing

Just as you can send your outline to PowerPoint from Word, you can send your presentation back to Word (File > Send To > Microsoft Word) to use that word processor's features to revise your notes and print them properly, with headers, footers, and other elements not found in PowerPoint.

This option gives you greater flexibility and more layouts for your handouts, and lets you easily edit the handouts before printing them.

You can even save a link between the presentation and the Word handout document so that the handout contents are automatically updated when changes are made in the presentation.

Use Slide Sorter as a Storyboard

A great PowerPoint tool is the Slide Sorter. Use it (View > Slide Sorter) to see thumbnails of your slides as your storyboard. Look at the titles and content of your slides in sequence to see if they truly flow naturally from one to the other, and delete or hide those slides that slow down the message that is most important for you to convey.

Figure 12.2. Slide Sorter View Can Act as a Storyboard and Show How Your Concepts Flow

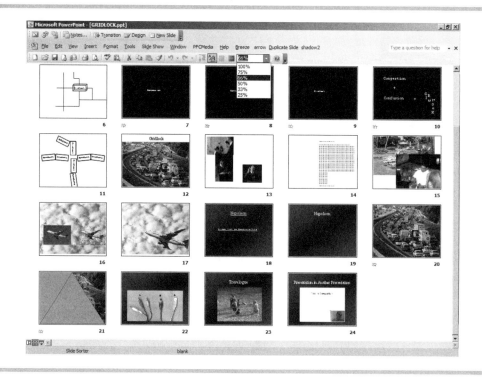

Take Advantage of Notes

Maybe you know intuitively that your slides are too busy but also that you're going to be held accountable for getting certain information into the presentation. Move the most complex or driest technical information to your Note pages and then print these pages as handouts. This lets you use your delivery to talk about the issues in a meaningful way and without boring your audience by reading through an overly long and detailed slide. You can always call attention to the handouts by saying, "A more detailed analysis of this issue and some resources are available in the handouts. Make sure you refer to this material before next week's meeting." You can quickly create notes from your bullets by copying and pasting them from the Slide window into the Notes panel in Normal view.

Preparing Your Slides on the Laptop

Two areas to focus on as you prepare your slides are writing better bullets and making your slides legible to all in your audience.

Write Better Bullets

There's a good reason why the items in PowerPoint slides are called *bullets,* and it's not because they are supposed to cause Death by PowerPoint.

Bullets are meant to express key concepts succinctly. Then the speaker amplifies on these points, saying interesting, profound, and meaningful things about the topic.

There are many theories about how many bullets are appropriate for a slide, but the key thing to remember is that each slide should be about only one topic.

Most presentation experts consider more than four or five bullets on a slide excessive, but it's really not the number of bullets but the way they're phrased that is most important. A bullet should never be a complete sentence, just a single, succinctly phrased important idea.

Some presentation theorists want to kill all bullets completely. If you like that idea, check out the work of Cliff Atkinson, author of *Beyond Bullet Points* (2005), at his Web site: http://www.sociablemedia.com.

Applying the PowerPoint design templates is a good way to avoid a font faux pas; they can help you match up pleasing design elements. Mixing multiple fonts is a good way to give your audience a subliminal headache and can be very annoying to people.

Make Sure Your Slides Are Legible

In terms of what the audience perceives, however, I can share some best practices with you based on experiences with several clients.

- First and most important, viewers need a sharp contrast between the text color and the slide background, light on dark is best for slides; dark on light is all right in some cases and should also be used for printouts.

- Darker blues and greens are good for backgrounds; yellow and white are good for text and data.

- Title font sizes should be no smaller than 36 regular.

- Text (bullet) font sizes should be no smaller than 28 regular.

- References, footers, and notations may be able to go down to a font size of 14, but check readability in your specific situation.

- Chart and dialogue labels and titles can range between 14 to 18 points, but the larger the better as long as these elements don't overwhelm the data.

- Line style for axes or arrows should be no less than 2¼ inches in width to be seen by a large audience.

Applying a Color Scheme is a good way to implement contrasting backgrounds and pleasing colors for elements (use the Accents in the Color Scheme dialogue box).

Have a Method for Using Personal Notes

Prior to a presentation you may find yourself writing notes on little pieces of paper, napkins, and Post-its. Then you fumble through them prior to the presentation or try to organize them as you're speaking, never getting them in the right order. Should you just type them up? What's the best way to keep personal notes handy?

Having your notes in typewritten form is probably even worse than the napkin strategy because you can't even wipe the sweat from your forehead with them. Everyone's preference is different, but the best technique I have found is to use index cards, which are easy to shuffle and organize. Some presentation experts suggest binding the cards together with a ring. This prevents loss and keeps them in order but also leaves them separate. Because they remain separate you can reorganize them for each speech and keep only the most important ones nearby. Don't lay out too many notes prior to your presentation. It tends to distract you from your flow, and you may fumble to find the right one at the right time.

Create a Presentation Roadmap with Anchor Objects and Bumper Slides

It's important to have a clear and coherent message structure to your presentation. This will keep people from shuffling through your handout and asking themselves, "Where the heck is he now?"

A great way to see this structure is to use a simple table to set off the different thematic sections of your presentation, and highlight each section a bit differently. Although a good graphic designer can come up with something much more dazzling, from a thematic perspective something simple, like the layout shown in Figure 12.3, can make your audience confident that you know where you're going and that they're likely to get there before lunch or sundown, as the schedule promises.

Figure 12.3. Presentation Roadmap: The Case for Widgets

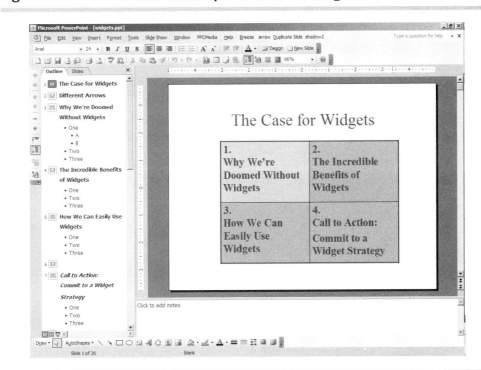

A *presentation roadmap* helps organize your material. A great way to introduce topics in your presentation is to use slides that foreshadow the topics visually, like a four-cell table or a set of circles that summarizes where you're headed.

Then at the beginning of each topic, you can highlight the appropriate graphical element and leave the others dim, which lets your audience know that you've organized your material, you've covered one or more topics, and now it's on to something new.

Creating slides like this is easy, because once you create one main concept slide, just use the Insert > Duplicate Slide feature of PowerPoint to reproduce it for each section you want to introduce, changing the duplicate slide each time to emphasize a new section. Then drag the introductory slide to the beginning of that topic in Slide Sorter View.

Don't use topic markers in short presentations or too frequently because your audience may think that you are condescending.

Appeal to the Different Cognitive Styles

Any presentation is essentially a learning experience for the audience, and it is to be hoped, for you as well. Participants should come away knowing more and having absorbed more information than they had when they arrived.

You might want to look at the many reference works on instructional design and learning theory. In essence they all say that different people absorb information through different primary senses: visual, auditory, or kinesthetic. Many presenters with PowerPoint appeal almost exclusively to the visual modality of their audience. Some simple techniques that enable you to appeal to other modalities, such as using your voice more effectively and getting your audience physically involved in some way, will help ensure you reach everyone with your message.

Remember that PowerPoint is just one widget in your presentation toolkit. Trainers, in particular, know the value of getting their audience involved through an event, a physical activity, or a game. This breaks up the monotony of a lecture, and the most successful trainers of this type call themselves *facilitators,* so they can charge more money. You can learn some of these techniques from books like *Games Trainers Play,* by John W. Newstrom and Edward E. Scannell (1980). A big part of these kinds of exercises is debriefing them to ensure that participants learn something, and PowerPoint graphics can be very effective during this phase.

If you can anticipate the results of your exercise, you can create slides that describe, for example, the typical group dynamics that your audience members have just experienced. Even more effective is eliciting these results directly from the audience and noting them on a flipchart or whiteboard.

Analyzing group behavior together stimulates discussion, creates energy, and provides audience members with the concrete feeling that they have gained substantial insight into a problem or issue.

Knowing the Presentation Room: Control the Room Layout

Depending on the purpose of your presentation, room layout and setup can be critical to its success. For example, are you going to influence people, inform them, or inspire them? Will they feel comfortable in the room or claustrophobic? Do they need to take notes, move around, look at each other? Do you want to encourage activities or interaction among the participants or remain above the fray?

Do you anticipate troublesome or antagonistic participants? If so you may want to assign seats (if possible) and move certain individuals out of a central or dominant position to other positions where you can keep them under control.

It's good news if you have event staff to handle the logistics. But if they are not familiar with the subtleties of promoting a comfort level for different types of presentations, it is up to you to do the research and take control of your environment. If you don't have such a staff, it is even more important that you familiarize yourself with the features of different layouts and make sure the appropriate setup is there for your presentation.

Getting Set Before the Presentation

Take these three preparatory steps immediately before your presentation.

Increase Your Energy Level

The fault, dear presenter, is not in the slides but in you. Audience energy is greatly a reflection of your own commitment and confidence. Audiences want to become involved and stimulated, and in the next section we'll talk about planning the slides themselves more effectively.

But before we go there, you need to get your own juices flowing. Usually, there is an adrenaline rush that comes with speaking publicly, and that should be a good start. But you should develop a routine that gets you *up*. Go off on your own for a minute if doing things like these makes you self-conscious, but clap your hands, bounce up on the balls of your feet, shadowbox like Sugar Ray Leonard, get your heart pumping. I walk briskly to the men's room and look into the mirror and tell myself, "You da man!" over and over again. (I have never revealed that before.) The bottom line is you need to find something that gets your energy level up, because your audience feeds off your energy.

Practice Eloquent Elocution

There is no quick fix for learning how to speak well—it's a matter of practice like any other important skill. Here are some main techniques to use:

- If you tend to speed up, learn how to breathe consciously and slow down.

- Stop and sip a glass of water to relax and clear your throat. (Make sure you have a glass handy.)

- Learn how to pause without panicking; a pause can help you regain your thoughts and is not a problem. If anything, it tells your audience that you are carefully weighing your words.

- Purge your delivery of nonwords: *uh, uh; you know, you know; OK, OK.*

- Get feedback from audience members in the rear of the room to find out if they can hear you.

- Practice speaking in front of a mirror or with a microphone while you have a toothpick in your mouth or chewing gum. Then repeat the material more clearly and distinctly with an empty mouth.

One of my most painful experiences was seeing myself on videotape when I first began to present—but it was also probably the most valuable learning tool I could have had. So, difficult as it may seem, get yourself videotaped and consult a qualified speaker coach. Even one or two sessions can make a dramatic difference in your self-confidence, how you are perceived by an audience, and how effectively you convey your message.

Meet and Greet Your Audience

If you're not busy plugging wires into the back of your laptop up until the beginning of your presentation, you should have plenty of time to actually meet the people you're talking to.

Really good presenters (and even some lousy ones) make it a point to say hello to members of your audience before their presentation begins, and even to ask what these individuals are most interested in hearing. Then they may even refer to an individual by name during the talk, and address his or her issues (perhaps with a slide or other relevant material). If you really have a problem with this, join Toastmasters and practice developing rapport with an audience. When people get to know you before the presentation, they'll find your slides much less annoying.

A good presenter is a good host. Ask if people are comfortable, if they can see the screen, and if the temperature of the room is OK. All of this reinforces the impression that you care about your audience and not just about getting through the PowerPoint slides.

Delivery Do's and Don'ts

These tips will help you perform effectively during the presentation.

Don't Point at the Screen

Walking to the screen and pointing to items inevitably makes you turn your back on your audience and then you lose contact with your participants. Most portable presentation mice come with a laser pointer that lets you point to the screen from a long distance away so you can maintain eye contact and your connection with your audience. PowerPoint 2003 also has a highlighter option that you can use during the slide show (even if you're a technical klutz). Change your pen to the highlighter and drag a swatch of color over the significant material.

Don't Use PowerPoint as a Teleprompter

Reading your slides is the worst thing you can do and the most annoying aspect of PowerPoint for most audiences—because you are boring them to death and wasting their time.

The ultimate transgression is to read your slides from the screen. This means you are turning your back on your audience while you're boring them to death and wasting their time. At least have the courtesy of facing the audience and boring them to death by reading from your laptop screen.

So place your laptop front and center and refer to its screen, or use a large monitor at the front of the stage.

Better yet, practice your material so that you anticipate the bullets and let them accentuate your points. This will enable you to maintain a connection with your audience.

I should also mention a product from Serious Magic called Visual Communicator (http://www.seriousmagic.com). This tool lets you insert PowerPoint slides into a video presentation and create a script to read from as you record the presentation. It still requires a lot of practice to be natural when reading the material, so just think about how condescending you appear as a presenter when you use your PowerPoint slides as a script in front of a live audience.

My Audience Isn't Looking at Me

If people are not looking at you during a presentation, take a good look at your slides—they're probably much too complex or busy, and you're probably putting them up there in their entirety while you're discussing the topic. Use Custom Animation or Animation Schemes to build the slides and strip all but the most important information out of your slides and bullets.

Use your slides to amplify and build your message. When you show a chart or graph, don't slap it up there all at once. Introduce the concept by showing the title and gridlines. Introduce the data series by category or in a fashion that helps you tell a story.

Walking to different parts of the room also refocuses attention on you and allows you to establish a closer connection, through eye contact and proximity, with members of your audience.

Do Get the Focus Back on You

Does this happen to you? People have stopped taking notes, and their eyes and body language show they are drifting. What can you do in PowerPoint to get their attention back?

First of all, congratulations on even noticing what your audience is doing. Many PowerPoint presenters are so focused on their own slides and terrified of the audience that they're oblivious to even the most obvious signs of boredom or impending rebellion.

The most obvious answer is to stop PowerPoint. Click the letter B on the keyboard to blank the screen temporarily. Begin an interactive discussion about the meaning of your last slide or the meaning of life itself. Ask if there are any questions. If possible, have someone turn on the lights.

The focus returns to you, and you have regained your audience's trust by showing them that you actually care that they're out there.

Do Escape from the Podium

Getting out from behind the podium is another matter of planning ahead. Ask the host or audiovisual (AV) staff to set up a small table on which you can put your laptop; the table should be placed where you can maintain eye contact with your audience and be closer to them.

If the projector is properly positioned at an angle, the front of the stage or room should be available as your domain. This will allow you to glance down to see the slides, and then look back at your audience—and even walk out and engage participants directly from time to time. Think of the podium as a trap that separates you from your audiences, inviting you to hide behind it for shelter and slouch against it for support.

Do Get Group Feedback

When you ask questions of your audience, don't let people's responses evaporate into thin air. Make notes or type the responses into the text editor. Using flipcharts, which let you use large markers and show that you're really working, or a whiteboard, you can accumulate feedback. Whiteboards are electronic marking surfaces generally used to share concepts during an electronic meeting among participants in different physical locations, but you can also use them to gather information. These products include software that lets you save the text to Word, Notepad, or even back to PowerPoint. (For a listing of whiteboard manufacturers, compiled from *Presentations* magazine, go to http://snipurl.com/bzna).

If you're a confident PowerPoint user you can use your lunch break or any other intermission to quickly compile a few slides that address points raised by your audience. For example, you can get data from the Web and paste it into a series of slides or provide hyperlinks to valuable resources. In any case, creating and showing a PowerPoint slide based on direct feedback signals to your audience that you care about participants' needs and take their comments seriously.

Don't Show Your Slides Too Soon

You can right-click on any PowerPoint 2002/XP or 2003 file or its shortcut, and you will see an option for Show. This will launch only the slide show and not the PowerPoint file; it does the same thing as saving a PowerPoint file as a *.PPS show file, which is another option. My favorite technique, however, is to simply click B and blank the screen until you're ready to present, keeping the focus on you instead of on PowerPoint. Only when you're ready, show the screen, and you should then be in your slide show—this also works well if you want to continue a show after a break or start a show somewhere after the first slide.

Do Elicit Questions

If you're just plowing through your slides, stopping to ask for questions only before lunch or a break, it tells your audience you just want to get through the material. Many PowerPoint audiences have been conditioned or numbed to just get through the slides without interruption. The room may be darkened and that further increases anonymity and reduces the feeling of group participation.

A good way to get interactivity going is by asking questions yourself and phrasing them in a way that stimulates give-and-take. Also, when a participant asks a question, make sure everyone has heard it and acknowledge the importance of the issue raised ("I'm glad you brought that up, John"). Never bluff an answer. If you don't know the answer, promise to get it and provide it at an appropriate time— before the end of the event or perhaps after you've been able to do more research.

In most cases audiences will be on your side if someone threatens your authority in a presentation, as long as you remain courteous and above the fray. You should always validate the importance of an individual's input but then point out that this time has been set aside for the presentation agenda. "If we're going to get through this section, I'll need to take that offline." If you say something like this, firmly but with a smile, the rest of your audience will be on your side. If possible, defuse the situation privately during a break by giving the person the individual attention he or she craves. Leaving yourself enough time after the presentation to handle troublesome issues lets you address them on a more personal level. It also leaves a better impression with your audience than your rushing out to catch a plane.

Don't Overstay Your Welcome

If you fear your presentation will be too long, there is an easy way to quickly edit it down. Take advantage of the PowerPoint feature that lets you use hidden slides. Go into Slide Sorter, select the slides you want to remove, and click the Hide Slide button (a slide with a line through it) on the toolbar. These slides won't be shown during the slide show but will still be available if you right-click and select Go to Slide.

This can also make you look like a genius. If someone asks a question related to the hidden material, you can say, "I hadn't intended to show that slide, but since you asked . . ." and show the hidden slide. Then just right-click again and select Last Viewed—you're back where you were when you answered the question. Another thing you can do is to create custom shows of various lengths from one longer presentation. You might name them to correspond to their various lengths. Going overtime when you're an invited presenter is a good way not to be invited back.

If you're going to hide slides, and it is a great technique for shortening a talk quickly and still looking smart when a question pops up, make sure you put titles on all your slides. (If you have slides that are all pictures or large videos, you can hide the title off screen or behind an object). With titles, finding a slide during a presentation is easy—right-click on your screen for a menu and click Go to Slide. A slide list will pop up, and you can find the slide by its title. Or, if you happen to know the number of a slide, you can just type it in with the number keys and jump there directly. Finally, you can type H, and PowerPoint should take you to the next hidden slide, but sometimes H is for Hope.

Beginning and ending your presentation on time creates a sense of trust between you and your audience and reinforces your professionalism.

Preparing for Potential Problems

Many of the technical problems presenters encounter are predictable and manageable. Here are some suggestions.

Placing the Projector Properly

Many conference rooms and most AV staff set up projectors in the center of the room—this is a big mistake. Projectors should be angled off to one side, making you the center of attention and making the slide show what it is meant to be, speaker support. Also remember that you can make the most of your forays to center stage by blanking the screen—just click B on the keyboard. You can also get products that will mask the image from falling on you while you're in front of the projector. (For example, check out the demo for Iskia at http://www.imatte.com/demo/flash.html)

Avoiding Projector Panic

Setting up equipment scares many PowerPoint users. There are many answers to your projector woes, but the quickest and most likely fix is screen resolution and scan rate. You may be trying to synch up to an older projector with a newer laptop. Right-click on Desktop > Properties > Settings. Decrease your screen size from 1024 x 768 to 800 x 600. Then click Advanced > Monitor. Decrease your Screen refresh rate to 60 Hz. In most cases this will make an older projector happy. But do review and check your slides too, because at the lower resolution some images and movies will appear much larger on the screen than you're used to seeing.

To accommodate the projector, some laptops are smart enough to adjust their screen size to a lower resolution. Some laptops (such as Sony) can do this by leaving the LCD screen size the same (1024 x 768) and putting the smaller screen inside it (800 x 600). The important thing is that the projector image is all right for your audience, and you may need to take a few minutes to make sure you can find your desktop shortcuts.

Sometimes you may find yourself in a venue where there is no way to align your projector directly with the screen, or the screen may be placed at a weird angle. This results in a distorted image. This is known as *keystoning,* and it can be corrected by a feature you can look for when you rent or buy a projector. Newer DLP (digital light processing) projectors have automatic keystone correction whereas older machines may have manual settings, either on the unit itself or on the remote, to adjust the trapezoidal image that results from such angular alignment. The keystone correction will generally be vertical or horizontal, depending on whether the image is wider on one side or wider at the top or bottom. (To learn more about these features in projectors, you can go to http://www.projectorpeople.com)

Obviously the more pronounced the keystone correction, the more the final image quality will suffer, so you should use this feature only when absolutely necessary. Your first task should be to go for optimal alignment of your projector and the screen.

Setting Up a Projector and Laptop

When you get to the venue the last thing you need is stress, and yet getting a laptop to work with a projector you're not used to can be very taxing. Here's the best way to do it.

- Connect the VGA output from the laptop to the VGA input of the projector.
- Turn on the projector. Sometimes you need to hit an additional button to leave stand-by and warm up the bulb.
- Turn on your laptop. If you're lucky you'll get a simultaneous display right away.
- Boot up your laptop into Windows.

- Look for the external display function key (FN toggle key) on your laptop. Typically, it is the F5 or F7 key, and it has three display settings:

    Laptop-only display

    Projector (external-only) display

    Simultaneous display

- Hit the FN toggle key once to see if the projector takes the image.

- Then hit the FN toggle key again, and you should get the simultaneous display you want.

For an excellent site with tips on setting up projectors check out Epson Presenters Online (http://snipurl.com/k88h) and its diagrams about projector set-up and related issues.

Avoiding TV Output

Audiences hate looking at a TV image of a computer screen—the quality cannot match VGA, for a host of technical reasons. Never use the video cable to connect to a projector either, because it's meant to take a VGA signal. The video input on the projector is meant to take a feed from a VCR or DVD player. For any presentation that you deem important, make sure you have a projector or large-screen computer monitor on which to show your PowerPoint slides.

Setting Up PowerPoint's Presenter View

If your laptop supports dual monitors, you can take advantage of PowerPoint's Presenter View. This means that instead of using a simultaneous display on laptop and projector, the projector shows the slide show but your laptop screen (or another monitor) shows a console that lets you navigate through your slides and also consult your notes and see what's coming up.

Presenter View is cool, but if you can run it you might just as well just use the Extended Desktop, which it requires to show the slide show on the second monitor (projector), and use your local screen for cheat notes, or consult Slide Sorter view in PowerPoint itself.

Only a very few laptops let you treat your projector literally as a second monitor and extend your desktop to it, which is required in order to use Presenter View.

You can buy a USB to VGA adapter from Tritton (http://www.trittontechnol ogies.com/products/TRIUV100.htm) to enable another VGA output on your laptop and extend your desktop. This will enable Presenter View (see Figure 12.4 for an example).

Figure 12.4. Presenter View Allows You to Navigate Through Your Slides, Consult Your Notes, and See What's Coming Up

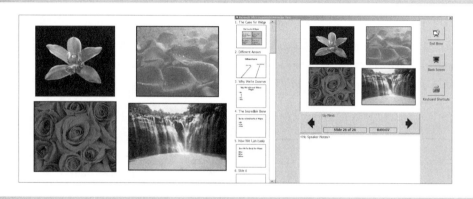

Watching Out for the Remote Freeze Frame

I've heard presenters tell me, "I've set up my projector perfectly and I get the simultaneous display I want, but when I get into my presentation, my image changes on my laptop but it doesn't change on the screen!" This happens when you hit the screen capture on the remote by mistake. Hit this key again to unfreeze it. Check the directions for your remote control mouse or the unit for the projector to understand all the keys.

Responding When Your Laptop Freezes

For all the advantages afforded by PowerPoint, it is still delivered on a computer, and every so often computers do malfunction. There are two aspects to dealing with freezes—the personal and the technical.

On the personal level, think of a freeze as an opportunity. It will take you out of your rhythm, and your best bet is probably to waste a bit of time rebooting the machine. (You can try Ctrl + Alt + Del, but your slide show will be gone even if your computer comes back, so bite the bullet and reboot.)

While you're rebooting, use the techniques we're discussing here to build rapport. Tell a story, answer questions, and go out into your audience and interact. Most important, understand that the members of your audience will be very empathetic with your situation, and if you deal with it resourcefully, they will love you for that.

In addition to being prepared to step away from your programmed show briefly, you should take these precautions against the dreaded freeze:

- Turn off all screen savers.

- Deactivate your antivirus software.

- Turn off power management.

- Run from an AC adapter, not a battery.

- Use only one mouse driver at a time (for a single portable device).

- Close all other programs, particularly Instant Messaging.

- Turn off any wireless adapter.

OK, you say, I've told my story and rebooted and gone through the checklist, and I keep on freezing. Isn't there some technical mumbo jumbo I can try to stop freezing in the future?

Most severe freezing issues relate to the video driver on your laptop. Make sure it's up to date and that it's the right driver, and do the same for your DirectX drivers. You can click Run on the Start Menu and enter "dxdiag" to check the status of your DirectX installation.

If necessary, you can also turn off (disable) DirectDraw and Direct3D under the display tab. You may need to reboot. Finally check with your computer manufacturer and graphics chip maker about any other fixes or updates.

Telling Stories

To prepare for any emergencies, such as screen freezes during your PowerPoint show, and also to build rapport with your audience and let them see you as a person and get comfortable, you should be armed with a few stories of various lengths to use for introductions, returns from breaks, and keeping some momentum going in the case of disaster.

The best stories are personal and should also relate to the topic at hand. Preferably, a story you tell your audience will also reveal a vulnerability or sensibility that may not otherwise be apparent. This builds an emotional bridge to your audience and opens the door for the dry, less intriguing stuff you'll probably present in PowerPoint.

For example, I tell audiences whom I'm training in PowerPoint about screen freeze incidents or how I inadvertently froze my projector image with the remote control—it puts us on the same level and wavelength and helps them realize that stuff like this happens to everyone.

In-the-trenches stories are great for training. For sales and marketing, success stories about the company's product or service and how it saved a client from a dastardly fate or solved a serious business problem are ideal.

There are also many other resources for business-related stories at the library and online, although these may lead to generic and dull material. Try to dig inside yourself for anecdotes and experiences that will resonate with your audience; turn off the PowerPoint and turn on your personality.

Preventing Your Portable Mouse from Going Crazy

Presentation mice are RF (radio frequency) devices and can be affected by other transmissions in the area. Particularly in hotels or convention centers, there may be conflicting devices in the area, so test yours thoroughly, and if you find a conflict, change its channel.

A crazy mouse is another reason for your audience to empathize with you. Do what Bud did in the episode of *Married with Children* where he loses the TV remote, and say, "You know, I seem to remember hearing that in the old days there were no TV remotes and there was actually a button to change channels directly on the TV. Maybe there's a button I can use directly on the laptop to advance my slides . . ." and then use the Arrow keys, or Pg Up and Pg Down, to go through the slides and bullets.

Handling Microphone Feedback

Feedback is generally caused by moving too close to the speakers or to another microphone. You can check this before your speech by trying the microphone from different areas of the room and noting any that are troublesome. Feedback might also result from having the levels (volume) set too high on either the microphone or the amplifier. In either case locate the volume control and lower it slightly.

Microphones are meant to be kept about the width of your hand from your mouth for optimal results. Feedback or screeching can also result if you let a hand microphone drift too far from your face and a sound technician suddenly raises the volume level to compensate. Do a sound check to thoroughly familiarize yourself with the equipment and the room.

Working with Audio

Besides the projector, perhaps the most difficult aspect of a presentation is the audio. You have two elements to contend with—your voice, which is probably amplified through a microphone into some loudspeakers, and any audio coming out of your laptop such as sound from video you may be playing out of PowerPoint.

If you don't account for on-board audio at a large venue, playing a video and expecting your audience to be able to hear the sound coming from tiny computer speakers can brand you as an amateur.

At a sophisticated venue, both of your *feeds* (microphone and computer output) go into a mixer, or switcher, preferably run by a technician for you. You need to cue this person when to switch from your vocal audio to the computer feed, and he or she should be able to connect the audio output from your computer (the speaker or headset output) to the input for the central audio in the room.

Obviously you need to do a thorough sound check before your speech to make sure there is no feedback from your microphone and to note any areas of the room that cause feedback.

In a less sophisticated environment, you may be on your own. Perhaps you're given a portable microphone hooked into the main sound system and left to set up your computer audio yourself. You should travel with a long audio cable and set of adapter plugs to connect your computer audio output to either the projector audio input, if someone has been smart enough to set that up for you, or directly to the amplifier going to the speakers.

If you're lucky the levels from your microphone and from your computer can coexist through the mixer. If you need to switch between audio sources, try to have an assistant do that for you, or time your breaks and Q&A so that you can go to the switcher and make the necessary adjustments.

Remembering to Shut Off Your Microphone

What if you go to the toilet and leave your microphone on, and the sound is sent back to your audience? Get in the habit of turning off the microphone whenever you stop showing slides or take a break. Most portables have a red light that is lit when the microphone is on and dark when it is off.

Getting Equipped with Plugs and Cables

These are the plugs and cables you should know about or have available when you present:

Audio

- RCA plug: the simplest and most common stereo and mono audio connector.
- 1/4-inch phone plug: connector for laptop audio (speakers and headset).
- Y cable or adapter: converts two channels of RCA into one phone plug and vice versa. Depending on your needs you may require different variations; get them at Radio Shack.
- XLR: the most common higher-end microphone and audio connector.

Video

- Composite cable and plug: lowest quality but adequate for connecting a VCR or video source to a projector.
- S-VHS: 4-pin plug and cable that provides higher quality for video connections. Remember that audio must be connected separately.
- DV-I: connectors and cables for higher-end LCD monitors and projectors.
- VGA: standard signal connector between laptop and projector. Consider having an extension cable, with plugs of the correct gender at either end, so you can move your laptop further away from podium.
- Component: split cables to multiple color inputs. Less commonly needed for most presentations.

Using a PC Microphone

Getting most PC or laptop microphones to work through external speakers, particularly while you also enable audio output through your software, is generally a losing proposition.

Check out the inexpensive USB amplifiers and sound systems made specifically for laptops by Creative Labs and Griffin Technology. The Griffin PowerWave is "the Swiss Army knife of sound" and will accommodate both your microphone and

PC audio, routing both to external speakers (http://www.griffintechnology.com/products/powerwave).

Presentation Checklist

You may not need everything here, but in terms of technical preparation, you should consider bringing these items with you to your presentation venue:

- One LCD projector capable of accommodating your particular laptop computer (1024 x 768 resolution)
- One 6-foot to 10-foot VGA cable to connect the computer to the projector
- One 12-foot front projection screen for the front of the room
- One podium on risers, to be placed off to one side of the screen
- One lavaliere microphone with cables for a house public address (PA) system
- One laser pointer
- One power strip for the podium extension cord

Before your arrival also make sure you have at least the following items available:

- Extension cord and surge protector (don't rely on batteries)
- Laptop power adapter (don't present on batteries)
- Your presentation loaded on a CD-ROM or DVD (kept separate from your laptop bag)
- Wireless mouse (extra batteries)
- Extra audio and video plugs and cables
- Any adapters necessary for an external monitor or CD or DVD devices
- All handouts and supplementary materials for your presentation
- Recovery CDs and software for your laptop (or a disaster DVD or overheads)
- Laptop manual
- Projector bulbs

Also consider these suggested items:

- External USB hard drive or ZIP drive containing the presentation
- Overheads with the presentation on them, to be used in a pinch

- Phone numbers of local laptop rental facilities that can provide a replacement computer

Rehearsal and Final Preparations

In addition to planning your delivery, rehearse it. These suggestions will help.

Rehearsal Is Not a Dirty Word

Most PowerPoint users fall into two categories: those who are creating the show for someone else (you have my sympathy) and those who are creating the show for themselves (you have no excuse).

At the very least use the Rehearse Timings (under Slide Show on the main menu). But be careful; this in itself can be a major annoyance if the file is saved, because the animations may play automatically during the presentation. But used properly, Rehearse Timings is a minimal way of checking the overall length of each slide along with what the speaker has to say, timing the bullets, and coming up with snappy material before the main event. The timer alone is worth the feature, because it shows you how long each slide lasts and the total length of the presentation.

A phenomenal rehearsal tool is Apreso from Anystream, which lets you easily videotape a speaker delivering a presentation with the PowerPoint slides, and then play back the presentation for brainstorming or constructive criticism. When the presenter is part of a team that wants input into the final message, check out Apreso at http://www.anystream.com. Serious Magic's Visual Communicator can also be used as an effective rehearsal tool.

Save Annotations

You can mark up a PowerPoint slide in various ways as you present, to accentuate a point or respond to a comment or question. Pen tools and highlighters are available to you for real-time annotation in the later versions of PowerPoint.

If you're using PowerPoint 2003 you will be given an option to save your annotations on the slides when you close the slide show. (If you anticipate doing this, save a backup version of the presentation without the annotations prior to presenting.) If you're using older versions of PowerPoint, you can hit the Print Scrn key and, at the earliest opportunity, paste the captured presentation screen into another PowerPoint slide or into Microsoft Word. Remember you can have only one screen grab in memory at a time using this function, so if you want to grab multiple screens, try using a screen capture program like SnagIt (http://www.tech smith.com). If annotations are a big part of your presentation, consider using a tablet PC or incorporating a whiteboard into your presentation.

Hide Your Bullets During Rehearsal

Many people use the bullets in a presentation to jog their brains and end up reading the slides. The only answer to this bad habit is to practice, practice, practice, and hone your message until you know what you want to say. This doesn't mean memorizing and being robotic—it's a matter of organizing your material in a way that builds and to which you, as the speaker, add significant value through your insights.

Otherwise your presentation is all about the slides, and your audience will snooze. One suggestion is to look at your presentation in Outline View and collapse the bullets. Now practice discussing the slides. Then reveal the bullets later on, to check how you did.

Use a Self-Running Show

What if you have information you want to present outside the main topic area or flow of your talk? You may really annoy your audience if you take a break and don't give them one.

How about presenting a self-running show for those who might be interested in it while you and the other participants take a break and race each other to the toilet? Just use the Rehearse Timings feature under Slide Show, and save your timings as a file with a new name. This file should run automatically, delivering information while you make your escape. It's still a good idea to say something like, "I want to present this material while we take a short break," and then to keep an eye on the show to make sure it's running and not stalled.

Get Instant Feedback

If you have the resources, consider using an automated response system (ARS), which is a set of keypads that lets audiences "vote" or give answers to multiple-choice questions. You can use this to create competition for the smartest respondents (and gauge how well people are retaining information). It's amazing how excited even the most self-important physicians, attorneys, and corporate executives can get when they have a chance to "finish first" and win a T-shirt.

ARS systems can be rented or purchased and vary greatly in price. Some come with animated results, like car races with sound effects, representing the data graphically, and requiring an expert to run. Others can be fitted into a small suitcase, connect directly to PowerPoint, and work in a conference room or boardroom.

If you can't use ARS, you could just do an informal poll of your audience and put a visual representation of the data into a datasheet to create a real-time PowerPoint chart.

Learn from Presentation Web Sites

Modeling oneself on the experts is the best way to learn any craft or profession. Fortunately, in the PowerPoint and presentations world there are resources available to give you ideas on how to approach any project. Here are some of the best:

- Indezine (Web site by Geetesh Bajaj, PowerPoint MVP): http://www.indezine.com
- *Presentations* magazine (particularly Speakers Notes): http://www.presentations.com
- InfoComm (particularly the ICIA and Presentations Council): http://www.infocomm.org
- United Visual tech tips (configure laptops and obtain projector specs): http://www.unitedvisual.com/2tips/2tips1.asp
- 3D slide elements as alternatives to boring bullets: http://www.perspector.com
- Above & Beyond CD—(*Ten Ways to Avoid Death by PowerPoint*): http://www.aboveandbeyond.ltd.uk

Summing Up

PowerPoint and other presentation programs are tools that you can use effectively to tell your story, whether for training or any business purpose.

Mastering these tools is an investment in time and patience, but if you've seen an effective presentation, you know it's worth the effort. This chapter cannot possibly be a complete guide to this technology, but I hope it will serve to point the way with hints and tips that can empower you to use these phenomenal tools in your own endeavors.

Key Points

- Few things annoy an audience more than self-centered presenters. First, take into account what your audience hopes for or expects to gain from giving you their valuable time.

- Look at the titles and content of your slides to see if they truly flow naturally from one to the other, and delete or hide those slides that slow down the message that is most important for you to convey.

- Move the most complex, driest technical information to your Note pages and print these pages as handouts.

- Bullets are meant to express key concepts succinctly, and you (or another speaker) are meant to amplify on these points and say interesting, profound, and meaningful things about the topic.

- Don't lay out too many notes prior to your presentation. It tends to distract you from your flow, and you may fumble to find the right one at the right time.

- Going out into your audience every so often or just walking to different parts of the room refocuses attention on you, and allows you to establish a closer connection, through eye contact and proximity, with members of your audience.

- Beginning and ending your presentation on time creates a sense of trust between you and your audience and reinforces your professionalism.

Appendix 1
ROI Formulas

Return on Investment

$$\text{ROI \%} = \frac{\text{Realized monetary benefits} - (\text{Total direct costs} + \text{Total indirect costs})}{\text{Total direct costs} + \text{Total indirect costs}} \times 100.$$

Benefit-Cost Ratio

$$\text{BCR} = \frac{\text{Total training benefits}}{\text{Total training costs}}.$$

Payback Period

$$\text{Payback period} = \frac{\text{Total training cost}}{\text{Total monthly benefits}}.$$

Note: Total monthly benefits = Total training benefits / 12.

Appendix 2
Using the ROI Calculator

THE ENCLOSED CD-ROM includes a return on investment calculator for you to use in evaluating your next major training project. This ROI calculator provides you with an opportunity to determine all your costs and benefits to arrive at a complete ROI calculation that you can present with confidence to management. This calculator structures and simplifies the process of calculating the financial returns from your investments in training. It can be used to

- Forecast potential returns
- Measure actual returns
- Analyze training programs
- Analyze training during a year
- Analyze internal and external training programs

To Use the Calculator

Access the CD-ROM and open the file "ROI Analysis Templates." Copy it onto your computer. Once you make changes to it, you will have to give it a new name in order to save it. You might want to use a name that links to the program you are analyzing.

Then, to conduct an analysis, simply fill in the cells in the worksheet under each section (Costs, Benefits, and Assumptions). Be careful, as some of the cells are self-calculating. All the formulas are in place to calculate the end results in the ROI Summary tab.

Steps in Conducting an ROI Analysis

The training ROI calculator uses two worksheets to take you step-by-step through an ROI analysis:

Assumptions (12-Month ROI Analysis tab)

This section lists the assumptions that will be used by the calculator in making its calculations. Assumptions include such information as number of working days in a year, salary amounts, overhead costs, payroll costs, class sizes, and costs for training facilities. When you have modified these assumptions so they are correct for your organization, you might like to save this file as a template that you can use time and again.

Costs (12-Month ROI Analysis tab)

The next step is to enter the costs associated with the program you are analyzing.

Benefits (12-Month ROI Analysis tab)

Then move on to enter the details of the benefits arising from the program.

Summary (Summary tab)

The calculator automatically provides you with a final report, including ROI percentage, payback period, and benefit cost ratio.

Appendix 3
Thinking Like
Management Review

Financial Reports and T&D

- How can training and development improve the organization's bottom line?
- What is a proper level of investment in training and development?
- What impact will an investment in training and development have on the organization?

The Balance Sheet and T&D

- How can we reflect the investment in training and development in the balance sheet?
- How has training and development contributed to increasing the value of the organization?

The Cash Flow Statement and T&D

- What is the actual cash requirement for the training and development initiative?

- Will the training and development initiative be part of the operating or investment activities?
- How will the training and development initiative be financed?

Financial Ratios and T&D

- How leveraged is T&D?
- How are you financing the T&D assets?
- What proportion of the assets is financed by external creditors?

Management's Concerns

- Minimize disruptions and unproductive time of employees.
- How will the training contribute to the objectives of the organization?
- What results can we expect the training program to deliver?
- Is an ROI measure required, and how will T&D measure it?
- What will the training program cost?

Getting Evidence of Results from Training

- Do we need to evaluate a financial return on investment?
- What other impact can we have directly on the business?
- What is the value of the training to the business?
- How do we effectively evaluate that training has met its objectives?
- How do we correct the situation if we're not meeting the objective of the training program?
- How do we see if the training provided a return on investment?

Basics of ROI Calculations

- Show us the costs involved in developing and delivering the training program?
- How does the ROI of the training program proposed compare to other alternatives?
- What are the expected and the post ROI results of the training program?

- How long will the investment made in the training program take to break even and become profitable for the organization?
- What is the benefit of the training versus the cost of it?

What an ROI Calculation Does Not Tell You

- What other benefits can we expect from the training program?
- How will the intangible benefits provide value to the participant or the organization?
- Can the value of the intangible benefits provide any monetary or financial returns?
- How will we know if the intangible benefits are realized or are genuine?

Communicating Results to Stakeholders

- How will the organization tangibly benefit from the training, beyond what you have presented?
- Can you further justify the required investment in the training program?
- How will the employees benefit in the long term from the training program?
- What makes this training program any better than what our competitors do?

Determining Whether to Use an Outside Vendor for T&D

- What resources are we lacking?
- Why are we lacking these resources?
- What are our options for obtaining these resources?
- How will these resources affect the business?

Making the Decision to Hire or to Outsource

- Have we objectively and equally evaluated both outsourcing and hiring?
- What are some of the expected challenges of bringing on additional employees?
- What is the financial impact of hiring additional employees?
- Will we be able to leverage the employees for other purposes?

- What stress is placed on existing employees if we do not hire?
- What impact will not hiring additional employees have on clients and other parts of the company?
- Are we seeing hiring as an additional cost or as an investment?

Preparing a Request for Proposal

- Is tendering an RFP our only alternative?
- Who needs to be involved in developing the RFP?
- What is the objective of the RFP?
- What challenges will we face in creating the RFP?

Selecting a Vendor

- Have we found the top vendors?
- Is our process fair and objective—immune to attacks from external sources?
- Did we verify the backgrounds and references of the top vendors?
- Do we have a secondary vendor in the event the first does not work out?
- What is the cost in relation to the value we will receive by using a vendor?

Appendix 4
Answers for Delivery Flexibility Scenario in Chapter Six

GIVEN THE SIZE of the budget overage (15% of the total project budget) that the CTO plans to recoup by canceling the planned training, those costs for the classroom experience may be burdened with travel, lodging and other peripheral expenses that may be avoidable. Andy should acknowledge the goal of the CTO, and commit to assisting the CTO in accomplishing it without losing sight of the original goal: a smooth transition to the new system. Andy should suggest that the cost to the company of replacing employees unable to adapt, unassisted, to the new technology will be extremely high.

Andy should remind the CTO of the training materials ready for use and suggest that they be distributed to the users accompanied by a clear communication directing them to log on to a series of Web based conference training calls. This information should contain easily understood information for a new Web user to navigate the log on to the conference site. Andy should propose breaking the training sessions down into modules that are manageable for the learners regarding the content covered and time commitment required by the learners. Properly structured, these modules would find learners putting the information immediately to work as they log off the Web training and return to their new PC screens. Andy should prepare the estimated costs for the training to review against the previous plan costs and send them with a proposed Training Web Based Conference Call Schedule for the CTO along with an Executive Summary suitable for sharing with the Executive Team [Richard Gasparotti, Senior Trainer, Sodexho Corporate Services].

The CTO needs to be persuaded that the rollout will be disastrous *if* the end users aren't provided training. First, people don't like change. I call it the FUD factor (Fear, Uncertainty, Doubt). They need to be persuaded that the new system is better, more efficient and more cost effective. One of the best ways to persuade them is get buy-in during training.

Second, if no training is provided, people won't know how to use the new system, which could be disastrous for the company's overall business strategies. The CTO needs to understand that not providing training upfront would result in training having to be provided later anyway with additional expenses due to lost productivity, poor service and delayed implementation.

If the CTO still won't budge, Andy does have the training materials. First, he could just distribute the training materials (least expensive, least recommended). Second, instead of training everyone, it may be necessary to drastically cut back and train one or two end users in each area to be experts. They could take the materials and knowledge back to their area and train other end users and serve as the expert for that group (more expensive, recommended). If this option was taken, it would be nice if Andy could leverage his improved relations with IT to ask them to provide technical support for end users by phone or email [Jennifer Olson, Instructor, Clarian Health Partners, Inc.].

1. Empathize (e.g., "You're between a rock and a hard place: The project is being squeezed from both ends—over budget, behind schedule and something's got to give.") Attempt a 15-minute face to face meeting to discuss consequences of cutting training.

2. Assuming the worst:

   A. Work with Marketing, Recruiting, Human Resources and Tech Development & Support to ensure that there is a firm, motivational communications plan for rollout. (Plan probably already exists but will need to be tweaked given cancellation of face to face training.)

   B. Bring executive team on board to spearhead the rollout through their various departments—Develop a motivational meeting plan for them to introduce the new system and the advantages of the change. (At large group meetings and in Direct Report staff meetings.)

   C. Develop a middle manager motivational meeting plan that they will deliver at a staff meeting prior to rollout in their area.

   D. Ensure that end users who have never worked on a PC attend a basic Windows course. (Hopefully from a different budget such as a generic training pool budget.)

   E. Hold train-the-trainer sessions for key players/subject matter experts who can act as trainers, mentors and coaches for their area. Also ensure that the technical support area is fully versed on the installation process, the system and trouble shooting. (Dependent upon CTO agreeing to this minimized cost per reward initiative.)

   F. Get together with the web master to discuss the feasibility of electronic learning as an adjunct to the rollout. (Bear in mind that these end users probably do not have a PC at their desk, since up to now they have been working on dumb terminals. Prior to rollout they will have to go to a computer resource center, if such a thing exists, to take advantage of the e-learning. Post rollout, they probably will not have time to take advantage of it.) Also to discuss electronic documentation and self-help screens.

   G. Make the most of the materials that have been developed. Middle managers distribute self-help materials at the staff meeting (as is or tweaked) as system rolls out in their area (e.g. user manuals, check lists, job aids, FAQs etc.). A training representative (those who were to do the training that has been cancelled) will attend the staff meeting to answer questions and/or to provide follow-up.

   H. Pray [Meliora Dockery, President, Capability on Demand].

First, the CTO has some valid points about people who are going to be using the system. Many will have had enough experience that they can muddle through at the beginning. However, there should be alternatives in place, perhaps on a voluntary basis, for those users who need more assistance and do not want to be left behind. Super-users and trainers can be enlisted to give some precise, targeted training. Tips can be posted on the intranets along with FAQs and recent problems and solutions. Training can be about open and frequent communication rather than formal classrooms. Needs will arise and a plan should be in place to meet those needs [Anne-Marie Armstrong, Instructional Design Consultant, Government Printing Office].

Appendix 5
Answers for Measurement Flexibility Scenario in Chapter Six

JILL NEEDS ANSWERS. All she has is a memo from the COO and some hearsay about her group's need to develop "consulting competencies." If Jill cannot get answers directly from the COO she should enlist the VP of training and organizational development to help her better understand what the COO and for that matter the rest of the executive team have in mind for her group. Parallel to her inquiries up the food chain, Jill should start engaging with her group to gather their ideas and impressions of the major changes facing them. . . .

[According to the industry competency model of the American Society for Training and Development (ASTD)] the first and most important key action associated with measuring and evaluating is to *identify customer expectations:*

Works with customer or stakeholders to determine why they are interested in measurement and what they hope to accomplish with the results; clearly

This appendix is a reprint of the discussion section of T. Gargiulo and J. Naughton, "Competency Challenge: What Would You Do?" *ASTD Links*, Apr. 2005. © ASTD, Alexandria, VA. All rights reserved.

defines research questions, expectations, resources available and desired outcomes of the measurement project; manages unrealistic expectations [ASTD Competency Model. © 2004. ASTD. All Rights Reserved].

If at all possible, Lewis needs to find a way to respectfully refuse to run the classes. There is much more at stake than training here. Once Jill understands the COO's expectations, Lewis can help her develop a measurement and evaluation plan with two phases. Phase I would identify the gaps between the company's objectives and the group's current capabilities. Phase II would measure the impact of whatever intervention is developed. From a design perspective, weaving consulting competencies into the training is an excellent strategy and one which Lewis would be wise to implement. . . .

Here is a summary of additional pieces of information Lewis might want to collect. These are not in any particular order:

- Examples of the KET team's work
- Why the decision was made to go to external customers
- Number of customers anticipated
- How is success going to be measured with external customers
- Changes in KET's organizational structure
- Job description of team members
- Team and individual goals
- Budget and timeline
- Baseline data on knowledge skills and results
- Information about external customers
- More information from the COO
- Scope definition of what the KET will provide to clients
- Business plan to support KET's new revenue goals
- Difference between selling KET services externally versus internally . . .

Be careful what you ask for. . . . Jill's survey assumes her team needs some kind of generic training skills. So, the data has little or nothing to do with the business change that she has been directed to initiate and implement. Her first step should be to get with the COO and other executives to understand the business opportunity and the challenges her group will face. It is from this analysis that she and Lewis can begin to assess what is needed for the KET team. If I were Lewis I would help Jill to focus on the Business Need and the changes that need to occur within KET to meet the business expectations. In my experience most of these changes will have very little to do with generic soft skills. Some training for the KET team may be necessary, but it is likely to be very specific and related to changing how they will do business and align them with the intent of the business change [Darryl Sink, president of Darryl L. Sink Associates].

Lewis has several objectives. First, he must show that the training function's new responsibilities will pay off for the company. Then, he must show how the new training will set the training staff up for success in their new ventures. Success can be monitored, by looking at how well the group achieves a variety of goals.

Lewis needs to show that the skills and competencies addressed by the training are important for the business. One important step is to clarify with senior leadership the new business model for the training function. For example, he could start with a business objective such as "growing the business" and show that the training staff's expanded role would contribute to business growth. The business of capturing best practices and sharing those practices with other organizations would become a revenue source for the organization. Lewis would need to review the market and show that there was a need for these services and prospects for selling them. Essentially, Lewis needs to leverage his business acumen and show his understanding of how the company's business operates. Then, Lewis would need to show that improving the staff's interpersonal and consulting skills would make them more effective in delivering their services. He might create a baseline measure of their skills and then follow up after the training to monitor improvement. Additional measures might be created around the new training function responsibilities. They could set goals for achieving financial outcomes, customer satisfaction, internal processes, and employee skills (all part of the HR Scorecard).

Here are a few pearls of wisdom from T&D colleagues. . . .

I know this scenario is supposed to be about measurement and evaluation . . . but there is a huge relationship piece that has to be worked on before anything else occurs. Jill needs to clarify her boss's expectations, and then Lewis and Jill need to sit down together to figure out what to do next. At this point, the measurement/evaluation focus seems premature. Success can't occur for either Jill or Lewis unless they work together on this challenge [Susan Afriat, Children's Hospital of Philadelphia, senior learning and OD consultant].

Lewis needs to identify Jill's performance objectives for KET so he can directly link his training to KET achieving those objectives. He also needs to know how Jill is going to measure KET's progress so he can align his training efforts with those metrics, and perhaps offer ongoing training throughout the fiscal year to help ensure that KET meets the fiscal year goal. Finally, throughout the process, Lewis should work with Jill to consider "what's next" after KET achieves this goal, so he can continue to be instrumental in developing and achieving future business objectives for KET and [the organization] [Bridget Wright, First National Bank of LaGrange, VP training & development].

This is exactly what we are beginning to undertake in our organization and it is essential to developing meaningful measures and gaining company buy in to initiatives and resources.

1. The company business objectives and specific measures and time-frames—so we could link the learning outcomes of training activities to the business objectives and determine measures for evaluation in particular level 4.
2. The position descriptions, competencies and key job responsibilities and activities for the roles that the T&D group would be working with in order to be able to develop measures for evaluation of level 2 and level 3 effectiveness. On the job measures will assess the impact of the training in the areas of performance and behavior change that contribute to the business objectives and are more meaningful than level one. Linking these inputs together in a learning impact map at design will assist in the development of a robust evaluation plan and measures that directly correlate with the business outcomes

[Teresa Weerasinghe, Yellow Pages New Zealand, content development manager].

This entire scenario seems to be putting the cart before the horse (not an uncommon situation in hierarchical business structures). "Measurement" implies that an assessment has revealed what items need to be measured. Jill and Lewis seem to be trying to measure without knowing what they are measuring or why it is important. Level 1 evaluations rarely result in useful data to ensure training is producing business-aligned results, and that seems to be all Lewis has gathered to date. Jill, as leader of the project, needs clear information about how her project aligns with and supports business goals. If she doesn't have access to the COO (which seems to be the case, given that her memo arrived from "senior management"), perhaps the VP of training can help her get this information. Lewis is currently acting in a "pair of hands" role—never a successful place to be. He needs to meet with Jill to find out how the training request she sent him aligns with department and business goals. Further, both Lewis and Jill need to move into consultative roles—something the business (per the grapevine) wants. Lewis and his colleagues should ask clarifying questions about that rumor, as well as request other department and business expectations so that they know what to measure. Once they have a clear vision of how their work aligns with the business, the plan will be easy to construct [Susan Butler, L. L Bean, Inc., learning developer].

Jill needs to meet with her boss to ensure she is on the same page. The training she wants to provide her staff is all good stuff; unfortunately, if it is not the skills that will help her staff be successful, what good will it do? In addition, she should take the time to have some in-depth discussions with her staff regarding the new direction. Jill could gather their input on what need to be successful and at the same time gain group buy in to the solutions that are created. Jill, with the help of T&D and HR (and any other department who might have knowledge), needs to sit down and take a look at the competencies necessary to serve external customers as opposed to internal customers. Wherever they find differences, this could be an area they focus training and coaching efforts. At the same time, they can look at what skills are already in place and how can they make them stronger. One final thought . . . when creating a training strategy surrounding the competencies, we have always had great success when we correlate them to a desired outcome. When you see this outcome, you will know that the training was successful [Michelle Drager, West Coast Bank, AVP employee development].

References and Suggested Reading

Atkinson, C. *Beyond Bullet Points.* Buffalo, N.Y.: Microsoft Press, 2005.

Bersin, J. "Business Process Outsourcing: Pros & Cons." *Chief Learning Officer,* Apr. 2005. Retrieved Mar. 2006 from http://www.clomedia.com/content/templates/clo_article.asp?articleid=910&zoneid=67

Biech, E. *Training for Dummies.* Hoboken, N.J.: Wiley, 2005.

Blake, G., and Bly, R. W. *The Elements of Business Writing: A Guide to Writing Clear, Concise Letters, Memos, Reports, Proposals, and Other Business Documents.* New York: Longman, 1992.

Brethower, D., and Smalley, K. *Performance-Based Instruction: Linking Training to Business Results.* San Francisco, Pfeiffer, 1998.

Bunzel, T. *Sams Teach Yourself Microsoft Office PowerPoint 2003 in 24 Hours.* Indianapolis: Sams, 2003.

Bunzel, T. *Solving the PowerPoint Predicament: Using Digital Media for Effective Communication.* Reading, Mass.: Addison Wesley, forthcoming.

Davidson, L. "10 Questions to Answer Before Turning to a Third-party Vendor." *Workforce,* Jan. 1998, *77*(1), 42.

Gargiulo, T. "Whose Training Is It Anyway?" *ASTD Links,* Dec. 2003. Retrieved May 2006 from http://www1.astd.org/news_letter/December03/links/whose_training_Nov.html

Gargiulo, T. *The Strategic Use of Stories in Organizational Communication and Learning.* Armonk, N.Y.: Sharpe, 2005.

Gargiulo, T. *Stories at Work: Using Stories to Improve Communications and Build Relationships.* Westport, Conn.: Praeger, 2006.

Gargiulo, T., and Naughton, J. "Competency Challenge: What Would You Do?" *ASTD Links,* Apr. 2005. Retrieved Apr. 2006 from http://www.astd.org/astd/Publications/ASTD_Links/2005/April2005/Comp_Chall_Apr05.htm

Hale, J. *The Performance Consultant's Fieldbook: Tools and Techniques for Improving Organizations and People.* San Francisco: Jossey-Bass, 1998.

Hale, J. *Performance-Based Evaluation: Tools and Techniques to Measure the Impact of Training.* San Francisco: Pfeiffer, 2002.

Hale, J. *Outsourcing Training and Development: Factors for Success.* San Francisco: Pfeiffer, 2005.

Investopedia. "Fundamental Analysis: The Balance Sheet." 2006a. Retrieved Mar. 30, 2006 from http://www.investopedia.com/university/fundamentalanalysis/balancesheet.asp

Investopedia. "Fundamental Analysis: The Cash Flow Statement." 2006b. Retrieved Mar. 30, 2006 from http://www.investopedia.com/university/fundamental analysis/cashflow.asp

Investopedia. "Fundamental Analysis: The Income Statement." 2006c. Retrieved Mar. 28, 2006 from http://www.investopedia.com/university/fundamental analysis/incomestatement.asp

Kaner, S., and others. *Facilitator's Guide to Participatory Decision Making.* Philadelphia: New Society, 1996.

Kaplan, R. S., and Norton, D. P. *The Balanced Scorecard: Translating Strategy into Action.* Boston: Harvard Business School Press, 1996.

Kirkpatrick, D. L. *Evaluating Training Programs: The Four Levels.* (2nd ed.) San Francisco: Berrett-Koehler, 1998.

Kirkwood, T., and Pangarkar, A. "The Inside Track." *CMA Management,* Mar. 2004. Retrieved Mar. 2006 from http://www.managementmag.com/index.cfm/ci_id/1486/la_id/1.htm

Kiser, A. G. *Masterful Facilitation: Becoming a Catalyst for Meaningful Change.* New York: AMACOM, 1998.

Kouzes, J. M., and Posner, B. Z. *The Leadership Challenge.* (3rd ed.) San Francisco: Jossey-Bass, 2002.

Laabs, J. J., and Sunoo, B. P. "Winning Strategies for Outsourcing Contracts." *Personnel Journal* (now *Workforce*), Mar. 1994.

Markel, M. *Technical Communication.* (8th ed.) New York: St. Martin's Press, 2006.

Mohr, A. *Financial Management 101: Get a Grip on Your Business Numbers.* North Vancouver: Self-Counsel Press, 2003.

Newstrom, J. W., and Scannell, E. E. *Games Trainers Play.* New York: McGraw-Hill, 1980.

Niven, P. R. *Balanced Scorecard Step-by-Step: Maximizing Performance and Maintaining Results.* San Francisco: Pfeiffer, 2003.

The Outsourcing Institute. *Outsourcing Index 2000.* Jericho, NY: The Outsourcing Institute, 2000.

Overfield, K. *Developing and Managing Organizational Learning.* Alexandria, Va.: ASTD Press, 1998.

Paradi, D. "Bad PowerPoint Presentations Survey." Retrieved Mar. 28, 2006, from http://www.communicateusingtechnology.com/pptsurvey.htm

Phillips, J. J. *Return on Investment in Training and Performance Improvement Programs.* (2nd ed.) Boston: Butterworth-Heinemann, 2003.

Phillips, J., and Stone, R. *How to Measure Training Results: A Practical Guide to Tracking the Six Key Indicators.* New York: McGraw-Hill, 2002.

Phillips, P. P. *The Bottom Line on ROI: Basics, Benefits, & Barriers to Measuring Training & Performance Improvement.* Atlanta: CEP Press, 2002.

Piotrowski, M. V. *Effective Business Writing: Strategies, Suggestions and Examples.* New York: Perennial Library, 1990.

Robinson, D. G., and Robinson, J. C. *Training for Impact: How to Link Training to Business Needs and Measure the Results.* San Francisco: Jossey-Bass, 1989.

Robinson, D. G., and Robinson, J. C. *Strategic Business Partner: Aligning People Strategies with Business Goals.* San Francisco: Berrett-Koehler, 2004.

Schwarz, R. *The Skilled Facilitator: A Comprehensive Resource for Consultants, Facilitators, Managers, Trainers, and Coaches.* (Rev. ed.) San Francisco: Jossey-Bass, 2002.

Stolovitch, H. D., and Keeps, E. J. *Training Ain't Performance.* Alexandria, Va.: ASTD Press, 2004.

Valenti, D. C. *Training Budgets Step-by-Step: A Complete Guide to Planning and Budgeting Strategically-Aligned Training.* San Francisco: Jossey-Bass, 2004.

van Adelsberg, D., and Trolley, E. A. *Running Training Like a Business.* San Francisco: Berrett-Koehler, 1999.

Wallace, G. W. *T&D Systems View.* Naperville, Ill.: CADDI Press, 2002.

Index

About the Author

TERRENCE L. GARGIULO has spent over fifteen years helping people working in training and development acquire the skills they need to be significant contributors to the businesses that have hired them. He holds a master of management in human services degree from the Florence Heller School at Brandeis University, and is a recipient of *Inc.* magazine's Marketing Master Award.

Among his past and present clients are GM, DTE Energy, Dreyers Grand Ice Cream, UnumProvident, the U.S. Coast Guard, Boston University, Raytheon, the City of Lowell, Arthur D. Little, KANA Communications, Merck-Medco, Coca-Cola, Harvard Business School, and Cambridge Savings Bank.

His previous books include *Making Stories: A Practical Guide for Organizational Leaders and Human Resource Specialists* (also translated into Chinese); *The Strategic Use of Stories in Organizational Communication and Learning; On Cloud Nine: Weathering Many Generations in the Workplace* (with Robert Wendover; also translated into Korean, and Spanish); and *Stories at Work: Using Stories to Improve Communications and Build Relationships.*

He is a frequent speaker at the international and national conferences of such organizations as the American Society for Training and Development (ASTD), International Society for Performance Improvement (ISPI), Academy of Management, and Association of Business Communications, and he is a field editor for ASTD. His articles have appeared in *American Executive* magazine, *Communication World,* the ISPI journal *Performance Improvement,* and *ASTD Links.*

He resides in Monterey, California, with his wife, Cindy; son, Gabriel; and daughter, Sophia. He is an avid scuba diver, passionate chef, and lyric baritone. *Tryillias,* an opera by Terrence Gargiulo and his father, was accepted for a nomination for the 2004 Pulitzer Prize in music.

Terrence Gargiulo can be reached by phone: 781-894-4381, or e-mail: Terrence@MAKINGTORIES.net

Also visit his Web sites: http://www.makingstories.net
http://www.oncloudnine.org

About the Contributors

ⒶJAY M. PANGARKAR is president of CentralKnowledge, a leader in comprehensive and measurable strategic learning solutions. He is recognized for his experience in the "business and strategy side of training," helping companies implement training evaluation and ROI strategies, developing balanced and performance scorecards, training and certifying new trainers and subject experts, and supporting those with responsibilities for managing the training function. He is a regular contributing writer for several prominent HR and training publications, is a recognized published author, is government accredited in professional learning, and delivers learning programs for professional organizations and business institutions. He is highly involved in the Montreal community, serving on the board of directors of nonprofit groups and committees. Nominated for the Ernst & Young/Canadian Business of the Year award, he is regularly interviewed by business and news media for newspaper articles and radio broadcasts. He is a founding member and chair of the Quebec chapter of the Canadian Society for Training and Development (CSTD), the founder of the Quebec ROI Network, a member of the CSTD national board of directors and the Canadian ROI Network, and is extensively involved with and speaks to the global learning and performance industry. He can be contacted at info@centralknowledge.com or www.centralknowledge.com or 866-489-7378.

TERESA **KIRKWOOD** is founding partner of CentralKnowledge, brings over eighteen years of industry and training experience to her work, and is recognized for her experience in helping companies implement training evaluation and ROI strategies, training new trainers and subject experts, and supporting those with responsibilities for managing the training function. She writes for several major HR and training publications, is a published author, is government accredited, and delivers learning programs for professional organizations and business institutions. She is exceptionally involved in community activities, including mentoring business start-ups for youth, and she regularly speaks to women's entrepreneurial groups. She was nominated for the Ernst & Young/Canadian Business of the Year award and is regularly interviewed by business and news media for newspaper articles and radio broadcasts. A founding member and vice chair of the Quebec chapter of the Canadian Society for Training and Development (CSTD), she has helped to establish the Quebec Training ROI Network and is a member of many CSTD development committees. She has also been invited to speak at learning industry and business conferences on topics related to learning strategies and entrepreneurship. You can contact Teresa at info@centralknowledge.com or www.centralknowledge.com or 866-489-7378.

TOM **BUNZEL** specializes in knowing what presenters need and how to make technology work. He has appeared on Tech TV's *Call for Help,* as Professor PowerPoint, and has been a featured speaker at InfoComm and PowerPoint LIVE as well as working as a technology coach for corporations and other organizations, including the Neuroscience Education Institute. He has written a number of books, the latest two being *Sams Teach Yourself Microsoft Office PowerPoint 2003 in 24 Hours* and *Easy Digital Music.* His other books are *Easy Creating CDs and DVDs, How to Use Ulead DVD Workshop, Digital Video on the PC,* and an update to the *Visual QuickStart Guide to PowerPoint 2002/2001.* He is contributing editor to *Presentations* magazine and writes a weekly column as the Office Reference Guide for InformIT.com. He can be reached through his Web site, www.professorppt.com

How to Use the CD-ROM

System Requirements

PC with Microsoft Windows 98SE or later
Mac with Apple OS version 8.6 or later

Using the CD with Windows

To view the items located on the CD, follow these steps:

1. Insert the CD into your computer's CD-ROM drive.

2. A window appears with the following options:

   Contents: Allows you to view the files included on the CD-ROM.

   Software: Allows you to install useful software from the CD-ROM.

   Links: Displays a hyperlinked page of websites.

   Author: Displays a page with information about the author(s).

Contact Us: Displays a page with information on contacting the publisher or author.

Help: Displays a page with information on using the CD.

Exit: Closes the interface window.

If you do not have autorun enabled, or if the autorun window does not appear, follow these steps to access the CD:

1. Click Start -› Run.

2. In the dialog box that appears, type d:\start.exe, where d is the letter of your CD-ROM drive. This brings up the autorun window described in the preceding set of steps.

3. Choose the desired option from the menu. (See Step 2 in the preceding list for a description of these options.)

In Case of Trouble

If you experience difficulty using the CD-ROM, please follow these steps:

1. Make sure your hardware and systems configurations conform to the systems requirements noted under "System Requirements" above.

2. Review the installation procedure for your type of hardware and operating system. It is possible to reinstall the software if necessary.

To speak with someone in Product Technical Support, call 800-762-2974 or 317-572-3994 Monday through Friday from 8:30 a.m. to 5:00 p.m. EST. You can also contact Product Technical Support and get support information through our website at www.wiley.com/techsupport.

Before calling or writing, please have the following information available:

• Type of computer and operating system.

• Any error messages displayed.

• Complete description of the problem.

It is best if you are sitting at your computer when making the call.

Pfeiffer Publications Guide

This guide is designed to familiarize you with the various types of Pfeiffer publications. The formats section describes the various types of products that we publish; the methodologies section describes the many different ways that content might be provided within a product. We also provide a list of the topic areas in which we publish.

FORMATS

In addition to its extensive book-publishing program, Pfeiffer offers content in an array of formats, from fieldbooks for the practitioner to complete, ready-to-use training packages that support group learning.

FIELDBOOK Designed to provide information and guidance to practitioners in the midst of action. Most fieldbooks are companions to another, sometimes earlier, work, from which its ideas are derived; the fieldbook makes practical what was theoretical in the original text. Fieldbooks can certainly be read from cover to cover. More likely, though, you'll find yourself bouncing around following a particular theme, or dipping in as the mood, and the situation, dictate.

HANDBOOK A contributed volume of work on a single topic, comprising an eclectic mix of ideas, case studies, and best practices sourced by practitioners and experts in the field.

An editor or team of editors usually is appointed to seek out contributors and to evaluate content for relevance to the topic. Think of a handbook not as a ready-to-eat meal, but as a cookbook of ingredients that enables you to create the most fitting experience for the occasion.

RESOURCE Materials designed to support group learning. They come in many forms: a complete, ready-to-use exercise (such as a game); a comprehensive resource on one topic (such as conflict management) containing a variety of methods and approaches; or a collection of like-minded activities (such as icebreakers) on multiple subjects and situations.

TRAINING PACKAGE An entire, ready-to-use learning program that focuses on a particular topic or skill. All packages comprise a guide for the facilitator/trainer and a workbook for the participants. Some packages are supported with additional media—such as video—or learning aids, instruments, or other devices to help participants understand concepts or practice and develop skills.

- *Facilitator/trainer's guide* Contains an introduction to the program, advice on how to organize and facilitate the learning event, and step-by-step instructor notes. The guide also contains copies of presentation materials—handouts, presentations, and overhead designs, for example—used in the program.

- *Participant's workbook* Contains exercises and reading materials that support the learning goal and serves as a valuable reference and support guide for participants in the weeks and months that follow the learning event. Typically, each participant will require his or her own workbook.

ELECTRONIC CD-ROMs and Web-based products transform static Pfeiffer content into dynamic, interactive experiences. Designed to take advantage of the searchability, automation, and ease-of-use that technology provides, our e-products bring convenience and immediate accessibility to your workspace.

METHODOLOGIES

CASE STUDY A presentation, in narrative form, of an actual event that has occurred inside an organization. Case studies are not prescriptive, nor are they used to prove a point; they are designed to develop critical analysis and decision-making skills. A case study has a specific time frame, specifies a sequence of events, is narrative in structure, and contains a plot structure—an issue (what should be/have been done?). Use case studies when the goal is to enable participants to apply previously learned theories to the circumstances in the case, decide what is pertinent, identify the real issues, decide what should have been done, and develop a plan of action.

ENERGIZER A short activity that develops readiness for the next session or learning event. Energizers are most commonly used after a break or lunch to stimulate or refocus the group. Many involve some form of physical activity, so they are a useful way to counter post-lunch lethargy. Other uses include transitioning from one topic to another, where "mental" distancing is important.

EXPERIENTIAL LEARNING ACTIVITY (ELA) A facilitator-led intervention that moves participants through the learning cycle from experience to application (also known as a Structured Experience). ELAs are carefully thought-out designs in which there is a definite learning purpose and intended outcome. Each step—everything that participants do during the activity—facilitates the accomplishment of the stated goal. Each ELA includes complete instructions for facilitating the intervention and a clear statement of goals, suggested group size and timing, materials required, an explanation of the process, and, where appropriate, possible variations to the activity. (For more detail on Experiential Learning Activities, see the Introduction to the *Reference Guide to Handbooks and Annuals*, 1999 edition, Pfeiffer, San Francisco.)

GAME A group activity that has the purpose of fostering team spirit and togetherness in addition to the achievement of a pre-stated goal. Usually contrived—undertaking a desert expedition, for example—this type of learning method offers an engaging means for participants to demonstrate and practice business and interpersonal skills. Games are effective for team building and personal development mainly because the goal is subordinate to the process—the means through which participants reach decisions, collaborate, communicate, and generate trust and understanding. Games often engage teams in "friendly" competition.

ICEBREAKER A (usually) short activity designed to help participants overcome initial anxiety in a training session and/or to acquaint the participants with one another. An icebreaker can be a fun activity or can be tied to specific topics or training goals. While a useful tool in itself, the icebreaker comes into its own in situations where tension or resistance exists within a group.

INSTRUMENT A device used to assess, appraise, evaluate, describe, classify, and summarize various aspects of human behavior. The term used to describe an instrument depends primarily on its format and purpose. These terms include survey, questionnaire, inventory, diagnostic, survey, and poll. Some uses of instruments include providing instrumental feedback to group members, studying here-and-now processes or functioning within a group, manipulating group composition, and evaluating outcomes of training and other interventions.

Instruments are popular in the training and HR field because, in general, more growth can occur if an individual is provided with a method for focusing specifically on his or her own behavior. Instruments also are used to obtain information that will serve as a basis for change and to assist in workforce planning efforts.

Paper-and-pencil tests still dominate the instrument landscape with a typical package comprising a facilitator's guide, which offers advice on administering the instrument and interpreting the collected data, and an initial set of instruments. Additional instruments are available separately. Pfeiffer, though, is investing heavily in e-instruments. Electronic instrumentation provides effortless distribution and, for larger groups particularly, offers advantages over paper-and-pencil tests in the time it takes to analyze data and provide feedback.

LECTURETTE A short talk that provides an explanation of a principle, model, or process that is pertinent to the participants' current learning needs. A lecturette is intended to establish a common language bond between the trainer and the participants by providing a mutual frame of reference. Use a lecturette as an introduction to a group activity or event, as an interjection during an event, or as a handout.

MODEL A graphic depiction of a system or process and the relationship among its elements. Models provide a frame of reference and something more tangible, and more easily remembered, than a verbal explanation. They also give participants something to "go on," enabling them to track their own progress as they experience the dynamics, processes, and relationships being depicted in the model.

ROLE PLAY A technique in which people assume a role in a situation/scenario: a customer service rep in an angry-customer exchange, for example. The way in which the role is approached is then discussed and feedback is offered. The role play is often repeated using a different approach and/or incorporating changes made based on feedback received. In other words, role playing is a spontaneous interaction involving realistic behavior under artificial (and safe) conditions.

SIMULATION A methodology for understanding the interrelationships among components of a system or process. Simulations differ from games in that they test or use a model that depicts or mirrors some aspect of reality in form, if not necessarily in content. Learning occurs by studying the effects of change on one or more factors of the model. Simulations are commonly used to test hypotheses about what happens in a system—often referred to as "what if?" analysis—or to examine best-case/worst-case scenarios.

THEORY A presentation of an idea from a conjectural perspective. Theories are useful because they encourage us to examine behavior and phenomena through a different lens.

TOPICS

The twin goals of providing effective and practical solutions for workforce training and organization development and meeting the educational needs of training and human resource professionals shape Pfeiffer's publishing program. Core topics include the following:

Leadership & Management

Communication & Presentation

Coaching & Mentoring

Training & Development

e-Learning

Teams & Collaboration

OD & Strategic Planning

Human Resources

Consulting

What will you find on pfeiffer.com?

- The best in workplace performance solutions for training and HR professionals

- Downloadable training tools, exercises, and content

- Web-exclusive offers

- Training tips, articles, and news

- Seamless online ordering

- Author guidelines, information on becoming a Pfeiffer Affiliate, and much more

Discover more at www.pfeiffer.com